Challenging the Growth Machine

STUDIES IN GOVERNMENT
AND PUBLIC POLICY

CHALLENGING THE GROWTH MACHINE
Neighborhood Politics in Chicago and Pittsburgh

Barbara Ferman

University Press of Kansas

© 1996 by the University Press of Kansas

All rights reserved

Published by the University Press of Kansas (Lawrence, Kansas 66049), which was organized by the Kansas Board of Regents and is operated and funded by Emporia State University, Fort Hays State University, Kansas State University, Pittsburg State University, the University of Kansas, and Wichita State University

Library of Congress Cataloging-in-Publication Data

Ferman, Barbara.
    Challenging the growth machine : neighborhood politics in Chicago and Pittsburgh / Barbara Ferman.
    p.   cm. — (Studies in government and public policy)
    Includes bibliographical references and index.
    ISBN 0-7006-0786-2 (alk. paper). — ISBN 0-7006-0787-0 (alk. paper)
    1. Neighborhood government—Illinois—Chicago. 2. Citizens' associations—Illinois—Chicago. 3. Political participation—Illinois—Chicago. 4. Neighborhood government—Pennsylvania—Pittsburgh. 5. Citizens' associations—Pennsylvania—Pittsburgh. 6. Political participation—Pennsylvania—Pittsburgh. I. Title. II. Series.
JS713.F47   1996
320.4748'11—dc20   96-16253

British Library Cataloguing in Publication Data is available.

Printed in the United States of America

10 9 8 7 6 5 4 3 2 1

The paper used in this publication meets the minimum requirements of the American National Standard for Permanence of Paper for Printed Library Materials Z39.48-1984.

To Bernie,
whose giving knows no limits

Contents

Preface   ix

Acknowledgments   xiii

List of Tables and Illustrations   xv

1. Governing Regimes, Urban Arenas, and Opportunities for Neighborhood Mobilization   1

2. The Changing Political Economy of Pittsburgh and Chicago   19

3. Regime Formation in Chicago and Pittsburgh: Electoral Arenas and Civic Arenas   44

4. Planting the Seeds of Discontent: Urban Renewal and the Neighborhoods   65

5. Challenge and Response: The Politics of Cooperation Versus the Politics of Confrontation   85

6. Chicago: The Barriers to Multidimensional Progressivism   111

7. Pittsburgh: The Limits of Consensus   124

8. Toward a Conservative Progressivism?   135

Notes   153

Bibliography   175

Index   185

Preface

As is often the case, this book began as something quite different from what it has become. Intrigued by the phenomenon of public–private partnerships, I set out for the city that had become a model of public-private cooperation, Pittsburgh. During a preliminary investigation in January of 1988, I steeped myself in the history of the Pittsburgh renaissance, the economic rebuilding that resulted from public and private efforts during the 1940s and 1950s and made Pittsburgh the unparalleled model of public–private partnerships.

My first trip to Pittsburgh, though a short one, yielded several strong impressions. First, the city's politics seemed tame. Having grown up in New York City, lived and conducted research in Boston and San Francisco, and (at that time) lived in Chicago, "tame" was not an adjective I would readily associate with politics. Second, for an old machine town that never went through a real reform period, Pittsburgh seemed to be dominated by a "good government," apolitical mentality.[1] Third, the status in Pittsburgh of community-based organizations (CBOs) was a further deviation from my experience. CBOs were key players in the city's associational life. They were recognized as being legitimate by political and civic leaders and had a cooperative relationship with city government. In the urban contexts that I knew, resistance and conflict tended to be the defining characteristics of the relationship between CBOs and city government. This was especially the case in Chicago, where, after a brief hiatus during the Harold Washington years (1983–1987), the old bunker mentality reclaimed center stage.

Another impression that has informed my overall perspective, while not directly incorporated into my study, centers around the structuring of research questions. Most of the academic and quasi-academic research conducted on Pittsburgh, by Pittsburgh researchers, is essentially devoid of politics. For the most part, it is policy-oriented and driven by technical, administrative, or managerial perspectives. By contrast, Chicago researchers have typically turned their intellectual queries toward the blood and guts of politics. This orientation did change somewhat during the Washington administration, as policy-oriented analyses were generated.

As I pondered these contrasts, I found my interests shifting until I finally jumped ship, dropping the public–private partnership focus and forging into an examination of the neighborhood experience in the two cities. Why were neighborhood-based organizations in Chicago viewed as obstructionist, especially by mainstream media and many civic leaders, while their Pittsburgh counterparts were seen as legitimate participants? What did the brief period of neighborhood incorporation under Harold Washington mean for the city's political system as a whole? Why was the period so brief?

The questions came fast and furious, some enduring, some dropping out to make way for new ones, some undergoing revision. But behind the changing research landscape, one nagging problem remained: the "big deal if neighborhood organizations are incorporated" syndrome. Or alternatively, as Richard J. Daley used to say, "What trees have you planted lately?" CBOs do not plant big trees. They do not have the resources, the capacity, and in most cases the desire to do so. And they are often defeated even in their attempts to plant small trees. Operating in a "big picture," "big project," "big money" world, CBOs have a kinship with Rodney Dangerfield: they get no respect.

I must confess that the nagging problem of the significance of CBOs came as much from my own soul-searching as it did from friendly critics. The limitations imposed on these organizations are enormous. Consequently, their results are often marginal from a citywide perspective. However, the results of a lot of mainstream economic development have been equally marginal, but the hype surrounding them has overshadowed the reality. CBOs have not benefited from such favorable press.

My own experience assuaged my doubts about the role of community organizations. Having lived all my life in urban neighborhoods, I knew intuitively that neighborhoods matter; they constitute the center of social activity and familial institutions, and therefore provide the moral fabric for society. Ironically, the media and civic leaders readily invoke the "breakdown of social and moral norms" as an explanation for the deterioration of our inner cities but just as readily dismiss those who push for more attention to urban neighborhoods, the place where these norms are learned and nurtured. If this breakdown plays such a significant role in urban deterioration, would it not be equally important to directly incorporate the neighborhoods within which community values could be learned in our vision of urban revitalization?

Community activists, because they do incorporate this line of thinking, often are perceived as a thorn in the side of politicians and policy makers. They remind us, however, that cities are important and that vital neighborhoods are critical to the overall health of the city. Studying their efforts to get this point across, and thus broaden the policy franchise, is the focus of this book. Put another way, the book is an effort to understand why some urban polities are more receptive to progressive initiatives than others.

The contrasting experiences of neighborhood organizations in Pittsburgh and Chicago provide bountiful material for exploring this question. They also require that we significantly expand the boundaries of urban analysis. Theories on urban politics have been extremely useful but narrowly conceived. Typically devoid of comparative dimensions, the studies upon which these theories are based omit critical contextual variables, particularly institutional and cultural ones. Thus, an important objective of this study is to expand the scope of urban analysis to include institutional and cultural factors. In addition, much of the research on urban politics follows a case study approach that focuses on a single municipality.[2] Although such studies are rich in descriptive detail, they can be severely limited in providing possible (or likely) implications of contrasting urban histories, institutions, and political cultures. A major objective of this study, then, is to take a more comparative approach that explicitly connects such urban contrasts to opportunities for progressive politics.

The book highlights the formative impact of each city's political history, institutional framework, and political culture on regime behavior and group mobilization. Institutional frameworks, through their patterns of resource distribution and decision-making norms, play a critical role in shaping the opportunities for and conditions of participation in the political system. Political culture, that is, the collective expectations of the population about the roles and behavior of their government and political system, also has an impact on the form and effectiveness of political participation.

Unfortunately, these key contextual factors have been underemphasized or ignored altogether in the major theories of urban politics; regime theory[3] and growth machine theory are often guilty of underemphasizing these contextual factors while public choice theory and its various iterations (e.g., "city limits" thesis) tend to ignore these factors.[4] The comparative analysis of Chicago and Pittsburgh shows how critical these contextual factors are in shaping the direction of politics and policy.

Viewing the city in terms of overlapping urban arenas is a useful corrective to these grave omissions. Local political systems are composed of numerous arenas (civic, electoral, intergovernmental, business, and so forth), each distinguished by a particular institutional framework and political culture. Although regimes typically are engaged in more than one arena, there is primarily one toward which the regime is oriented. In Chicago, for instance, the electoral arena is primary, whereas in Pittsburgh it is the civic sector. This difference goes a long way toward explaining the varied fortunes of neighborhood and other organized interests within the two cities.

The concept of urban arenas facilitates the comparative analysis of cities, a relatively undeveloped feature of both regime and growth machine theory. A comparative perspective can also illustrate the forms of political mobilization that are possible under different institutional arrangements and permit us to develop some generalizations about the prospects for progressive policy at the local level.

This study also departs from much of the literature in urban politics by focusing on nonelite actors. Urban scholarship tends to disproportionately examine the behavior of economic and political elites who constitute governing coalitions (regime theory) as well as that of the rentiers who constitute the growth machine.

Incorporating neighborhoods into urban analysis adds an analytical dimension that is absent from many scholarly studies. It also provides a normative dimension currently lacking in the marketplace conception of the city that drives much urban policy. We can begin to examine questions of participation, citizenship, and quality of life, the fundamentals of a polity, a human city, and a humane society. Although downtown areas house significant amounts of economic activity, neighborhoods serve vital social and political functions. Just as the human body requires a multitude of healthy organs to function properly, so too does a city. The failure of neighborhoods to serve these functions threatens the health of cities, even when they contain reasonably viable downtowns. This study attempts a more holistic and balanced view of large cities, arguing that neighborhoods are integral to what cities are and can be.

Acknowledgments

Long-term projects are never really the product of one person. Without the intellectual and moral support from colleagues and the humor, warmth, and encouragement of friends, such works would be unbearable. Fortunately, I have received more than my fair share from all.

Intellectually, I have benefited from the helpful comments of numerous colleagues. Larry Bennett, Brian Corbin, Bill Grimshaw (whose work on Chicago politics supplied me early on with a good education), Robin Jones, Bernie Mennis, Ted Muller, and Clarence Stone all read parts of the manuscript. Robin Jones pulled double duty, keeping me updated on Pittsburgh while I resided in Chicago and then in Philadelphia. (Let us never forget popcorn, big hair, and "Is it Sunday yet?") I am particularly indebted to Rich DeLeon. As one of the reviewers for the University Press of Kansas, Rich provided a wealth of suggestions, comments, and criticisms that helped me to improve this book in immeasurable ways.

During the course of my research in Pittsburgh, Joel Tarr was extremely helpful, providing me access to resources I would not have known existed. Alberta Sbragia was also very generous, sharing with me her own files on Pittsburgh. Frank Zabrowski of the University of Pittsburgh's Hillman Library kindly made the Renaissance Oral History Collection available to me during off hours. During my first research trip to Pittsburgh, Simon Reich and Linda Myers-Reich provided me with a researcher's dream—a clean, comfortable, free place to stay. Thanks, guys.

In Chicago I benefited from that wonderful tradition of politics being a spectator sport. You can't pass too much time without talking politics. I gained many insights from my numerous conversations with Paul Barrett, Larry Bennett, Marcia Edison, Bill Grimshaw, Loomis Mayfield, and Andy McFarland. The Municipal Reference Library (now the Municipal Reference Collection in the Harold

Washington Library) and the Chicago Historical Society were gold mines of information staffed by people whose dedication and knowledge are truly amazing.

In addition to reading just about everything I could get my hands on, I relied on a series of interviews in Pittsburgh and Chicago. While confidentiality prevents a listing of names, I would like to express my deepest thanks to those individuals who took time out from very busy schedules to give me information, insights, assessments, and further leads.

My Temple colleague, friend, and gym partner, Robin Kolodny, provided support in numerous ways: easing my transition from Chicago to Philadelphia, explaining Temple University to me, and just being there. Thanks, friend. A Summer Faculty Research Grant and a semester Study Leave from Temple University supported my work on completing the manuscript. Thanks also goes to Scott Snyder of Temple University for preparing the neighborhood maps.

Fred Woodward, director of the University Press of Kansas, provided support and encouragement at every step of the way. Melinda Wirkus and Susan Schott, also of the Press, treated my manuscript with great professional care.

Finally, to my best critic and biggest supporter, Bernie Mennis, for sharing it all.

Tables and Illustrations

TABLES

1.1 Regime Theory and Urban Arenas: Components of Analysis   7
1.2 Institutional Framework   8
2.1 Basic Population Characteristics: Chicago and Pittsburgh   21
2.2 School Enrollments by Race: Chicago and Pittsburgh   22
2.3 Population by Age, Chicago and Pittsburgh, 1990   30
2.4 Mayoral Administrations: Chicago and Pittsburgh   37
6.1 New Hires by Race and Gender, Chicago   116
6.2 Mayoral Appointments by Race, Chicago   117
8.1 Governing Regimes: Pittsburgh and Chicago   137
8.2 Institutional Framework: Chicago and Pittsburgh   138
8.3 Political Culture: Chicago and Pittsburgh   140

ILLUSTRATIONS

1.1 The Mediating Role of Governing Regimes and Urban Arenas in Local Decision Making   11
2.1 Neighborhood Map by Race, Pittsburgh   24
2.2 Neighborhood Map by Race, Chicago   26

1
Governing Regimes, Urban Arenas, and Opportunities for Neighborhood Mobilization

If the city is a text, how shall we read it?
—Joyce Carol Oates

In 1988, neighborhood activists in Pittsburgh celebrated as the Pittsburgh Partnership for Neighborhood Development (PPND) was established. This centralized administrative and funding mechanism was the culmination of more than two decades of struggle by neighborhood organizations for incorporation into the larger governing regime. One year earlier, neighborhood organizations in Chicago had mourned the untimely death of Harold Washington, the city's first progressive, pro-neighborhood, and African American mayor. Like their counterparts in Pittsburgh, Chicago's neighborhood organizations had battled for years against the orientation and exclusivity of the "growth machine." The brief period of hope offered by the Washington administration was shattered with his passing as the city's politics returned to the familiar pattern of rewarding friends and punishing enemies and policy was reoriented toward downtown megaprojects. On both counts, Chicago's neighborhood organizations were big losers.

Why did the neighborhood experience vary so significantly in these two cities? Why did Pittsburgh's governing regime, while initially resistant, ultimately accommodate neighborhood demands for inclusion? Why did Chicago's governing regime vehemently resist similar demands? Why were Harold Washington's efforts at broadening the franchise turned back after his death and politics in Chicago so quickly returned to its traditional practices?

* * *

THE POLITICS OF URBAN POLICY

Implicit in these questions is the view that much of urban policy is contested ground. While the external political economy (e.g., federalist structure and global capitalism) imposes severe constraints on cities and the types of policies they can pursue, these constraints often are mediated through local political systems. Many fine case studies have demonstrated that within this overarching structure there is "space for reform."[1] Variation occurs among urban places. Certain cities do engage in redistributive policy, do seek to regulate and control capital, and do from time to time question the wisdom of unfettered development. Other cities clearly do not. What accounts for this variation among cities or within the same city over time? A common theme to all answers to this question is the role that local political systems play in mediating larger structural forces.

Richard DeLeon's study of San Francisco illustrates how the political success, albeit temporary, of a progressive coalition translated into policies that limited the prerogatives of capital: zoning legislation, linkage fees, building regulations designed to protect the aesthetics of San Francisco, and finally Proposition M, "the most restrictive growth-control legislation of any large U.S. city."[2] These policies are testimony to the latent power of local political forces to modify what appear to be structural imperatives.

Similarly, linkage policies in Boston, which sought to tap some of the city's service-sector growth and employ it for progressive purposes, resulted from political battles between community groups and the real estate and development communities.[3] Rather than trust in classical economic theory, which argues that the benefits of growth trickle down, community activists developed sufficient political power to regulate the benefits down.

At times progressive coalitions have also successfully challenged the ownership prerogatives of private capital. Swanstrom's examination of Cleveland shows how Mayor Kucinich, with the help of a progressive coalition, maintained municipal control over the city's major electric utility.[4] The city of Hartford, under the progressive leadership of city council leader Nicholas Carbone, became part owner in several key downtown developments that were then used as leverage to encourage minority and resident hiring.[5] In Santa Monica a majority progressive coalition on the city council enacted stringent rent control legislation.[6]

This sampling of cases reiterates the point that market activities and their consequences can be politically contested. When they are, policy is often the result of political struggle within the city. This relationship makes variation among cities intriguing for the opportunity it provides to examine the preconditions for, as well as limits to, policy change.

This book is an attempt to understand the politics of policy change through an examination of the contrasting experiences of Chicago and Pittsburgh. Even more specifically, it is an effort to understand why some urban polities are more conducive to progressive initiatives than others.

Borrowing from numerous works (including those by Clavel, Clavel and Kleniewski, Krumholz and Clavel, and Nyden and Wiewel), the picture that emerges of a progressive political system is one characterized by inclusionary governing coalitions, public participation in planning, a concern for equitable policies and balanced development, and a greater focus on neighborhoods.[7] According to these criteria, Pittsburgh's political system generally has been more progressive than Chicago's; within Chicago, the Washington administration (1983–1987) was without question the most progressive administration in the city between 1955 and the present.[8] These contrasts point to several broad areas of inquiry that inform the overall analysis: First, why are some political systems more amenable to neighborhood inclusion in decision-making activities than others? Second, what forms does neighborhood mobilization take, why does it take such forms, and how does that affect chances for inclusion? Third, what are the obstacles to progressive governance? Finally, it is essential to examine the issue of neighborhood participation; while my sympathies are clearly on the side of neighborhood inclusion, there are many critics of "backyard populism" and many reasons to be critical.

URBAN REGIMES AND URBAN ARENAS

In exploring these areas of inquiry, it is necessary to disassemble the broad and somewhat amorphous concept of urban "political system" into more manageable analytical constructs. Regime theory, by focusing on the informal arrangements that coalesce in order to govern within a particular city, provides a fruitful starting place. According to regime theory, the American political economy is characterized by "a division of labor between market and state."[9] Public and legal powers, as well as overall responsibility for citizen well-being, are concentrated in the state, while ownership and control of productive assets are typically in private hands. At the local level, where governmental authority is the most constrained and fragmentation is a defining characteristic, the division is especially problematic. Effective governance, defined as the ability to make and carry out policy, necessitates a bridging of this divide. The concept of an "urban regime" captures this bridging process. By bringing together economic and political elites, a regime constitutes the "informal arrangements by which public bodies and private interests function together in order to be able to make and carry out governing decisions."[10] Since cooperation is fundamental to this relationship but is not automatic, the questions of "who cooperates and how their cooperation is achieved" are central to understanding how a city is governed and its overall policy orientation. Hence, two critical components of regime analysis are the composition of the governing regime and the accommodation process among its elements.

Regime theory has served as an important corrective to the pluralist ("politics is everything") and the determinist ("politics is irrelevant") schools of analysis. In so doing, it has reorganized how we think about urban politics. In successfully challenging key assumptions of the pluralist and determinist paradigms, regime theory has allowed, indeed forced, us to examine other critical aspects of urban politics. Rejecting the pluralist notion that there is an autonomous state that sufficiently empowers government to make and carry out policy, regime theory poses the question "What makes governance possible?" Parting company with the pluralist conception of distinct spheres of economic and political activity, and with the determinist's view that politics is subordinate to economics, regime theory suggests a two-way relationship between politics and economics.[11] Answering the question of what makes governance possible thus forces us to explore the conditions under which economic and political actors come together and encourages us to grapple with issues of cooperation and collective action.

In rejecting the state autonomy argument and the instrumentalist's view that all activities are dictated by the prevailing mode of production, regime theory also promotes an alternative conception of power. Instead of the social control model of power that characterizes these two paradigms, Stone suggests a social production model. Where coercion (power over) figures prominently in the social control model, cooperation (power to) is the reigning factor in social production.[12] When we consider that regime theory has given us an alternative way of viewing authority, governance, and power—three of the most important issues in any polity—we can begin to appreciate its critical impact on the study of urban politics.

As useful as regime theory has been, there is still more work to be done. Much more attention must be given to the critical role of institutional and cultural factors in influencing political organization and decision making. As currently constituted, though, regime theory may draw too much attention to the mediating impact of city-specific regimes. According to regime theory, policy choices are best understood as the result of the coalitional needs of the governing regime. Regime change is essentially a maintenance strategy, and policy, a mechanism for empowering regime members. The potential in regime theory for equating the regime with the overall political system is enormously tempting.

The incorporation of institutional and cultural variables allows us to resist the strong gravitational pull that coalition-centered analysis can have, but it still may leave us with more than we can analytically digest. Chicago and Pittsburgh, for instance, have many of the same institutions (i.e., political party, political machine, ward organizations) and city agencies (i.e., planning, urban renewal and redevelopment, housing). Nevertheless, these similar entities operate differently and exhibit varying degrees of importance within the two cities. How do we avoid addressing these differences in anything but a descriptive fashion?

The concept of "arenas" provides an organizational solution. Arenas are "spheres of activity"[13] that are distinguished by particular institutional frameworks and underlying political cultures that lend a structure to these activities.

Local political systems are made up of numerous arenas—electoral, civic, business, intergovernmental. Which institutions within the city are prominent and how they operate depends largely on which arena is the primary home of activity; a brief comparison between the civic and electoral arenas illustrates this point. Civic arenas tend to be dominated by private, nonprofit institutions that distribute resources on a collective basis and foster a cooperative culture. Electoral arenas are often dominated by partisan[14] institutions that distribute resources on a market exchange basis and, in so doing, create highly competitive environments. At the level of the specific institution, we can also see the impact of arenas on operating styles. Pittsburgh's housing department, heavily influenced by the salient position the civic arena enjoyed in that city, engaged in innovative programs and partnerships with the private sector. Chicago's housing department, under the sway of the electoral arena, was essentially a patronage operation prior to the Washington administration (see chapter 5).

Arenas can thus be said to have a distinct logic. They operate according to certain norms, rules, and principles derived from the institutional and cultural frameworks they embody.[15] These norms, rules, and principles shape the types of relationships that develop (e.g., vertical or horizontal; highly or loosely structured), the form that political mobilization and organization takes, the types of conflicts that can be aired, the opportunities for leadership, and the policy options that can be considered.

Although a regime typically is involved in more than one arena, there is a primary one toward which the regime's power is oriented. This orientation is heavily influenced by the regime's principal objectives (e.g., political power, economic growth). If the regime is powerful enough, the entire political system will be shaped by the logic and culture of the particular arena it favors.

The significance of arenas tends to be underemphasized in much regime analysis. Partly, this results from method; regime analysis typically is conducted through a single case study. It also stems from the implicit assumption that power is rooted disproportionately within the business community. While this may be the case structurally (i.e., the private sector commands most of the economic resources, and governmental authority is highly fragmented), it does not necessarily follow that at the level of the individual regime power relations always will resemble this pattern. The interests of business can be well served in a regime dominated by political elites. This was certainly the case for Chicago under Richard J. Daley.

Finally, regime theory underestimates the significance of arenas because of the disproportionate emphasis it places on the activities and behavior of elites within the city. As this study shows, however, the issue of who dominates the regime is critical to other, nonelite interests within the city (e.g., neighborhoods, racial minorities) since it influences the arena in which most activity will occur. The particular arena that comes to characterize politics within a city has important implications for the ability of other interests to access and influence the policy-making process. Consequently, the balance of power between political and economic elites within a particular regime is not to be assumed but needs to be empirically tested because of its implications for the type of arena that will be dominant. Once we accept that such variation in regimes exists, the issue of arenas becomes quite relevant. To reiterate, the key elements constituting governing regimes, political elites and business elites, are predisposed toward working in different arenas. This has serious consequences for neighborhood organizations since in order to participate they must negotiate the institutional and cultural terrain of the dominant arena in their municipality.

The relationship between arenas and their institutional and cultural frameworks is mutually reinforcing. In the electoral arena, for instance, the continued distribution of resources on an individual exchange basis strengthens the underlying logic of competition. This logic, in turn, feeds back into and strengthens institutional behavior and practice. This relationship between institutional frameworks, political culture, and the arenas that house them has critical implications for political change. Groups seeking incorporation essentially have three choices: they can use the logic of the dominant arena to make their case, which is what happened in Pittsburgh; they can seek to change the underlying logic of the dominant arena, which was the unsuccessful strategy employed in Chicago; or they can shift operations to another arena if the first two options are not viable.

This interactive feature distinguishes my use of the concept of arenas from its use elsewhere in the policy literature. Efforts by Theodore Lowi and more recently by Paul Peterson to develop policy typologies have been essentially unidirectional.[16] Their argument that policy shapes politics implicitly assumes that government is an autonomous actor, unaffected by the power of organized interests. A more accurate depiction would be one in which both politics and policy move back and forth between dependent and independent variables, but even this picture is limited because it assumes that policy and politics occur in an organizational vacuum. We know, for instance, that the same policy can result in very different political relations in different cities. Similarly, not all cities have the same policies. Thus, we are forced to go beyond the "policy causes politics" or "politics causes policy" explanations. The concept of arenas as used here permits a broader examination by calling attention to such intervening factors as institutional structure, cultural attributes, decision-making rules, and patterns of resource distribution.

In addition to mediating policy and political mobilization, the institutional and cultural frameworks of the specific arena may contribute to some degree of regime alteration. This broader conception of urban governance moves us away from the stilted unidirectionality of the policy arenas concept and from regime theory's focus on internal coalitional dynamics. Regime theory is expanded to more seriously consider the balance of power among regime members and the objectives of the regime, which in turn will influence the primary arena of operation. By linking regime theory to the concept of urban arenas, we can focus on

GOVERNING REGIMES   7

Table 1.1. Regime Theory and Urban Arenas: Components of Analysis

Governing regime[a]	Arena
Composition (who)	Logic
Accommodation process (how)[b]	Institutional framework
Objectives (what)	Political culture
Principle arena of activity (where)	

[a] The various components of the regime, in particular the "how" and the "what," influence the selection of arenas.
[b] Balance of power among regime members.

the critical elements of the institutional framework and the political culture that contribute to shaping the direction of the city's politics and policy. This linkage will provide a way to compare cities, a latent but as yet undeveloped dimension of regime theory. The comparative perspective can illustrate what forms of political mobilization are possible under different institutional arrangements. Finally, we will be able to develop some generalizations about the prospects for progressive policy at the local level. Table 1.1 illustrates the broad contours of the analysis.

Institutional Framework

The inclusion of arenas in the analysis forces us to pay more attention to institutional frameworks than is typical in regime analysis, which tends to focus more on informal governing arrangements than on formal structures and their influence on political behavior. While Elkin has emphasized the centrality of institutional arrangements in his typology of urban regimes, he noted that the "consequences" of institutional variation over time had not been investigated.[17] Such an investigation can illuminate the relationship between institutional structure (or framework) and the forms of political mobilization and interest representation that can develop within a given polity.[18]

As used here, the institutional framework refers to the larger environment within which specific institutions operate. This environment contains critical elements that collectively set the tone for how particular institutions operate, thereby shaping expectations of acceptable forms of behavior. These elements include decision-making rules, patterns of resource distribution, degree of formalization, general orientation, and governing orientation. Table 1.2 displays some of these critical elements and their possible characteristics.

Each of these elements is critical to some aspect of group formation and demand articulation. Decision making and formalization affect access and information; orientation and resource distribution influence the issues around which it is feasible to organize; governing orientation influences the choice of tactics. These individual elements combine to form a larger pattern. Assuming that institutions are "devices for achieving purposes,"[19] it follows that the elements within them

Table 1.2. Institutional Framework

Element	Characteristic
Orientation	Geographic
	Electoral
	Functional
	Programmatic
Degree of formalization[a]	High/low
Decision making	Open/closed
	Consensual/conflictual
Resource distribution	Individual/collective
	Targeted/dispersed
Governing orientation	Social control/social production

[a] Refers to the number of institutions within the overall framework and the degree of formal procedures/requirements within individual institutions.

will be coherently linked. For example, we are not likely to find an institutional framework characterized by open and consensual decision making that also engages in social control (i.e., coercive behavior) practices.

These patterns are critical because they shape our perceptions regarding acceptable forms of behavior. Since perceptions are important determinants of actions, these patterns and the institutional frameworks that house them serve as opportunity structures, empowering certain types of activities while constraining others. Thus, institutional frameworks play a critical role in shaping the opportunities for, and conditions of, participation in the political system.

Political Culture

The form and effectiveness of political participation are also shaped by the predominant political culture, by which I mean the collective expectations of the population about the roles and behavior of their government and political system. In the broadest sense, all U.S. cities operate within the political culture of liberal democratic capitalism which shapes our expectations about the roles of the public and private sectors. The market, as Lindblom has asserted, not only imprisons policy but severely constrains intellectual thought and scholarly research.[20] This political culture, to the extent that it reinforces structural factors, especially the "privileged position of business" in capitalist society,[21] constrains progressive policy initiatives.

The emphasis on individualism within the larger political culture constitutes yet another limitation to progressive efforts. In a recent book review essay, John Gray eloquently writes, "The ruling American culture of liberal individualism treats communal attachments and civic engagement as optional extras on a fixed menu of individual choice and market exchange."[22] This logic undergirds much of the mainstream thinking on urban policy. Although many scholars feel that public choice theory and the "city limits" thesis[23] have been adequately picked apart, their grip on local policy remains firm. In fact, I would extend Gray's observation to say that when "communal attachments" and "civic engagement" seek to alter the workings of the market, they go from being "optional extras" to obstructionist enemies.

This larger political culture, within which all cities operate, is mediated by local political cultures that may create further obstacles for progressive policy or may enhance the possibilities for such policy. Although the larger political culture renders civic engagement and communal attachments as "optional extras," some local political cultures encourage civic participation. All things being equal, this type of culture would provide a more supportive environment for progressive policy initiatives than one characterized by individualistic and market-oriented behavior.

Local political cultures can be especially important at the institutional level, where most policy change is implemented. Robert Putnam's work on Italy's regional governments is particularly instructive here.[24] In 1970 the Italian government established fifteen regional governments that had the same constitutional structures and mandates but that varied significantly in overall effectiveness, political practice, and democratic governance.[25] Since institutional structure clearly was not the explanatory variable, other reasons were sought. After empirically testing the role of civic community (as measured by civic engagement, political equality, solidarity, trust and tolerance, and active associations) and socioeconomic modernity, Putnam concluded that civic community was a much better predictor of institutional performance than was economic development. Moreover, he concluded that civic community often explained economic development and not the other way around.

Putnam's findings have enormous implications for how we think about policy and political change. The role of institutions in shaping political interactions and resource opportunities would lead one to conclude that institutional change is a necessary and sufficient condition for overall policy change. This would especially be the case if we are seeking to broaden the franchise to accommodate more groups and/or a wider range of interests. Such a conclusion is tempered, however, by the potential impact of political culture. As Putnam's findings in Italy suggest, changing the structure or function of an institution while leaving the underlying political (and institutional) culture untouched may amount to nothing more than moving boxes on an organizational flow chart.

This somber conclusion suggests that we view political change as a long-term, comprehensive, dynamic process that must incorporate political education; it requires alteration in values, perceptions, expectations, and ultimately behavior. Hence, political change is an ongoing process that will feature progress as well as regress. And, the greater the disjunction between the changes being sought and the existing political culture, the more arduous the task and the longer the time required for actual change. As described in this book, this disjunction between political culture, as rooted in institutional structure, and policy change was one of the biggest obstacles facing the Washington administration in Chicago.

In exploring the impact of political culture on the nature and effectiveness of neighborhood mobilization, this study focuses on social capital, underlying values, and civic attachment. Borrowing from Putnam, social capital refers to the "features of social organization, such as trust, norms, and networks that can improve the efficiency of society by facilitating coordinated actions."[26] The social organizations in this study are the governing regimes in the two cities and the arenas in which they principally operate. According to Putnam, the higher the stock of social capital, the easier it is to achieve voluntary cooperation among members of a community. In comparing Pittsburgh and Chicago, we should find a positive correlation between social capital and social production.

Overall behavior will also be influenced by the underlying values within a political culture. Does the local political culture enhance the tendency toward strong individualism found in the larger political culture, or does it contain values of communalism and collective enterprise?

Finally, what is the nature of civic attachment? Civic attachment, as used here, refers not to the number of organizations or groups within a given society but to the sense of attachment these groups feel toward the larger governing regime. Groups that feel alienated from the governing regime are more likely to pursue an adversarial course of action than are groups that have a strong sense of attachment to the regime. Thus, civic attachment affects the form that mobilization takes and, even more specifically, the strategies and tactics that are adopted.

Urban Arenas, Institutional Frameworks, and Political Culture

Although discussed separately, institutional frameworks and political culture interact, thereby reinforcing each other and the underlying logic of the arena in which they are found. Putnam's examination of the regional governments in Italy demonstrated this interactive quality. His treatment of institutions as both independent (shaping political behavior) and dependent (being shaped by history) variables underscores this relationship. In a study of neighborhood mobilization in the United States, Jeffrey Henig has also advanced this connection. Examining cases from Chicago and Minneapolis, Henig concludes that neighborhoods with preexisting organizational ties, strong social bonds, strong geographic identification, and "habits of cooperation" facilitated the "sociable" as opposed to the atomistic aspects of the individual.[27] Although Henig does not use the labels "institutional" and "cultural," his findings can easily be categorized in these terms. Although his unit of analysis was the neighborhood and mine is the city, the comparison of Pittsburgh and Chicago illustrates a similar integration of institutional and cultural factors. Figure 1.1 illustrates the components of the comparative examination of Pittsburgh and Chicago. The various components of the governing

GOVERNING REGIMES   11

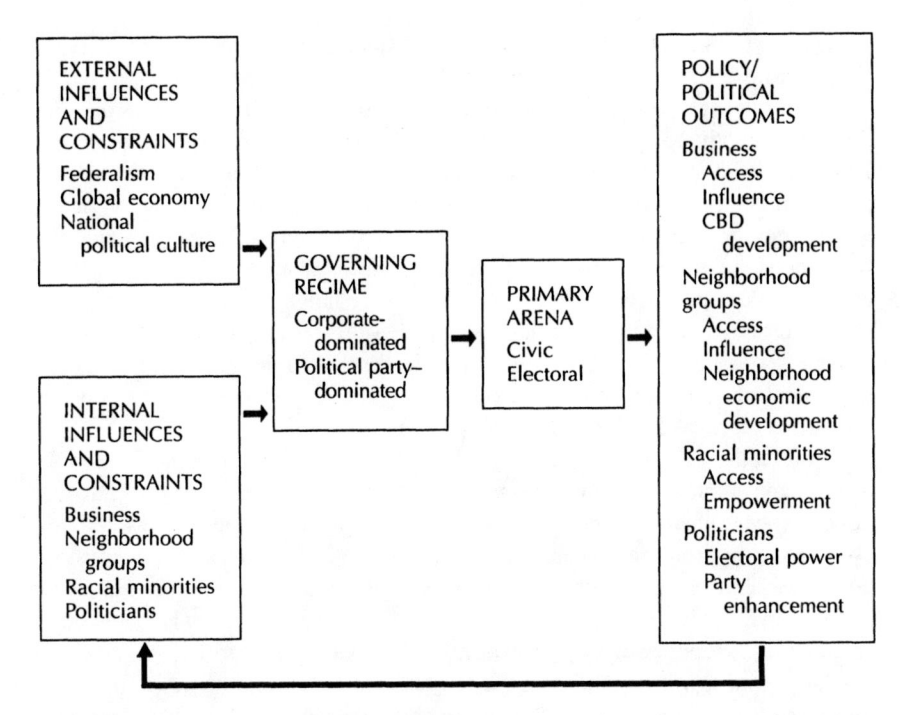

```
┌─────────────────┐
│ EXTERNAL        │
│ INFLUENCES      │
│ AND             │
│ CONSTRAINTS     │
│ Federalism      │
│ Global economy  │
│ National        │
│  political      │
│  culture        │
└────────┬────────┘
         │
         ▼
┌─────────────────┐     ┌──────────┐     ┌─────────────────┐
│ GOVERNING       │     │ PRIMARY  │     │ POLICY/         │
│ REGIME          │ ──▶ │ ARENA    │ ──▶ │ POLITICAL       │
│ Corporate-      │     │ Civic    │     │ OUTCOMES        │
│  dominated      │     │ Electoral│     │ ...             │
│ Political party-│     └──────────┘     └─────────────────┘
│  dominated      │
└────────▲────────┘
         │
┌─────────────────┐
│ INTERNAL        │
│ INFLUENCES      │
│ AND             │
│ CONSTRAINTS     │
│ Business        │
│ Neighborhood    │
│  groups         │
│ Racial minorities│
│ Politicians     │
└─────────────────┘
```

POLICY/POLITICAL OUTCOMES:
Business — Access, Influence, CBD development
Neighborhood groups — Access, Influence, Neighborhood economic development
Racial minorities — Access, Empowerment
Politicians — Electoral power, Party enhancement

Figure 1.1. The Mediating Role of Governing Regimes and Urban Arenas in Local Decision Making.

regime, in particular the balance of power between political and economic elites and, accordingly, the primary regime objectives, will influence the selection of arenas (e.g., electoral or civic) through which most political activity occurs. The institutional and cultural attributes of the selected arena serve to mediate group demands (form, content, and outcome) as well as regime policies.

CHALLENGING THE GROWTH MACHINE: THE CASE FOR NEIGHBORHOOD POLITICS

The previous discussion has argued that regime analysis has been a very useful tool for examining urban policy but that it must be expanded to include a consideration of the dominant arena in a particular municipality. This expansion is especially important when examining the opportunities for political participation available to nonelites. Thus, two questions arise. First, does it make any difference to interests challenging the governing regime which arena is dominant? The comparison of Pittsburgh and Chicago in the following chapters will shed considerable light on this issue. But perhaps even more fundamental is the question of why urban analysts should be concerned at all about the activities and effectiveness of such nonelite interests as neighborhood organizations. It is to this issue we now turn.

In exploring challenges to the governing regimes, this study focuses primarily on neighborhood groups or community-based organizations (CBOs) (here the terms are used interchangeably). Within policy-making circles, the neglect of neighborhoods has been severe. Imprisoned by market ideology, captured by vested economic interests, and egged on by a booster media, city policy makers have focused their attention on the central business district and the few neighborhoods deemed "gentrifiable." CBOs have challenged this "growth machine" orientation and have sought to broaden the geographic and substantive scope of policy making and to bring more interests into the policy-making process. According to the criteria set out earlier, these organizations constitute a force for progressive politics at the local level.

Politically, CBOs serve valuable functions. Through their economic development and community organizing activities, they bring ordinary citizens into the policy process, thereby exposing them to the complexity of local issues and decision-making processes. Understanding what the issues are and appreciating their complexity is becoming more important. As the U.S. economy continues to "streamline," "downsize," and "restructure," the public will have to be educated about the increasingly prevalent trade-offs between priorities. At the local level, the issue is not, nor should it be, neighborhoods versus downtown. Both are necessary; alone they are not sufficient to rendering a city vital. Rather, the costs, benefits, and trade-offs of decisions must be viewed from the perspective of balanced development so that rational and fair decisions can be made and compensatory mechanisms employed when the larger public interest requires that particular interests be sacrificed. Decisions made behind closed doors reflect the interests of those on the inside; neighborhoods often rise or fall as a result of those decisions.

CBOs have also been instrumental in promoting more balanced policy initiatives. In his study of linkage policies in Boston, San Francisco, and Santa Monica, for instance, Dennis Keating concludes that one of the critical factors in adopting such policies is the existence of political support from progressive politicians and "candidates backed by neighborhood organizations."[28] At the national level, pressure from community activists has resulted in the passage of numerous neighborhood-oriented policies and programs: the Community Reinvestment Act (CRA), Community Development Block Grant (CDBG), Comprehensive Housing Affordability Strategy (CHAS),[29] Community Outreach Partnership Center (COPC), and Empowerment Zones.

A common theme to these policies, and a belief held by those who advocated for them, is the view that cities consist of interdependent parts. Although downtown areas house significant amounts of economic activity, neighborhoods constitute the center of social activity and familial institutions. To paraphrase Evans and Boyte, neighborhoods are the soil in which the "free spaces" between our private lives and the large, impersonal institutions that surround us can grow. It is within these "free spaces" (voluntary associations rooted in community life) that we find the potential for civic virtue, for the realization of the common good, and for the fulfillment of the democratic promise.[30]

Incorporating neighborhoods into urban analysis thus adds a normative dimension currently lacking in the economic development or marketplace conception of the city. We can begin to examine questions of participation, citizenship, and quality of life, the fundamentals of a polity, a human city, and a humane society.

Even if one does not accept this broader view of the city, which I would argue is a grave mistake, the reality is that cities are home to millions of people, the majority of whom neither work nor live downtown. A policy orientation focused almost exclusively on downtown, and thus catering to a minority, has serious political, social, and ethical costs. CBOs have been the most vociferous proponents of this argument and consequently are a thorn in the side of many downtown-focused politicians and policy makers. To many others, they are a reminder that cities, neighborhoods, and people matter.

In arguing for a strong neighborhood presence in policy discussions, I am not seeking to uncritically romanticize all neighborhood initiatives or all CBOs. The development of "free spaces," as Boyte himself has noted, is often preempted by the "cynical language of narrow interests."[31] All too often, these interests are expressed in racial terms. Many of the early "neighborhood improvement associations," for instance, formed to keep blacks out of their neighborhoods, a development that, unfortunately, is still not confined to the history books.

Even when race is not the overriding factor, many CBOs still tend toward a narrow parochialism that is usually geographic in nature. The "urban trenches" that Ira Katznelson unearthed in his study of New York City did not disappear with the political machines that nurtured them. The tug of community is still strong enough to separate political man from economic man, thus impeding efforts to forge larger, class-based movements.

Such parochialism also helps to nurture the "siege mentality" that is so characteristic of many urban neighborhoods. Whether it is threats of gentrification, disinvestment, or the death and destruction of crime- and drug-ravaged streets, many urban dwellers see their neighborhoods as imperiled entities precariously existing in openly hostile territory. It is not long before an "us versus them" mentality takes hold. While the idea of an external enemy helps to organize a neighborhood (indeed this was the organizational approach of Saul Alinsky), it makes it difficult to forge any alliances beyond the neighborhood.

This "enclave consciousness," which Sidney Plotkin argues is endemic to the American notion of community, also features a strong sense of neighborhood independence. While this can foster feelings of pride and encourage participation in the life of the community, it can also create a false sense of separation from the rest of society.[32] The cry of "neighborhood schools for neighborhood children," which was loudly sounded in several Boston neighborhoods in the 1970s, was at once an appeal to neighborhood pride and independence and a way of opting out of the larger school integration movement.[33]

The interaction between enclave consciousness, neighborhood independence, and external threats, to the extent that it becomes pathological, can create a city of "geographical islands of autonomy."[34] Clearly, this is not in the interests of a larger neighborhood movement, which is precisely what is required if individual neighborhoods are to experience true empowerment. Given the relative political weakness of individual neighborhoods, it is only through collective enterprise that they can be strengthened. It also represents a contradiction in ideological terms. If neighborhoods command loyalty from residents on the basis of communal ties, then the city as a whole should command similar loyalty from neighborhoods. To the extent that CBOs promote enclave consciousness, they are doing a disservice to this larger movement in both political and ideological terms.

Another criticism often leveled at neighborhoods and their organizational representatives is that they are reactionary; they do not promote any positive visions but only obstruct other people's plans. In defense of the obstructionist role, it should be noted that neighborhood residents have typically mobilized against policies or developments that would have had a devastating effect on their neighborhood. Urban renewal is perhaps the best example of a policy that destroyed many low- and moderate-income neighborhoods in the name of saving them. Moreover, as chapter 4 shows, local decision making, especially regarding site selection for urban renewal projects, was often a political rather than a "rational" process, with the results reflecting the balance of power among local elites. Poorer neighborhoods were not part of or important to this elite circle, and thus often had to assume the role of victim—usually at steep costs.

While not so much a criticism as a caution, there is also a strong potential for the populist rhetoric that accompanies many community-based initiatives to backfire on the proponents. The emphasis on grassroots participation and local decision making can easily became an excuse for governmental neglect. When the term "community empowerment" was used in the 1960s, it meant community control of government programs, an unnerving feature to political conservatives. During the 1980s, many of these same conservatives embraced the notion of community empowerment, reinterpreting it to mean the replacement of government obligation with local voluntarism. The Reagan and Bush administrations, for instance, touted the virtues of local communities while at the same time cutting much of the federal aid these communities so desperately needed.

These issues point to some very real tensions in community organizing. While we tend to applaud expressions of community attachment, loyalty, and local citizenship, these attributes can be a formidable obstacle to the formation of progressive urban regimes to the extent that they promote a fierce enclave consciousness. This phenomenon is exacerbated when issues of race, class, or resource distribution are involved. Richard DeLeon's typology of the "three lefts" is instructive here. His examination of liberals, environmentalists, and populists—the groups that comprise San Francisco's "three lefts"—indicates the difficulties of coalition building in the face of diverse and at times competing objectives, constituencies, and turf. The three lefts were able to come together to form a progressive "antiregime" but have not been able to overcome internal differences to a degree sufficient enough to form a proactive regime. Indeed, even the antiregime coalition showed serious signs of rupture.[35]

In Chicago, a city much less diverse than San Francisco, race was clearly the most divisive issue in Washington's progressive coalition. As chapter 5 shows, some neighborhood groups used Washington's own pro-neighborhood platform to camouflage their racial objectives. Although the effort was fairly transparent to many, it still created enormous difficulties for Washington and placed severe strains on his coalition.

Swanstrom's analysis of Kucinich in Cleveland has also demonstrated the connection between populism and racism, albeit in a different spirit than in Chicago. Faced with a tough reelection campaign, Kucinich appended sharp racial overtones to his populist, neighborhood appeals.[36] Frank Rizzo, the champion of white working-class neighborhoods, also relied heavily on race to woo electoral support in Philadelphia, the City of Brotherly Love.

This study neither resolves nor ignores the tensions inherent in backyard populism. It proceeds on the premise that challenges to the growth machine represent a promising corrective to the narrow preoccupation of many urban policy makers with the central business district. As the major source of this challenge, CBOs have often transcended the "reactive" stage to produce alternative paradigms for economic development. Moreover, many of the tensions that characterize community-based initiatives and community organizing are endemic to democratic political systems in general—for example, localism versus globalism, inclusionary versus exclusionary practices, conservative versus liberal tendencies.

Consequently, in response to the earlier question (Why study neighborhood organizing efforts?), the answer is both normative and practical. Normatively, neighborhood challenges to the growth machine allow us to examine efforts to broaden the policy franchise so that more interests within the city are positively served by government decisions. Practically, they enable us to examine the nagging and persistent problems of democratic politics and governance. Studying these efforts in the context of the analytical framework established here will permit us to identify the impact of urban arenas and their institutional and cultural attributes on the opportunities for political participation by nonelite interests within the city.

THE STUDY

Pittsburgh and Chicago provide a good testing ground to examine the influence of institutional frameworks and political culture on policy development and political organization. On the surface the two cities have had very similar regimes,

Pro-growth in orientation, the regimes have pursued economic development strategies centered around downtown physical development. Similarly, both cities boast a plethora of highly talented and politically sophisticated CBOs. Despite these similarities, the regimes responded quite differently when confronted with neighborhood demands for resources and inclusion in policy-making activities. In Pittsburgh the response was quite favorable, resulting in neighborhood incorporation that ultimately changed the nature of the regime. In Chicago the response was resistance as political elites tried desperately, and usually successfully, to protect the status quo.

Understanding the different responses requires that we look at the formative impact of each city's political history, institutional framework, and political culture on regime behavior and group mobilization. Chapters 2 and 3 provide the historical and contextual basis for understanding the development paths of the two regimes and their implications for progressive politics. We will see how the distinct history of each city's development interacted with demographic, economic, and political factors to promote and shape two distinct arenas—one conducive to neighborhood demands for incorporation and the other prone to frustrate neighborhood and progressive policy initiatives.

Chapter 2 provides the basic profiles of the two cities. While sharing much common ground (e.g., strong industrial base followed by massive economic restructuring, entrenched political machines, employment and population loss, development-oriented regimes), a point worth emphasizing is their difference. As will be discussed in greater detail, Pittsburgh has enjoyed much more stability than Chicago in terms of its racial and ethnic composition and its elite structure. Historically, Pittsburgh's highly centralized business community produced an undisputed set of leaders who headed the city's informal governing arrangements for many years. The city has also demonstrated remarkable stability in its political and neighborhood leadership. Chicago, by contrast, has been sharply divided by race, has a much more fragmented business community, and since Richard J. Daley's death in 1976 has experienced significant political upheaval. The relative stability that characterizes much of Pittsburgh's environment has allowed elites there to be more accommodational, whereas elites in Chicago perceived a need to impose order on a rapidly changing environment.

The dissimilar behavior of elites in the two cities is also explained by who the respective elites were and where their power was rooted. Chapter 3, in chronicling the development of the pro-growth regimes in the two cities, pays particular attention to the distinct accommodation processes in Pittsburgh and Chicago. We will see that the pro-growth regimes structured power very differently, which significantly affected institutional development and the particular channeling of resources.

The behavior of elites, the type of institutions created, and the pattern of resource distribution shaped the opportunities for neighborhood mobilization. Chapter 4 highlights how these opportunities differed in the two cities by looking at the first serious challenges to the growth machines. Pittsburgh's elites demonstrated expansionist or accommodationist tendencies, which set a precedent for future cooperation between CBOs and the governing regime. It also solidified the pattern of channeling resources through institutions in the civic arena, thus paving the way for a unidimensional progressivism centered around neighborhood empowerment. In Chicago the governing regime resisted challenges to its neighborhood development plans, setting in motion an acrimonious course of relations between neighborhoods and the governing regime. Progressive efforts, consequently, assumed a more confrontational and multidimensional tone in a city where the electoral arena was dominant.

The implications, for neighborhoods, of these distinct patterns are more fully developed in chapter 5, which focuses on mayoral efforts to incorporate neighborhoods into the policy-making schema. The chapter emphasizes how the political and institutional dissimilarities between the two cities helped to shape different mayoral strategies. Under two neighborhood-oriented mayors, Pittsburgh's governing regime moved, in evolutionary fashion, toward incorporating neighborhoods in the larger corporatist structure. In Chicago, one mayor retreated from pro-neighborhood beginnings while another marched furiously toward neighborhood incorporation, setting off a revolution in the process. The chapter also emphasizes the divisiveness of the race issue in Chicago and its negative impact on the neighborhood movement.

Chapter 6 explores the difficulties in building and sustaining multidimensional progressive regimes. Harold Washington's efforts to radically change the form and content of Chicago city government underscore the relationship between institutional structures and political, or institutional, culture. This relationship renders change a long-term process. Maintaining the political base of support for such change, however, is difficult, especially when a shrinking pie further diminishes the available opportunities, thus drawing particular attention to how the pie is sliced. When racial divisions are added to the equation, the results can be particularly explosive.

Chapter 7 examines the limits to consensual politics in Pittsburgh. When the Steel Valley Authority (SVA) sought to reopen steel mills under worker-ownership arrangements, it posed a direct challenge to the power of key members of the governing regime. Tracing the SVA's unsuccessful efforts underscores the larger structural barriers to progressive change. It also reveals the unidimensionality of Pittsburgh's progressivism and the difficulties in deviating from established patterns of the dominant civic arena.

The book concludes with an examination of the prospects for progressive politics at the local level.

While I have tried to maintain a somewhat orderly chronology of events, this book is not meant to be a recent political history of Chicago and Pittsburgh. Thus, there is movement across time periods when conceptualization requires it. Moreover, since the point is to explore neighborhood challenges to the growth machine orientation, this book focuses on the formation, execution, and results of those challenges. In both cities the formative period of neighborhood organizing begins with urban renewal. In Pittsburgh the next two stages encompass the Flaherty and Caliguiri years (1969–1988). The Masloff administration (1988–1994) represented, in terms of our examination, a continuation of Caliguiri. The Murphy administration (1994–present) has juggled some individuals and organizations, but as of 1996 the larger system of neighborhood incorporation is still intact. In Chicago there was a brief period of neighborhood incorporation under Harold Washington (1983–1987). While not totally disenfranchised, neighborhoods, as legitimate components of the policy agenda, lost considerable ground following Washington's death. In terms of general patterns, the overall climate of adversarial relations between CBOs and city government, and between CBOs and the machine orientation of many ward organizations, still characterizes Chicago politics.

2
The Changing Political Economy of Pittsburgh and Chicago

> *Just as physics teaches that it is sometimes useful to treat light as a particle and other times as a wave, so political analysis may find it useful to treat power sometimes in terms of the social-control model and other times in terms of the social-production model.*
>
> —Clarence Stone

On one level the stories of Pittsburgh and Chicago are quite familiar. Both are older industrial cities that experienced large population losses and a mass exodus of manufacturing jobs in the post–World War II period. In response, business and political elites carried out economic development strategies geared toward the new service-based economy. Both cities had entrenched political machines with significant clout in the city, region, and state. The economic and political conditions explain both why the two cities embarked on major economic development campaigns and how they were able to create strong pro-growth regimes in the first place. What they fail to explain is why the two regimes responded differently to specific development projects (see chapters 3 and 4) and to neighborhood demands. While a large part of this difference can be explained by the different accommodation processes between political and economic elites and the consequent institution building that took place (see chapter 2), it must be remembered that elites do not operate in a vacuum. Rather, their actions are shaped by and in turn help to shape the environment in which they operate.

A close look at the patterns of demographic change, the impacts of economic restructuring, and the evolution of the political machines will show marked differences between the two cities. In Pittsburgh these changes did not have the same wrenching effects that they did in Chicago. In fact, Pittsburgh's overall demography, its elite structure, and its institutional, political, and neighborhood leadership have exhibited remarkable stability. Supportive of and interacting with this stability is a political culture that emphasizes civic responsibility, cooperation, and a strong dose of deference. Chicago, by contrast, has been sharply divided by race, has a much more contested elite structure, and, since Richard J. Daley's death in 1976, has experienced significant political upheaval. The longstanding identification of politics with crass material exchange and of government with overt favoritism has shaped a political culture characterized by mistrust and cynicism. The relative stability that characterizes much of Pittsburgh's environment and a political culture that promotes civic-minded relations and cooperative behavior have allowed and encouraged elites there to be more accommodational than their counterparts in Chicago, who perceived a need to impose control on a rapidly changing environment.

DEMOGRAPHIC CHANGE

For both cities the demographic picture is one of significant decline. For Chicago the 1990 census came like a one-two punch; first, its population dipped below the 3 million mark, declining from 3,550,404 in 1960 to 2,783,726 in 1990. Second, Chicago was forced to cede its famed "second-city status" to Los Angeles. The statistics were equally grim for Pittsburgh; between 1950 and 1990 the city lost nearly half of its population (676,806 to 369,879). Behind these aggregate data, however, lie two dissimilar stories: substantial diversity and change in Chicago, and a relative absence of diversity combined with significant stability in Pittsburgh.

With a population that is 39 percent African American, 19.6 percent Hispanic, and 3.7 percent Asian, Chicago is clearly more diversified than Pittsburgh, which has a comparatively smaller African American population (25.8 percent), a nearly invisible Hispanic population (0.9 percent), and an only slightly larger Asian population (1.6 percent) Even these numbers do not reveal the full extent of Chicago's diversity; Chicago's Hispanic population, for instance, is composed of Mexicans (352,560) and Puerto Ricans (119,866), the two traditional groups, Cubans (approximately 16,000), and a wide array of newer immigrants from South and Central America, the Caribbean, and Spain. Similarly, the Asian population includes Chinese, Vietnamese, Cambodians, Hmongs, and Koreans. These ethnic differences are further reflected in language patterns; nearly 30 percent of Chicagoans speak a language other than English at home, compared with only 8.5 percent for Pittsburgh. And, despite Chicago's sizable Hispanic population, Spanish accounts for only a little over half of the 29.1 percent.

In addition to greater diversity, Chicago's population experienced much quicker change. The African American population, which until quite recently was the fastest-growing, went from 22.8 percent of the population in 1960 to 35.7 percent in 1970 to 39.83 percent in 1980. The comparable figures for Pittsburgh

Table 2.1. Basic Population Characteristics: Chicago and Pittsburgh

Population	Chicago		Pittsburgh	
1992	2,768,483		366,582	
1990	2,783,726		369,879	
1980	3,005,072		423,959	
Decrease 1980–1992	−7.9%		−13.5%	
White, 1990	1,263,524	(45%)	266,791	(72%)
Black	1,087,711	(39%)	95,362	(25.8%)
Hispanic	545,852	(19.6%)	3,468	(.9%)
Mexican	352,560		926	
Puerto Rican	119,866		711	
Asian	104,118	(3.7%)	5,937	(1.6%)
Foreign born	16.9%		4.6%	
Language other than English	29.1		8.5	
Spanish	17.4		1.3	
Median age	31.3		34.6	
Education				
High school graduate or more	66.0%		72.4%	
College degree or more	19.5		20.1	
Median family income	$30,707		$27,484	
Median household income	26,301		20,747	
Per capita income	12,899		12,580	
Below poverty:				
Families	18.3%		16.6%	
Female-headed households	38.9		38.9	
Persons	21.6		21.4	
Children	33.6		32.2	
65 and older	15.9		14.4	
Unemployment, 1991	8.4		5.4	

Source: U.S. Bureau of the Census, *City and County Data Book*, 1992

were 16.7 percent in 1960, 20.2 percent in 1970, and 24 percent in 1980. Chicago's Hispanic population doubled in size in the decade between 1970 and 1980 (7.4 percent to 14.05 percent) and then increased another third by 1990 (19.6 percent), while the 1980s saw a significant increase in the city's newest immigrant group, Asians (2.3 percent in 1980 to 3.7 percent in 1990).

The racial and ethnic differences between the two cities have a significant impact on their politics. In Chicago, racial conflict and, to a lesser though increasing extent, ethnic division have become the defining characteristics of the political system. These conflicts are most salient in the areas of housing, education, and electoral politics.

The size and rapid growth of Chicago's African American population combined with their geographic concentration placed enormous pressures on the housing market. Historic discrimination created sizable ghettos on the city's South and West Sides. As restrictions were lifted, middle-class African Americans began their exodus from the ghetto. Unfortunately, pent-up demand and limited supply became an attractive combination for unscrupulous realtors who played on racial fears of whites and, in the process, hastened racial turnover of neighborhoods. Some areas in Chicago went from all white to all black in a mere ten years. The reality and fear of racial change further hardened racial attitudes in many of the city's white ethnic neighborhoods. A particularly contentious issue historically was the siting of public housing. As a result of white intransigence and city council control over the site selection process, almost all of the "family" public housing projects were built in black areas.[1]

While Pittsburgh is not a shining example of racial integration, it does not exhibit the same type of segregation found in Chicago. According to the 1990 census, for example, eighteen of the city's ninety neighborhoods had African American populations in excess of 75 percent of the local population, compared with twenty-six of Chicago's seventy-seven neighborhoods. Even more telling is the spatial configuration in the two cities. As the maps indicate, Pittsburgh's black areas are not, for the most part, contiguous as they are in Chicago. With a smaller African American population to begin with, the spatial separation of Pittsburgh's black neighborhoods further reduces the perceived threat of a "black invasion" that permeates many of Chicago's white ethnic neighborhoods. It also tends to heighten neighborhood identification over racial identification for many African Americans, thus further diluting race as a political issue and as an organizing principle.

Another area in which race has played a much more prominent role in Chicago than in Pittsburgh is education. Data on public school enrollments tell much of the story (see Table 2.2). In Chicago, whites are a rapidly decreasing minority in the public schools. Between 1960 and 1983 the percentage of the Chicago school population that was white decreased by 66 percent; in Pittsburgh, by contrast, there was a 23 percent drop.

These differences, of course, mirror the larger patterns of racial change in the two cities. The interaction of these environmental factors with the larger school integration movement that was unfolding during this period shaped two very distinctive responses. In Chicago the response was unequivocal resistance; Daley

Table 2.2. School Enrollments by Race: Chicago and Pittsburgh

Year	CHICAGO			PITTSBURGH[a]	
	White	Black	Other	White	Black
1960	55.2%	42.1%	2.7%	62.8%	37.2%
1966	46.6	50.9	2.5	62.5	37.5
1970	34.6	54.8	10.6	60.1	39.9
1976	24.9	59.4	15.6	54.6	45.4
1980	18.6	60.8	18.5	50.1	49.9
1983	16.3	60.7	22.9	48.5	51.5

[a] Pittsburgh only records in two categories: white and black.
Sources: Pittsburgh: Office of Student Management; Chicago: Paul Kleppner, *Chicago Divided: The Making of a Black Mayor* (DeKalb. Northern Illinois University Press, 1975).

backed a school superintendent who was vehemently opposed to integration, thus further hardening the city's racial divisions. In Pittsburgh, economic and civic elites took the lead role in responding to demands for school desegregation. Through the establishment of magnet schools, the development of numerous grant programs to upgrade the quality of public education, and a series of meetings with parents, educators, and members of the business and foundation communities, these civic elites managed to diffuse the race issue, restore public confidence in the school system, and prevent massive white flight.[2]

The conciliatory and accommodational approach taken by Pittsburgh's elites was quite consistent with their overall behavior. Similarly, the resistance of Chicago's political elites to African American demands was becoming quite characteristic of that city's politics. Perhaps more important, though, elites in Chicago were operating in an environment of rapid racial change and in an arena (electoral) that made them very vulnerable to constituent pressures. The perception that it was "only a matter of time," combined with the need to secure white electoral votes, encouraged policy makers to engage in what essentially amounted to holding actions. In Pittsburgh, by contrast, there was a sense of urgency surrounded by possibility. The African American population's relatively small size and slow growth meant that massive white decline was not an inevitable outcome. Under such conditions, intervention, rather than a temporary stopgap, could shape the future direction of the schools. Similarly, the failure to act could have negative consequences. Finally, Pittsburgh's elites operated primarily in the civic arena, where they did not have to worry about electoral fallout. Thus, Pittsburgh's civic elites had much greater incentive to undertake constructive action.

The battles in Chicago over neighborhoods, housing, and schools have often come to an ugly head in the electoral arena as control over city hall is seen as tantamount to control in these other areas. As the school integration, fair housing, and civil rights movements came together in the 1960s, race replaced class as the foundation of Chicago politics. The increased salience of the race issue was positively correlated with the increased electoral power of African Americans; between 1960 and 1980 the percentage of the voting age population that was black nearly doubled (20.2 to 38.7 percent) while the percentage that was white shrank from 71.7 to 48.3 percent.[3] In addition, geographic concentration paid off electorally; between 1968 and 1976 the number of African American ward committeemen went from nine to fourteen.[4] In Pittsburgh, by contrast, geographic dispersal has diluted black electoral strength. In 1985, for example, no African American was elected to the city council—the first time in twenty years. Though largely the result of infighting among black ward committeemen, this situation signified a deeper political weakness within the black community. Under such conditions, African Americans are hardly perceived in a threatening manner by white voters.

Ethnic division also distinguishes Chicago politics from Pittsburgh politics. Issues of affirmative action and contract set-asides pit members of different ethnic

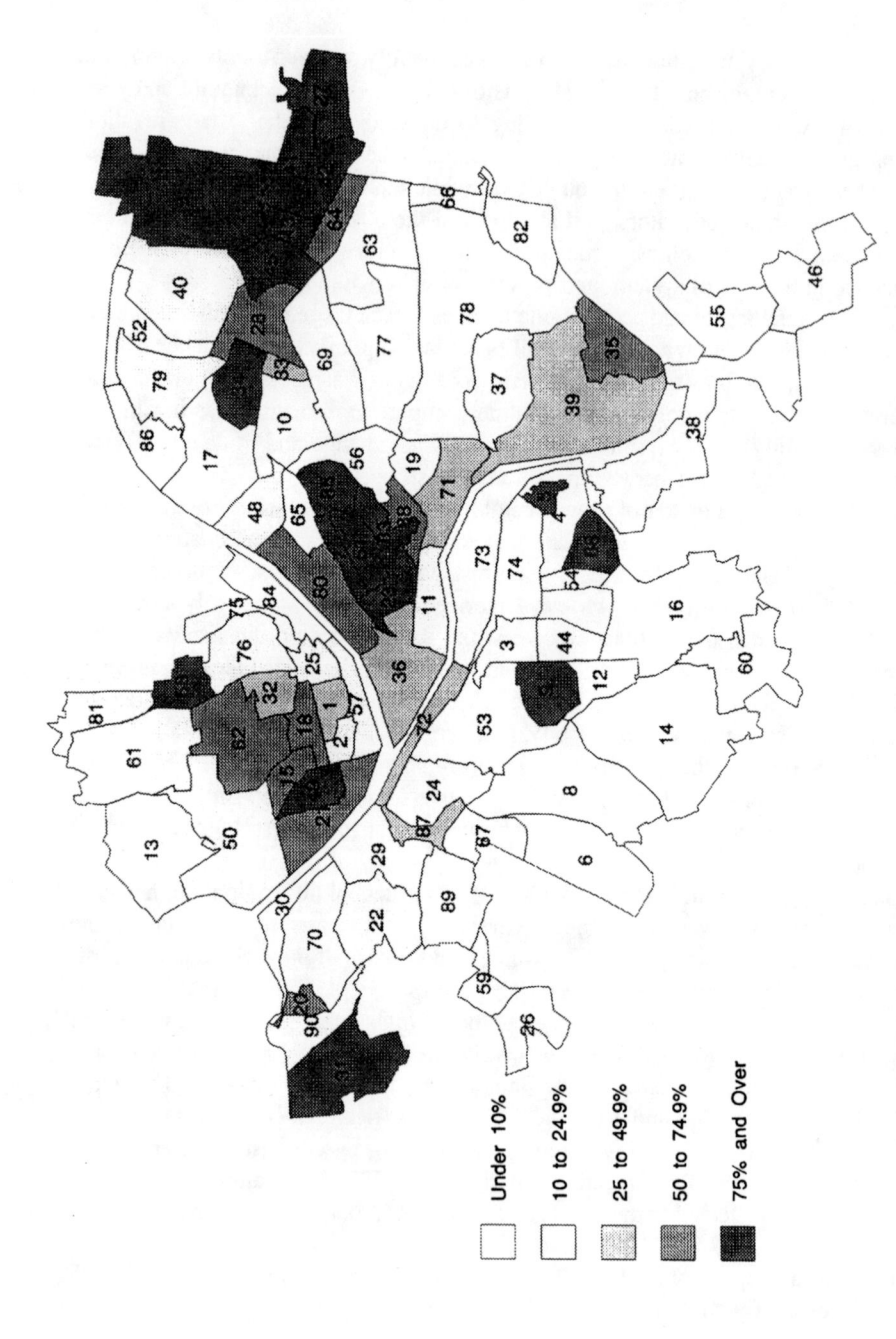

Figure 2.1. Neighborhood Map by Race, Pittsburgh. (*Source:* Social Science Data Library, Temple University. 1990 U.S. Census data, Summary Tape File 1.)

KEY TO PITTSBURGH NEIGHBORHOOD MAP

	Neighborhood	Total Population	Percent Black		Neighborhood	Total Population	Percent Black
1	Allegheny Center	1,262	35.02	46	Lincoln Place	3,841	0.00
2	Allegheny West	654	22.63	47	Lincoln-Lemington-Belm	6,644	87.13
3	Allentown	3,600	8.25	48	Lower Lawrenceville	2,650	13.96
4	Arlington	2,210	4.89	49	Manchester	3,077	85.54
5	Arlington Heights	1,497	92.92	50	Marshall Shadeland	7,903	17.70
6	Banksville	4,769	2.66	51	Middle Hill	2,829	98.59
7	Bedford Dwellings	2,317	97.37	52	Morningside	3,973	4.20
8	Beechview	9,323	3.53	53	Mount Washington	10,700	3.30
9	Beltzhoover	3,338	82.38	54	Mount Oliver Neighborhood	620	6.45
10	Bloomfield	10,405	6.17	55	New Homestead	1,008	9.92
11	Bluff	3,220	19.78	56	North Oakland	10,836	9.40
12	Bon Air	1,006	1.49	57	North Shore	273	13.55
13	Brighton Heights	8,580	3.32	58	Northview Heights	2,746	95.70
14	Brookline	15,441	0.98	59	Oakwood	1,099	3.09
15	California Kirkbride	1,156	67.73	60	Overbrook	4,456	0.79
16	Carrick	11,625	0.66	61	Perry North	4,927	12.42
17	Central Lawrenceville	5,867	2.57	62	Perry South	6,303	50.36
18	Central Northside	3,723	55.63	63	Point Breeze	5,909	4.45
19	Central Oakland	5,406	6.68	64	Point Breeze North	2,513	67.77
20	Chartiers City	569	69.95	65	Polish Hill	1,610	9.88
21	Chateau	9	55.56	66	Regent Square	1,090	0.83
22	Crafton Heights	4,558	12.77	67	Ridgemont	590	0.17
23	Crawford-Roberts	2,459	95.40	68	Saint Clair	1,960	88.83
24	Duquense Heights	2,786	1.47	69	Shadyside	13,385	7.81
25	East Allegheny	3,088	11.53	70	Sheraden	6,654	7.24
26	East Carnegie	605	9.26	71	South Oakland	3,368	34.23
27	East Hills	4,505	95.01	72	South Shore	44	25.00
28	East Liberty	7,973	58.21	73	South Side Flats	6,177	2.75
29	Elliott	3,009	6.88	74	South Side Slopes	5,672	1.59
30	Esplen	518	7.14	75	Spring Garden	1,753	0.68
31	Fairywood	2,951	88.28	76	Spring Hill-City View	3,288	16.48
32	Fineview	1,907	44.31	77	Squirrel Hill North	11,500	3.66
33	Friendship	1,976	33.81	78	Squirrel Hill South	14,968	2.91
34	Garfield	6,327	76.51	79	Stanton Heights	5,085	22.50
35	Glen Hazel	793	63.68	80	Strip District	275	66.91
36	Golden Triangle/Civic Arena	3,785	30.17	81	Summer Hill	1,203	13.55
37	Greenfield	8,485	2.11	82	Swisshelm Park	1,540	0.45
38	Hays	537	0.74	83	Terrace Village	5,073	98.29
39	Hazelwood	6,456	26.44	84	Troy Hill	2,742	0.04
40	Highland Park	7,029	16.94	85	Upper Hill	2,590	84.44
41	Homewood North	5,331	97.52	86	Upper Lawrenceville	3,328	0.87
42	Homewood South	4,811	97.67	87	West End	441	44.90
43	Homewood West	1,369	97.52	88	West Oakland	1,938	67.75
44	Knoxville	4,971	22.91	89	Westwood	3,282	2.50
45	Larimer	3,992	83.62	90	Windgap	1,603	17.03

25

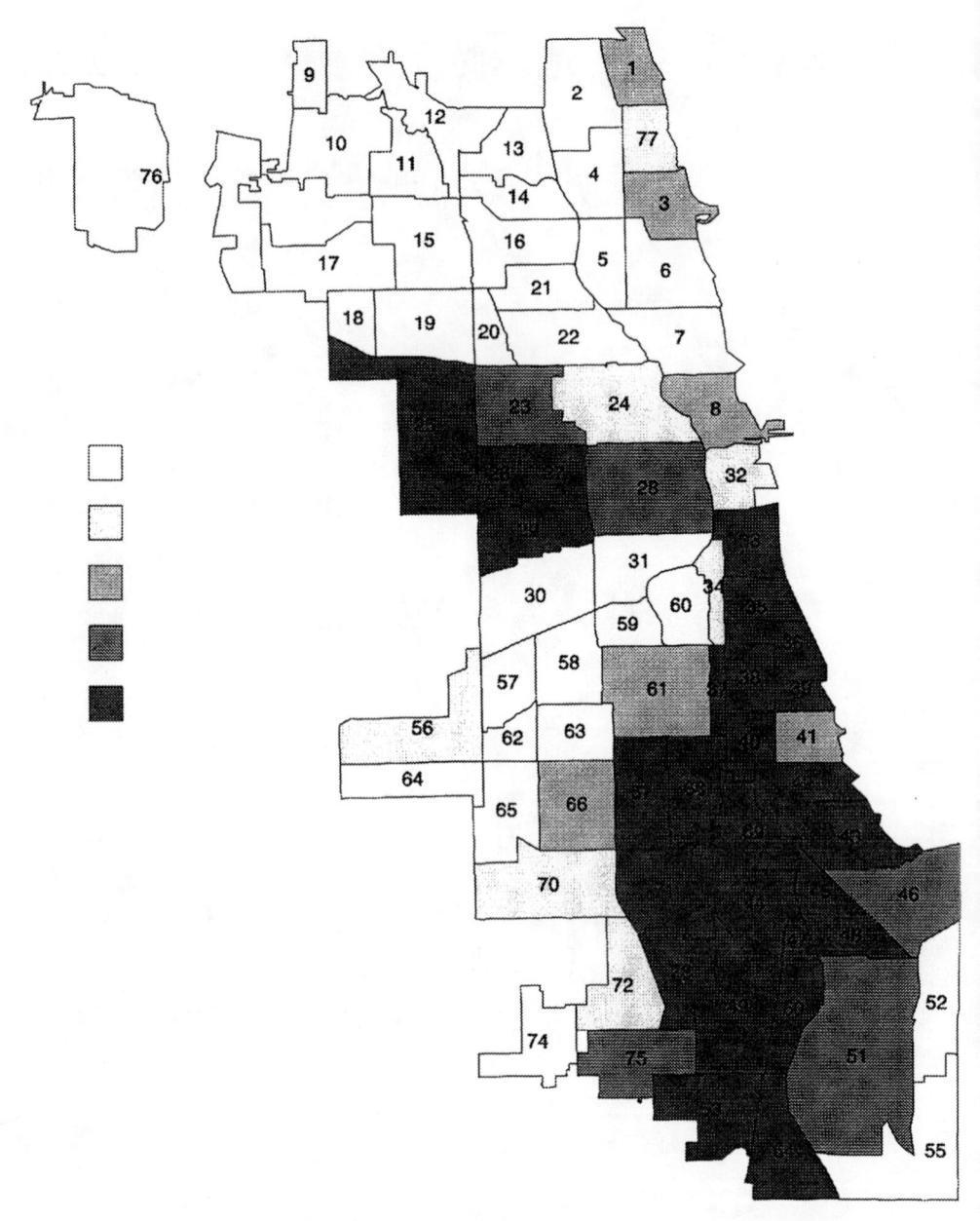

Figure 2.2. Neighborhood Map by Race, Chicago. (*Source:* Social Science Data Library, Temple University. 1990 U.S. Census data, Summary Tape File 1.)

KEY TO CHICAGO NEIGHBORHOOD MAP

Name	Total Population	Percent Black		Name	Total Population	Percent Black
1 Rogers Park	54,708	28.9	63	Gage Park	26,957	5.1
2 West Ridge	65,374	3.3	64	Clearing	21,490	0.0
3 Uptown	58,313	25.6	65	West Lawn	23,402	0.3
4 Lincoln Square	44,891	2.7	66	Chicago Lawn	51,243	26.5
5 North Center	33,010	3.3	67	West Englewood	52,772	98.4
6 Lake View	91,031	6.4	68	Englewood	48,434	99.2
7 Lincoln Park	61,092	6 1	69	Greater Grand Crossing	38,644	99.2
8 Near North Side	50,078	28.8	70	Ashburn	37,092	10.0
9 Edison Park	7,972	0.0	71	Auburn Gresham	59,808	99.1
10 Norwood Park	37,557	0.1	72	Beverly	22,385	24.2
11 Jefferson Park	23,649	0.1	73	Washington Heights	32,114	98.8
12 Forest Glen	17,655	0.1	74	Mount Greenwood	19,179	1.3
13 North Park	16,236	0.9	75	Morgan Park	26,740	64.7
14 Albany Park	49,501	3.4	76	O'Hare	11,236	2 8
15 Portage Park	56,513	0.3	77	Edgewater	60,703	19.9
16 Irving Park	50,159	1.0				
17 Dunning	36,957	0.4				
18 Montclare	13,105	0.4				
19 Belmont Cragin	54,255	1.3				
20 Hermosa	23,131	2.0				
21 Avondale	35,579	1.3				
22 Logan Square	82,605	6.8				
23 Humboldt Park	67,573	50.5				
24 West Town	87,703	10.6				
25 Austin	114,079	86.9				
26 West Garfield Park	24,095	99.2				
27 East Garfield Park	24,030	98.9				
28 Near West Side	46,197	67.0				
29 North Lawndale	47,296	96.4				
30 South Lawndale	81,155	8.9				
31 Lower West Side	45,654	1.1				
32 Loop	11,954	20.3				
33 Near South Side	6,828	93.5				
34 Armour Square	10,801	22.2				
35 Douglas	30,652	91.6				
36 Oakland	8,197	99.4				
37 Fuller Park	4,364	98.6				
38 Grand Boulevard	35,897	99.4				
39 Kenwood	18,178	76 7				
40 Washington Park	19,425	99.4				
41 Hyde Park	22,900	37.4				
42 Woodlawn	27,473	96.0				
43 South Shore	54,438	97 8				
44 Chatham	36,779	99.1				
45 Avalon Park	11,711	98.0				
46 South Chicago	40,776	62.1				
47 Burnside	3,314	96.7				
48 Calumet Heights	17,453	92.4				
49 Roseland	56,493	98.8				
50 Pullman	9,344	78.9				
51 South Deering	17,755	59.1				
52 East Side	20,450	0.1				
53 West Pullman	39,846	94.0				
54 Riverdale	10,821	97 9				
55 Hegewisch	10,136	0 7				
56 Garfield Ridge	33,948	12.8				
57 Archer Heights	9,227	0.0				
58 Brighton Park	32,207	0.1				
59 McKinley Park	13,297	0.2				
60 Bridgeport	29,877	0 1				
61 New City	53,226	41.3				
62 West Elsdon	12,266	0.0				

groups against each other for slices of a shrinking pie (see chapter 6). Issues of culture and language create heated contests for control over culture-transmitting institutions such as the schools.[5]

The patterns of demographic change in Pittsburgh and Chicago have had very different impacts. The striking characteristic of Pittsburgh's demographic change is population loss but political continuity. In Chicago, demographic change has altered the balance of power among racial and ethnic groups. While difficult to measure, there is also the psychological dimension for whites of making up less than 50 percent of Chicago's population. The issues raised and fears generated by this turn of events play out in the electoral arena, which has become extremely volatile. In short, demographic change in Chicago has become a source of much instability and conflict. These factors have encouraged many political leaders to try to impose a stability on the electorate, often by resorting to social control mechanisms. The ethnic and racial divisions also impede efforts to build and sustain progressive coalitions.

ECONOMIC CHANGE

Pittsburgh and Chicago are attempting to be postindustrial cities. Their shift in the basis of capital accumulation from manufacturing to services embodied a series of changes that benefited some and proved quite painful to others. The collapse of the steel industry, the decline of manufacturing, and the recession of the early 1980s had major social and economic consequences for Pittsburgh and Chicago: population and job losses, neighborhood deterioration, and an unequal distribution of costs and benefits as minorities and the poor bore a disproportionate share of the costs. As with the demographic changes, the implications of these changes varied for the two cities.

Chicago

Long heralded as the industrial capital of the Midwest, Chicago began losing manufacturing jobs after World War II, with the most precipitous declines occurring between 1972 and 1983 (40.7 percent).[6] In the meantime, the city pursued a pro-growth strategy of downtown office construction and selective neighborhood revitalization. Consequently, service-sector employment surged from 17 percent of total employment in 1950 to 27 percent of total employment in 1980, as did downtown real estate values. Yet the gain in service-sector jobs (57,000 between 1963 and 1982) did not offset in numbers or salaries the 232,000 manufacturing jobs lost during that same period.[7] Neglected by this economic development strategy were the displaced workers and older neighborhoods where industrial decline took its initial toll. Disinvestment and redlining completed the process of deterioration. Consequently, Chicago has a glistening downtown area surrounded by expensive residential towers, while vast tracts on the city's South and West Sides reveal the social and economic costs of uneven development; high unemployment, excessive poverty, and physical abandonment have replaced the factories that fueled the industrial heartland.[8]

The bifurcated nature of the service economy and the loss of high-paying manufacturing jobs have led to industrial retention efforts within the city. The pressures for real estate development in selected neighborhoods have generated many conflicts over land use. Underlying these conflicts is a fundamental rejection by neighborhood and labor advocates of the identification of economic development with real estate development, services, and tourism, which has characterized the approach of many of the city's official and unofficial policy makers. In their place, many community and labor activists have pushed for balanced development, job creation, and neighborhood revitalization. While these battles are often characterized by the media as "neighborhood versus downtown," they actually embody a somewhat looser confederation of interests: blue-collar workers, industrial-based unions, grassroots community organizations, progressive policy activists, minority neighborhoods, and white ethnic neighborhoods. While in their separate battles these groups may all be challenging the same "growth machine," their overall perspectives, interests, incentives, and stakes can vary considerably, making coalition building among them extremely difficult.

Pittsburgh

In a 1944 *Wall Street Journal* survey, Pittsburgh was classified as a city with a bleak future and limited prospects for growth.[9] In 1985 Rand McNally ranked Pittsburgh as the nation's most livable city.[10] Clearly, much had changed. As in Chicago, most of the change is to be found in the occupational base and the overall population.

Once the steel capital of the United States, Pittsburgh saw those fortunes disintegrate with the collapse of the American steel industry. While the cyclical nature of the manufacturing sector shows job loss as a long-term trend, the real crunch for the Pittsburgh area occurred between 1979 and 1988; 100,000 jobs were lost, accounting for a 44 percent decline in manufacturing employment.[11]

While the city and region were losing high-paying manufacturing jobs, policy makers embarked on an energetic campaign to attract service and high-tech jobs. Although the service sector is the fastest growing, it has not been able to compensate for losses in the manufacturing sector either in numbers of jobs created or in wages paid. During the same period in which 100,000 manufacturing jobs were lost, for instance, only 35,473 service-sector jobs were added.[12] The wage picture is equally sobering; in 1990, average annual wages for manufacturing in the Pittsburgh area were $36,989, compared with only $24,442 in the service sector.[13] Further, several studies indicate that it is at best difficult for displaced manufacturing workers to make a transition to the service sector.[14] As for high tech, the other highly touted component of Pittsburgh's new economy, the results have been even more dismal. Employment in the various high-tech occupations increased by roughly 2,000 jobs between 1976 and 1986.[15]

Pittsburgh's historical reliance on the steel industry and its supplier and client sectors, and the failure of the service and high-tech sectors to sufficiently compensate for manufacturing's decline, have resulted in very skewed population losses (Table 2.3). The greatest exodus has been among younger people and families, who leave in search of employment opportunities. The median age in Pittsburgh and Chicago is quite different (34.6 and 31.3 years, respectively). The distribution across categories shows a much higher concentration of persons aged 55 and older in Pittsburgh than in Chicago (27.5 percent and 20 percent, respectively). Moreover, nearly one-fifth of Pittsburgh's population is 65 and over, compared with just over one-tenth for Chicago. In fact, Pittsburgh's concentration of elderly persons is one of the highest in the country.[16] From an economic development perspective, this is especially troublesome since it makes it more difficult to attract business to an area that is losing its labor force; between 1980 and 1990, for instance, Pittsburgh's labor force declined by 11 percent.[17]

Although Pittsburgh's economic crisis was more serious than Chicago's, owing to its less diversified economy, for several reasons the political spillover was not as severe. First, a significant amount of the economic dislocation took place in the Mon Valley outside of Pittsburgh. In Chicago the economic dislocation took place in city neighborhoods. Consequently, deindustrialization is more hotly contested within Chicago than within Pittsburgh, although the Steel Valley Authority has strongly challenged plant closings in the Mon Valley (see chapter 7). Second, even when deindustrialization hit city neighborhoods, as in the city's North Side, these areas tended to be geographically and socially isolated from the rest of the city. Third, the exportation of Pittsburgh's labor force serves to artificially depress the unemployment rate. As the table indicates, Pittsburgh's unemployment rate in the years 1980, 1986, and 1991 has been lower than Chicago's;

Table 2.3. Population by Age, Chicago and Pittsburgh, 1990

Age	Chicago	Pittsburgh
Median	31.3	34.6
Under 5	7.8%	6.2%
5–17	18.2	13.7
18–24	11.5	14.0
25–34	19.3	16.9
35–44	13.9	13.2
45–54	9.3	8.5
55–64	8.1	9.6
65–74	6.9	10.1
75 and over	5.0	7.8

Source: U.S. Bureau of the Census, *City and County Data Book*, 1992.

even more important, Pittsburgh's rate has decreased significantly whereas Chicago's has exhibited only a moderate decline.[18]

	Chicago	Pittsburgh
1980	9.8%	9.2%
1986	9.3	7.4
1991	8.4	5.4

The disproportionate loss of younger, more professional workers also removed potential pressures on the real estate market. Pittsburgh has not had a significant problem with gentrification. Chicago, by contrast, with a sizable professional class, has experienced much gentrification, which has set off many neighborhood battles. The loss within Pittsburgh of this younger cohort and the consequent concentration of older cohorts have also had a conservatizing effect on the entire city. Many older persons are living on pensions, often in houses with no mortgages; typically, though not always, they are less piqued by salient political issues. Finally, pro-growth policies were carried out in Chicago in an environment already exhibiting significant animus as a result of earlier redevelopment battles between neighborhoods and ward organizations. Pittsburgh's early redevelopment efforts, by contrast, forged a very favorable image for the city's elites (see chapter 3).

Perhaps of greatest significance for Pittsburgh is the weakening of its corporate leadership and the consequent shift in corporate culture. Takeovers, mergers, and the overall hard times faced by many U.S. corporations have forced many chief executive officers to abandon their civic commitment for a more inward-looking posture. The mid-1980s takeover of Gulf Oil, the quintessential good citizen of Pittsburgh, sent shock waves through the corporate community. The dampening effect of the new corporate culture on civic commitment was acutely evident when Robert Pease, the executive director of the Allegheny Conference on Community Development (ACCD), Pittsburgh's leading business-backed civic association, retired in 1990 after twenty-two years at the helm. The search for a successor for the top position within Pittsburgh's civic community and corporatist structure was given over to a national corporate headhunting firm. Explaining this decision, the chief executive officer of Pittsburgh Plate and Glass, the head of the ACCD's search committee, confessed that he was "too busy."[19]

In short, many corporations have lost the interest and power to actively engage in city-building efforts. The change in corporate culture is especially problematic in a city like Pittsburgh, where the corporate sector was held in such high regard. Richard King Mellon and the ACCD were the city's visionary leaders. It was Mellon's commitment to remain in Pittsburgh and his ability to persuade other corporate leaders to follow suit that literally saved the city in midcentury. By the 1980s, however, even Mellon Bank had joined the disinvestment bandwagon (see chapter 7). In Chicago there was no corporate entity to suffer a comparable legitimacy loss because none had ever attained such a leadership position in city politics and planning. Instead, the city's policies merely hardened the cleavages between CBOs and the pro-growth regime.

POLITICAL CHANGE

Like most of the older industrial cities, Chicago and Pittsburgh were governed by strong political machines that wielded considerable influence within local, state, and, in the case of Chicago, national politics. These machines employed a divergence strategy of governance, creating distinct electoral and policy sectors. In the former, the machine practiced a politics of the individual based on a material exchange of jobs for votes and on ethnic loyalties. Issues were typically avoided because they contained the potential for division and conflict. The abundant supply of discretionary resources allowed the machine to maintain a forced army of patronage workers and a sufficient cadre of voters. This means of securing the vote provided the machine with the discretion to practice an elitist style of policy politics. Typically, bankers, businessmen, and labor leaders were the principal beneficiaries of the machine's policy process, which was centered around major economic development projects.[20]

Contained within this divergence strategy of governance are the two models of power that Stone describes; social control was practiced primarily in the electoral sphere as patronage jobs and the enforcement powers of local government were used to "reward friends and punish enemies." Social production was much more characteristic of elite politics, where the resources of public and private actors were melded in cooperative fashion to plan and execute major projects. The nature of the power relations in the two spheres differed largely as a result of the tasks involved and the resource base of the actors. Execution of large-scale economic development projects is a much more complex task than securing votes. Second, key business and labor leaders had more resources and power than any individual voter; unlike voters, they could not be politically muscled into submission (see chapter 4).

Maintaining social control over the electorate therefore requires that electoral politics be kept on an individual basis—hence, the machine's incentive to squash any organizing efforts outside of the ward organizations. It also requires continued access to an ample supply of material benefits and an electorate that will readily accept such benefits.

While they had similar beginnings, the machines in Pittsburgh and Chicago evolved in different directions. An unwillingness to share power and a resistance to change characterized the Daley machine, while the Lawrence machine in Pittsburgh yielded to other players and institutions, thus beginning a slow retreat from dominance. In Chicago the machine maintained control over both electoral and policy processes. As the supply of discretionary resources declined and large segments of the electorate began to reject the machine's two-tier resource distribution system, however, the machine's traditional mechanisms of social control were seriously weakened. Rather than renegotiate its relationship to the electorate, the machine fought back, substituting symbolic appeals for the decline in material resources. The machine became the defender of white racial interests, thus injecting a high level of conflict into the entire political system.

In Pittsburgh, by contrast, confronted with a similar challenge, the machine withdrew from key parts of the policy process. The creation and expansion of a viable civic-sector arena shifted important resources away from the machine. Thus, the two-tiered system of social production and social control gave way to social production as the machine weakened significantly vis-à-vis the institutions in the civic arena. This development was a major boon to the neighborhoods.

Much of the difference between the directions of the Lawrence and Daley machines can be traced to the accommodation between political and economic elites, a subject that is fully discussed in chapter 3. For now, I will provide an overview of the changes in political organization and their implications for politics—especially neighborhood politics—in the two cities.

The Changing Face of Chicago Politics: The Unraveling of the Daley Machine

Chicago under Daley was long viewed as "The City That Works." It had a booming downtown, labor peace, fiscal soundness accompanied by high bond ratings, a powerful political machine that could deliver in state and national elections, a relatively quiescent black community, and numerous black elected officials. Despite these perceptions, problems were brewing in Chicago. A combination of challenges from within the political machine, a decrease in discretionary resources, and electoral shifts ruptured the regime's accommodation process. Although the most visible signs appeared after Daley's death in 1976, there were cracks in the machine during his administration.

Politically, 1972 was a watershed year in Chicago. A slate of independent candidates, from both the Republican and Democratic Parties, combined extensive media use with vigorous campaigning to win numerous offices, including the governorship. African American congressman Ralph Metcalfe broke with his lifelong mentor—Richard J. Daley—over the issue of police brutality in the African American community. Edward Vrdolyak, as leader of the Young Turks in the city council, demanded more say in legislative matters. Nationally, the Democratic Party sent a strong message when it refused to seat the Daley delegation for noncompliance with the newly enacted McGovern rules. In the courts, political firing was declared unconstitutional in the first of the Shakman decrees.[21]

The Daley machine thus suffered serious challenges on several key fronts: its ability to win elections; its control of the African American vote; its control over its own members in the city council; its traditional "special status" within the national Democratic Party; and its supply of patronage. Although Daley won another election, albeit with sharp vote reductions, these events signaled a changed political landscape.[22]

The Politics of Group Mobilization

The most fundamental change was in the organization of the electorate. The issueless and individual politics of the machine were being replaced by controversy and group mobilization. Neighborhood displacement (see chapter 4), growing discontent with the machine among blacks, and racial conflict weakened the machine's hold over the electorate. The simultaneous mobilization of different constituencies provided the foundation for a multidimensional progressive movement.

Within the machine, battles over the distribution of power were equally wrenching. Forgetting the wisdom of their recently departed leader, Richard J. Daley, who admonished them to "hang together after I'm gone or you'll hang separately," aldermen pursued their individual desires for power, thus confirming the prediction. And this was all occurring in the context of shrinking discretionary resources.

Despite marked changes in the political landscape, Daley's two successors—Bilandic and Byrne—continued the machine's divergence strategy of governance. In so doing, they sharpened the divisions within Chicago, enhanced the adversarial tone of its politics, and effectively ruled out any possibility of compromise, making a confrontational orientation aimed at regime overthrow the only viable alternative for those advocating progressive change. Two of the sharpest cleavages within Chicago's political system centered around the issues of race and neighborhood resources.

Racial Politics. The rupture in the accommodation process was particularly evident in the governing regime's relationship with the African American community. As early as the mid-1960s, there were signs that race was becoming the foundation of electoral politics in Chicago. White middle-class voters increased their support for the machine, while African Americans, who had been the most loyal supporters, began withholding their support. The first development is unusual for machine politics, which typically is most appealing to voters of lower socioeconomic status who respond to the material incentives that are provided. The emerging middle-class base of the machine was not odd, however, given the new direction in Chicago politics. With the decline in discretionary resources and the changing demographics of the city, the machine replaced diminishing material incentives with the symbolic appeal of race as a social control mechanism. The machine was becoming the defender of white racial interests.

By appointing anti-integrationists to the Chicago Housing Authority and the school board—two pivotal institutions in the battle for racial equality—Daley sent a clear message to white voters. The message was even louder in his refusal to negotiate the police brutality issue and near deafening in his "shoot to kill" orders issued during the riots following the assassination of Martin Luther King Jr.

The "circularity of politics and policy" that characterizes a regime's accommodation process[23] was undermining the Daley regime. While African Americans had yet to find an alternative to Daley, they had begun to withhold their support.[24] This development, although downplayed by the machine, foreshadowed a more serious development: the split between black machine politicians (elites) and black voters (masses). While the former did benefit from supporting the machine, the African American community received little or no benefit and thus had little to lose by breaking with the machine. The "selective incentives" and "insider privileges" that are extended to elites did not reach the masses. Nevertheless, the governing regime was not about to address the collective issues of race and discrimination lest it risk losing its white support.

Despite the signs of change, the machine continued to take the African American vote for granted. The selection of Bilandic to finish Daley's term was the first in a long series of actions that angered and mobilized the black community. While the rules of succession were unclear, many African Americans felt that black city councilman Wilson Frost, as president pro tem of that body, was the rightful heir. Although Frost was given the powerful position of finance committee chair, it was seen by the African American community as another slap in the face.

The last slap that the black community took from the machine came during the blizzards of 1978–1979, which blanketed the city with several feet of snow. To expedite mass-transit rush-hour service to outlying (white) areas, the transit authority bypassed several inner-city (black) stations. The black community retaliated at the polls when it helped Jane Byrne defeat Bilandic, and hence the machine, in 1979. While Bilandic had the support of black elected leaders, Byrne had the support of voters, winning fourteen of the sixteen predominantly black wards.[25]

The split between African American leaders and African American voters signified a major shift in Chicago's electoral politics, highlighting the need for a new accommodation process. Byrne won the battle by exploiting this contradiction but lost the war when she too ignored the new political reality. Through personnel and labor actions, which included reneging on campaign promises, and her endorsement of a ward remap that diluted the power of African Americans and Hispanics, Byrne very quickly alienated the black community (see chapter 5). Once again, the black community registered its discontent at the polls, contributing to major electoral defeats for Byrne's slate in the 1980 Illinois primary races.[26] The real payback, however, came in the mayoral primary of 1983 when Jane Byrne and Richard M. Daley split the white vote, thereby paving the way for the city's first African American mayor—Harold Washington.

Neighborhood Politics. While the machine has often been portrayed in romantic terms as the champion of the neighborhoods,[27] a closer look reveals a highly imbalanced system in which insider elites—usually business and labor leaders—receive substantial rewards, while residents in the poor inner-city wards receive more basic and less costly forms of patronage.[28] In Chicago, Daley's fiscal conservatism, his support of downtown projects, and his own philosophy of limited government led to a highly inequitable system. Neighborhoods were shortchanged as capital resources were targeted almost exclusively toward the downtown area.

The failure of ward organizations to serve the neighborhood often led to alternative organizing efforts. Perceived as threats to the ward organizations, and thus to the machine, these efforts were fiercely resisted. As an astute political reporter observed, "The only thing a Democratic committeeman hates more than a Republican voter is a neighborhood organization [since] many of these organizations were formed as alternatives to ward organizations that weren't doing their jobs—delivering neighborhood services."[29] Basil Talbott, the *Sun-Times* reporter, had captured the contradiction of machine politics; it was not the best representative of its constituency, and at times, as in the case of urban renewal, it was as an outright enemy (see chapter 4).

As with the African American community, neighborhood developments were creating a chasm between elites (political leaders) and masses (voters). The former were distributing individual material benefits, while the latter were beginning to seek collective policy benefits. The balance of power in many neighborhoods was starting to shift.

The pace escalated in the 1970s as the increase in media campaigns and the decrease in patronage weakened the ward organizations. Additionally, the fallout from economic restructuring and the recessions in the seventies and eighties, which saw the collapse of the steel industry on the city's Southeast Side and the closing of manufacturing plants, helped to galvanize communities around major issues of employment and neighborhood economic development. Demands for affordable housing and quality education were soon added to the list. CBOs, not ward organizations, were the logical beneficiaries of this shift in neighborhood politics and priorities.

As the problems mounted, coalition-building efforts took root, resulting in the formation of groups like the Chicago Association of Neighborhood Development Organizations (1979) and the Chicago Rehab Network (1977). Thus, the 1970s saw significant organizing within communities around policy issues and across communities around common problems. Implicit in these efforts was an acknowledgment that the machine was not "taking care of business."

However, politics often has more than one logic. Enter the second contradiction. While the neighborhoods were seriously shortchanged by the twin practices of selective incentives and insider privileges, in white neighborhoods the machine could maintain allegiance on ideological grounds; it had become the "great

Table 2.4. Mayoral Administrations: Chicago and Pittsburgh

Chicago	Pittsburgh
R. J. Daley (1955–1976)[a]	Lawrence (1945–1959)[b]
Bilandic (1976–1979)	Barr (1959–1968)
Byrne (1979–1983)	Flaherty (1969–1977)[c]
Washington (1983–1987)[a]	Caliguiri (1977–1988)[a]
Sawyer (1987–1989)	Masloff (1988–1994)
R. M. Daley (1989–present)	Murphy (1994–present)

[a] Died in office.
[b] Lawrence won the governorship and thus left the mayor's office.
[c] Flaherty left to work in President Carter's administration.

white hope." Racial politics were used in the electoral arena to offset neighborhood disenchantment. Borrowing from Schattschneider and Key, one can say that the racial cleavage and the economic cleavage were in competition for the voter's attention.[30] These crosscutting cleavages have dominated electoral politics from the late seventies through the present, putting governance on a shaky foundation while presenting enormous obstacles to the development of multidimensional progressive coalitions like the one that elected Harold Washington in 1983 and 1987.[31]

A comparison of the changing mayoral administrations in Chicago with those in Pittsburgh (Table 2.4) highlights some of the instability within Chicago's political system. Since Richard J. Daley's death in 1976, Chicago has had five mayors, compared with three for Pittsburgh during the same period. Chicago has had even more elections as a result of the deaths of two mayors in office (Richard J. Daley and Harold Washington). Thus, its five mayors account for seven elections between 1976 and 1995. Finally, each of these elections took a serious toll on the city's political system as they represent deep-seated conflicts between machine factions (Bilandic vs. Byrne, 1979; Byrne vs. Daley, primary election 1983), between white and black (Washington vs. Byrne vs. Daley, 1983 primary; Washington vs. Epton, 1983 general election; Washington vs. Byrne, 1987 primary; Washington vs. Vrdolyak, 1987 general election; Sawyer vs. Daley, primary election 1989; Daley vs. Evans, general election 1989; Daley vs. Davis, primary election 1991; Daley vs. Pincham, general election 1991; Daley vs. Gardner, 1995), and between progressive and machine politicians (Washington primary elections, 1983 and 1987; primary elections, 1989 and 1991).

Pittsburgh: The Reform Revolution That Wasn't, The Machine That Isn't

Pittsburgh's machine was somewhat of a hybrid. In contrast to Chicago's political system, which remained untouched by reforms until 1972 (first Shakman decree), Pittsburgh's (Democratic) machine coexisted with reforms designed to "rationalize governmental authority against fragmentation."[32] A business-backed charter reform effort in 1911 resulted in a strong mayor–council system that gave the mayor formal authority over the budget, city departments, and council legislation. It also restructured the city council to a nine-member at-large body.

This structural dimension was reinforced by the dominant position of business elites in Pittsburgh's governing regime. The existence of competing logics (one economic, one political) and, more importantly, of competing resource bases (the civic arena as represented by the ACCD and the electoral arena represented by the machine) strongly influenced the nature of political behavior and the direction of machine politics. The development and subsequent expansion of the civic arena shifted control of key resources away from the machine, thus weakening its significance in the city's political system. Social production, as opposed to social control, was becoming the dominant mode of power relations within the city. These developments were further reinforced by Lawrence's sharp party–government distinction, a concept that has eluded Chicagoans.

The precedent established by Lawrence was continued by his successors as the city's political system moved toward a convergence strategy of governance; resource distribution channels for business elites and for neighborhoods were becoming one and the same. As this third sector increased in power and significance, the political machine became less relevant than its Chicago counterpart. Consequently, politics in Pittsburgh never acquired the adversarial and confrontational character that has come to define Chicago politics.

The dismantling of Pittsburgh's machine can be viewed as a progression from the silent transfer of power under the Barr administration (1959–1969) to assault under Flaherty (1969–1977) to indifference under Caliguiri (1977–1988). Joseph Barr, Lawrence's handpicked successor,[33] initiated the silent transfer of power with a careful allocation of federal resources to professional and civic organizations. The board of education, which was under the jurisdiction of the court of common pleas, received most of the Manpower Demonstration and Training Act dollars and a substantial portion of the city's antipoverty allotment.[34] The Allegheny Council for the Improvement of Our Neighborhoods (ACTION-Housing, Inc.), which had been set up by the ACCD, assumed major planning and implementation roles in the antipoverty program (see chapter 4). The Community Action Board (oversight board) contained powerful businessmen, including the executive vice president of Pittsburgh National Bank and the assistant to the president of Mellon Bank, both of whom were also members of the highly exclusionary ACCD executive committee.[35] Barr's conscious steering of resources away from the political machine suggests that programmatic, rather than patronage, concerns drove at least part of his decision making. This contrasts sharply with the Chicago experience, where federal programs were manipulated, co-opted, and when necessary reshaped to serve machine purposes.[36]

Barr's silent transfer of power turned into an all-out assault in the hands of his successor, Peter Flaherty. When Barr chose not to run again in 1969, Flaherty, a city council member who came up through the Democratic Party ranks, sought the office. Quickly breaking with the party and the growth machine, Flaherty ran on a platform of "nobody's boy," promising to sever the close ties with the ACCD and the political machine. Making good on both promises, Flaherty distanced himself from the ACCD, promoting neighborhood as opposed to downtown development, while dismantling the machine through major cuts in personnel, thus depleting its patronage reserves (see chapter 5).

When Flaherty left the mayor's office to work in the Carter administration (1977), city councilman Richard Caliguiri served the remainder of the term. Another independent, Caliguiri took the office on the condition that he would not seek reelection. After a change of heart and without taking part in the Democratic primary, Caliguiri ran in the general election on the Pittsburgh-for-Caliguiri ticket. Campaigning on the slogan "It's another Renaissance," Caliguiri became the second mayor to defeat the machine.

Unlike Flaherty, Caliguiri did not attack the political machine and the growth machine. If anything, Caliguiri's Renaissance II can be described as indifference and healing; he ignored the political machine while pledging his support to economic growth and the ACCD. Continuing in the Flaherty tradition, however, economic development had a new partner: the neighborhoods. Caliguiri strengthened the formal linkages between city government and neighborhood organizations and increased the flow of resources to those organizations (see chapter 5).

In contrast to Chicago's political landscape, which was besieged by conflict of fairly intense proportions, by 1980 Pittsburgh was uniting around an expansion of its corporatist system and a shrinking of its political machine. This new accommodation process represented a victory for planning and a loss for electoral politics. The inherent structural bias emphasized cooperation over conflict. Structures, like victories, however, benefit some while harming others. Nowhere was this more evident than in the politics of group mobilization, where a unidimensional progressivism was taking root.

The Politics of Group Mobilization

In her analysis of neighborhood politics in Pittsburgh, Louise Jezierski suggested, "A dual-state structure consisting of an electoral sphere and a quasi-state sphere typical of partnerships allows the state to avoid the constraints of the electoral system."[37] We can thus argue that as the quasi-state sphere expands its control over resources, the electoral sphere becomes less significant and thus less of a constraining factor on the state. Ultimately, planning could largely replace electoral politics, disenfranchising those interests that are represented through the electoral arena. While my expansion of Jezierski's point is clearly theoretical, one can see the political dilemmas of this "dual-state structure" by examining neighborhood and racial politics in Pittsburgh.

Neighborhood Politics. There was significant opposition when Pittsburgh's redevelopment activities were extended to the neighborhoods. Although protests did not stop the Lower Hill urban renewal project, the first residential one in

Pittsburgh, they did stimulate further neighborhood organizing. In many corners of the city, neighborhood groups emerged to fight the urban renewal bulldozer and to demand a role in local planning activities (see chapter 4).

While not entirely satisfactory to the neighborhood groups, the ACCD did make some gestures toward accommodating the new demands. ACTION-Housing, Inc., a private, nonprofit organization set up by the ACCD in 1957 to address the issue of affordable housing, did seek neighborhood input, albeit on a limited basis. The Urban Extension program, an outgrowth of ACTION, expanded the concept of neighborhood planning, as program planners worked directly with neighborhood activists, sometimes even setting up local planning groups (see chapter 4). The real coup, however, was Flaherty's election in 1969. The long years of organizing and advocacy efforts had paid off; the neighborhoods had an ally in city hall. Through departmental reorganization and policy changes, Flaherty gave official recognition and institutional legitimacy to CBOs. These ties were strengthened as community development corporations (CDCs) began working closely with the planning department, the Urban Redevelopment Authority, and local foundations on major neighborhood development projects. Caliguiri extended these linkages, committing additional resources to the neighborhoods (see chapter 5).

In 1988, with the incorporation of the Pittsburgh Partnership for Neighborhood Development (PPND), the city's largest CDCs, in keeping with corporatist tradition, had received their own peak association. In many ways the neighborhood analogue of the ACCD, the PPND brings together the city's leading CDCs, foundations, city government, and the business community to serve as a centralized planning and funding mechanism for community economic development (see chapter 5). Thus, while many CBOs in Pittsburgh began in an adversarial role, most ended up embracing the corporatist structure. Consequently, they narrowed their focus around economic development while the governing regime acquired a unidimensional progressive orientation.

Racial Politics. The increased importance of the civic arena vis-à-vis the electoral arena changed the nature of protest, coalition building, and strategizing, all of which benefited the neighborhoods. African Americans, by contrast, faced major obstacles in their efforts to access either the electoral or the civic arena as a route toward empowerment.[38]

Although Pittsburgh's machine practiced its own version of paternalistic politics, unlike Chicago it never aspired, nor was it perceived, to be "the great white hope." Consequently, it did not provide the African American community with incentives for racial mobilization. With a much smaller and older black population, Pittsburgh did not experience the racial threat the way Chicago did. The absence of electoral pressures for a race-based politics from Pittsburgh's white community goes a long way toward explaining the different behavior patterns of the two machines.

Geography has also impeded black organizing efforts. Unlike in Chicago,

African Americans in Pittsburgh are not concentrated in any one area. The Lower Hill, which had the largest concentration of blacks, fell victim to the urban renewal bulldozer in the mid-1950s. Whereas in Chicago such incidents resulted in massive public housing, which geographically concentrated blacks, the Pittsburgh experience was one of dispersal. Only three neighborhoods lack public housing, and only five public housing projects are predominantly African American.[39] By contrast, forty-three of Chicago's seventy-seven community areas have no public housing,[40] while nearly 90 percent of Chicago's housing projects are predominantly African American.[41] Moreover, the five wards controlled by black ward committeemen contain 54 percent of Pittsburgh's black population, with the remaining population scattered throughout the city.[42] Pittsburgh's topography, which features steep hills and countless bridges, creates natural boundaries that reinforce territorial, as opposed to racial, identification.

The African American community has also experienced significant political infighting, which, when combined with the weak resources in the ward system, further impedes black political development. In 1985, battles among black ward committeemen resulted in a failure to slate a black for the city council; for the first time in more than twenty years, Pittsburgh had an all-white city council. A subsequent legal challenge led to Pittsburgh's conversion to a district-based system (see chapter 5).

Perhaps even more damaging is the toll that political infighting has taken on the other, and more resource-rich, route to empowerment: the civic arena. Attempts to establish CDCs in all-black, as opposed to more integrated, neighborhoods have been much less successful. The Hill District—almost all black and one of the most impoverished areas in the city—has long struggled to deal with economic problems.[43] The CDC that it set up, however, was consumed by factionalism. Some of the board members, along with the president, the organization's director, and the assistant director, broke away and formed another organization—Hill CDC II. But even this organization was racked by internal strife as the board president orchestrated the ouster of the director and assistant director. In the summer of 1990 a new director—Stanley Horn, from Chicago—had been brought on board. While much optimism surrounded his recruitment, the turbulent political waters of the Hill District capsized these promising beginnings as well. Horn resigned in 1993.

The experience of the Hill CDC contrasts sharply with the longevity of personnel in Pittsburgh's other CDCs. In turn, this has caused local funders to adopt somewhat of a wait-and-see attitude (i.e., "when they get their act together we'll fund them"). This reluctance probably has a racial dimension as well; the foundations do not want to be perceived as being paternalistic. But, even if unintentional, there is an implicit paternalism in the wait-and-see attitude. By contrast, the foundations did work with the local chamber of commerce to set up, from the top down, the East Liberty Development Corporation, Inc.; the East Liberty neighborhood is integrated and still maintains a sizable white population.[44]

The purpose here is not to single out African American organizations in

Pittsburgh as particularly prone to factionalism, since that is a characteristic of many organizations, but to highlight the dilemma that blacks face in Pittsburgh. Racial issues can only be dealt with on a citywide level, yet there are too many obstacles to citywide black organization. Most important, the "dual-state structure" rewards territorially based organization; it is here that economic resources can be accessed. Thus, the electoral arena is not a viable arena for African Americans and the civic arena is not set up to accommodate racial issues.

Ironically, the very success of the neighborhoods in organizing has made it that much more difficult for blacks to organize. As Stone found in Atlanta, cities often have distinct patterns of civic cooperation.[45] Usually imposed by the groups with the most resources, these patterns dictate acceptable norms of behavior. In Pittsburgh the powerful institutions within the corporatist structure accepted, and then encouraged, the formation of neighborhood organizations centered around local real estate development and a modus operandi that stressed cooperation and consensus. This is a unidimensional progressivism whose boundaries are territorial in nature and cooperative in method. Calls for black political organization violate both of these rules.

Perhaps the most tragic part of the story is that Pittsburgh, precisely because it lacks the invidious racial conflict that dominates Chicago's electoral politics, probably could accommodate a more progressive stance on racial issues. In fact, Pittsburgh's elites did take a progressive stand on race in the area of education and, as shown in chapter 4, in the area of housing as well. On the other hand, the civic-sector arena has not been forthcoming with resources for black political organizing or empowerment. I would argue that this omission stems less from any overt racist behavior than from a strong adherence to the norms of civility and conflict avoidance that are at the heart of Pittsburgh's civic-sector arena.

URBAN ARENAS

Political systems contain numerous arenas for interaction, with each distinguished by a particular logic, institutional framework, and political culture. Taken together, these factors shape perceptions, expectations, and ultimately behavior. Thus, which of these arenas is the predominant one becomes crucial. In Chicago the electoral arena has remained the primary one for neighborhood groups and minorities, while in Pittsburgh the civic-sector arena has become the major channel for resource distribution. Consequently, the two cities exhibit markedly different political cultures.

In Chicago the predominance of the electoral arena resulted in the development and strengthening of institutions (ward organizations) that dealt largely in the distribution of material incentives on an individual basis. This practice tended to encourage a market-oriented behavior based on the principle of exchange. The machine's preoccupation with social control reinforced this individualistic behavior by discouraging any kind of group mobilization. Skewing the distribution of resources in favor of rewarding friends and punishing enemies, the political machine transformed the system of resource distribution into a source of conflict and adversarial relations. This was particularly acute between neighborhood organizations and the ward organizations, where a zero-sum relationship formed. This relationship, combined with the system of resource distribution, contributed to shaping a political culture characterized by deep cynicism and mistrust.

In Pittsburgh the civic sector was overtaking the electoral arena as the distribution center of resources sought by neighborhoods. The institutions that were set up (ACCD, the Urban Redevelopment Authority, ACTION-Housing, Inc., the planning department) operated according to a very different logic than ward organizations. Concerned primarily with economic development, these institutions conformed more to the social production than the social control model of power. Resources were channeled in ways that encouraged collective association, civic engagement, and communal attachment. With a reward structure that was favorable to collective organizing at the community level, power-dependent relationships formed between CBOs and the institutions within the civic sector. These relationships established a pattern of nonconflictual, accommodative behavior. In contrast to Chicago, Pittsburgh's political culture is characterized by a strong sense of civic-mindedness, trust, and cooperation.

CONCLUSION

The patterns of demographic, economic, and political change have shaped an environment in Pittsburgh that is conducive to cooperative relations and accommodative behavior by elites. Neighborhood organizations have been major beneficiaries of this environment. In Chicago, these changes encouraged elites to resist demands for change and for a broadening of the policymaking franchise. The biggest losers have been community-based organizations and minorities.

3
Regime Formation in Chicago and Pittsburgh: Electoral Arenas and Civic Arenas

Social context and history profoundly condition the effectiveness of institutions.
—Robert Putnam

Chicago and Pittsburgh have been governed by "pro-growth" regimes since the middle of the twentieth century. A close look at how these regimes were formed illustrates the significant relationship between the balance of power among elites and the fashioning of arenas through which the regime operates. The domination of Pittsburgh's development regime by economic elites resulted in the establishment of a powerful civic arena organized around collective economic objectives. In Chicago the political elite–dominated regime operated principally in the electoral arena, which was organized around the objective of winning elections and the practice of dispensing individual benefits. These variations are significant for the role they played in shaping the political systems in the two cities. In chronicling the formation of the pro-growth regimes, this chapter explores some of the reasons why the structuring of power varied and, more important, the impact of that variation on institutional development and political culture in the two cities.

ECONOMIC RESTRUCTURING IN PITTSBURGH: CORPORATISM AND THE GROWTH MACHINE

Pittsburgh's economic restructuring was spearheaded by a pro-growth regime composed of the city's economic and political elites. Spurred on by the crisis associated with the city's economic decline, Republican businessmen, led by financier Richard King Mellon, allied with Democratic politicians, led by Mayor David Lawrence, to systematically address Pittsburgh's economic problems. Using public bodies and public power, this coalition created a corporatist decision-making structure that institutionalized the growth machine.[1]

The urgency and obviousness of the problem—Pittsburgh was drowning in its rivers and choking on its smoke—certainly facilitated early efforts. The real boost, however, came from Richard K. Mellon, whose wealth, influence, and associations were unparalleled in Pittsburgh. The combination of Mellon's power and the crisis situation in Pittsburgh left Lawrence with few viable options. By tying his political fortunes to Pittsburgh's economic rebuilding, Lawrence subordinated machine-specific political objectives to collective economic ones as the basis of the regime. This particular structuring of power resulted in a sharp party–government distinction as significant institution building occurred outside of the political machine's control. Public authorities and private, nonprofit organizations, set up by this new regime, were filling the space between party and government, creating a powerful civic arena that would become the center for the distribution of resources.

Hard Times in Steel Town

Once the steel capital of the United States, by the mid–twentieth century, Pittsburgh had fallen on hard times. Demand for steel, which had been artificially boosted by World War II, fell back to Great Depression levels in the war's aftermath. Decentralization within the steel industry—the relocation of production from the east to the west—combined with the industry's technological lag and loss of competitive edge, pointed to the conclusion that Pittsburgh needed to diversify its economy.

The decline of its dominant industry dealt the city a double blow. Not only did the future for steel look bleak, but the entire city, albeit a direct result of the success of the steel industry, had a dismal and dreary pall to it. The great blast furnaces that supported generations of steelworkers extracted a heavy price from the landscape. Streetlights had to replace the sun's rays, which simply could not pierce the permanent shroud of dark smoke.

Like many cities, Pittsburgh had invested very little in its infrastructure. Consequently, its housing stock was seriously inadequate, its sewage system absent in large parts of the city, and it underwent significant annual flooding. On Saint Patrick's Day in 1936, the rivers rose twenty-one feet above sea level, submerging the downtown streets for several days. The final toll was 47 people dead, 2,800 injured, and 67,500 left homeless, as well as $50 million in property damage.[2]

To say that Pittsburgh was not a desirable location begs the point. In the *Wall Street Journal*'s 1944 survey of the prospects of 137 cities, Pittsburgh received the lowest classification, D; its future was bleak, with little prospect for growth.[3] Even worse, some of Pittsburgh's most powerful corporate headquarters—Westinghouse, Alcoa, and the major giant itself, U.S. Steel—were in the initial stages of relocation. As a result, Pittsburgh's downtown real estate, which accounted for a disproportionate amount of tax revenue, exhibited a sharp decrease in value; between 1936 and 1946, the valuation of Pittsburgh's downtown real estate decreased 28 percent, compared with 21 percent for the city as a whole.[4]

With the city facing the need for economic diversification, a deteriorating downtown, and corporate disinvestment, it is hardly surprising that efforts to stem the tide of economic decline focused on downtown. What is surprising is that these efforts brought together a Republican financier, and one of the wealthiest men in America (Richard King Mellon) and a Democratic political boss and powerhouse in Pennsylvania politics (David Lawrence). This merger of public and private power planted the seeds for Pittsburgh's Renaissance I, the city's highly celebrated economic restructuring program.

One Man a King, One Man a Mayor: Regime Origins in Pittsburgh

As with any great tale, the proliferation of legends over time makes disentangling the truth a cumbersome task. Such was the case with Richard King Mellon's decision to rebuild Pittsburgh. Some stories credit his wife's refusal to live in a city as filthy as Pittsburgh and his refusal to "lose such a wonderful wife."[5] Others place Mellon's businesslike pragmatism at center stage; he preferred to keep his financial empire centralized in Pittsburgh, where it would be under his watchful eye.

Regardless of which legend one adopts, there are certain indisputable points. First, Mellon did make a commitment to rebuilding Pittsburgh. Second, the nature of the commitment was shaped by the crisis situation that faced the city. Third, Mellon's economic clout was unparalleled in Pittsburgh as well as in Pennsylvania, and he could compete with nearly anyone on a national scale. Finally, as Mellon perceived it, there was a strong convergence between the city's economic health and the health of his financial empire. During this period, Pennsylvania did not allow statewide banking, which made Mellon dependent for deposits on Pittsburgh and surrounding communities.

Richard King Mellon, nephew of Andrew Mellon, who made billions largely through the finance of manufacturing ventures, inherited the family empire in the mid-1930s. At the age of thirty-eight, Richard K. Mellon headed the family's three-billion-dollar enterprise, sat on the boards of more than twenty corporations, and, through the Mellon Bank and Trust Company, which at that time boasted the most assets of any Pittsburgh bank and ranked fifth in the entire country, had controlling interests in Gulf Oil, Koppers Corporation, Pittsburgh Plate and Glass, Pittsburgh Consolidation Coal, and Westinghouse.[6]

Mellon's concern over and determination to do something about Pittsburgh's economic decline were temporarily suspended by World War II. When the war ended, however, Mellon turned his attention and, more important, his economic and political clout to solving the problem. With the establishment of the Allegheny Conference on Community Development (ACCD) in 1943, Mellon set in motion a process that would permanently change Pittsburgh's economic base and physical landscape.[7]

Consisting of the CEOs of Pittsburgh's top corporations, the ACCD was a business-backed civic organization set up to address the city's long-term economic decline. In essence, however, it was an extension of corporate power—more precisely, of Mellon's corporate power. Membership on the executive committee, the ACCD's decision-making arm, was limited to CEOs. A nonsubstitution rule (CEOs could not send proxies in their place) ensured that Pittsburgh's "yes and no people" were at the table.[8] Clearly, this was to be a decision-making body. The executive committee was also governed by a rule of unanimous consent; no decision would be adopted without it. Democratic though this may sound, one must not forget that Mellon controlled most of these corporations, a factor central to the success of Renaissance I.

The existence of the ACCD and the resources it could command gave the corporate sector a strong voice: the ACCD convened the city's key economic players; it generated, or provided the funding for, numerous studies, reports, and plans; it provided the impetus and often the seed money for spin-off institutions; and it lent an "apolitical, technical" color to economic development strategies. Despite its enormous economic clout, the ACCD lacked formal public authority. It could generate all the plans it wanted, but without political support they would remain just plans. While Mellon and the ACCD benefited from the support of a Republican governor—Edward Martin—politics at the local level was another matter. The Republican machine that had governed Pittsburgh, like its counterparts in many other industrial cities, was toppled in the New Deal Democratic sweep.

In 1933 Democrat William McNair was elected mayor. By 1936 the mayor's office, the county board of commissioners, the city council, and the governor's office were controlled by Democrats. A driving force in this Democratic coup was David Leo Lawrence. Elected chair of the Allegheny County Democratic Committee in 1920 and named state party chair in 1934, Lawrence was fashioning a powerful Democratic political machine in western Pennsylvania and in the process was becoming one of the most powerful Democrats in the state.

By 1945, however, the Democratic coup was unraveling. A series of scandals, in which Lawrence was indicted but never convicted, and internal battles among leading Democrats had resulted in a resurgent Republican Party. In 1938 Republicans recaptured the governor's mansion and regained control over the statehouse. Four years later they captured the Senate.[9] After an eight-year hiatus, the Republicans resumed control in Harrisburg.

The political scene in Pittsburgh was equally troublesome; the Democratic Party had been strained by the chaotic administration of McNair and the lackluster performance of his successor, Cornelius Scully. Scully's narrow margin of victory as an incumbent in 1941 (3,163 out of more than 220,000 votes cast) convinced many in the party, including Scully, that a new candidate was needed. In 1945 David Lawrence, who had never held elective office, agreed to run for mayor.

With the full backing of the Democratic organization, the primary would be a shoo-in. The general election, however, promised to be another story. Twelve years of poor Democratic leadership, Lawrence's reputation as a "boss," the scandals, and the severe economic and infrastructure problems plaguing the city were causing many to reconsider their party loyalties.

Lawrence's problems were compounded by the Republican governor's announcement, two weeks prior to the election, of his intentions to fund the Point State Park redevelopment package. Assembled by Mellon and company, this package called for environmental improvements and a complete renovation of the historic Point State Park on the western edge of the central business district. Lawrence was caught between a rock and a hard place. If he took the strictly partisan route and attacked the governor's plan, he risked being viewed as a political hack, an image he was desperately trying to overcome. If he endorsed the plan, he ran the risk of being called a sellout to Republican and, even worse, big business interests.

After consultations with political advisers and analyses of 1941 mayoral election returns, which showed a decided weakness in middle- and business-class support, Lawrence came out in full support of the program, saying that it was about time the governor did something for Pittsburgh. Lawrence even fashioned his own seven-point program that promised a cooperative approach between the mayor and the business community, a prominent role for the ACCD, and an emphasis on economic diversification and revitalization of the central business district.[10]

The pitch was successful; Lawrence won the election by fourteen thousand votes, making significant inroads in middle-class wards and among professionals and businessmen. Lawrence's victory in 1945 solidified Democratic control over Pittsburgh's politics. This secure hold was aided by Republican businessmen, who traded local political power for economic power. Though not formally endorsing Lawrence in subsequent elections, Republican businessmen refrained from endorsing his Republican opponents. Organizationally the trade was significant as the exit of the Republican Party from local politics meant the loss of a "loyal opposition." Lawrence won reelection three times, setting a precedent for Pittsburgh, and then was elected governor in 1958. The Democratic Party has yet to lose a mayoral election.

Through his control of the Democratic Party machinery, Lawrence brought considerable clout to the mayor's office. Additionally, he operated in a political system conducive to centralization. Pittsburgh's charter was the result of a business-backed reform effort in 1911, which created a strong mayor–council system that gave the mayor formal authority over the budget, city departments, and council legislation. The charter also replaced the bicameral, one-hundred-plus-member legislature with a nine-member at-large city council.

Expeditiously applying his political skills, Lawrence brought Pittsburgh's political system firmly under his control. During his thirteen years as mayor, Lawrence secured near-unanimous votes from the city council on every major issue and saw less than six minor requests defeated; most of these passed in resubmission.[11]

Tying his political fortunes to Mellon's economic revitalization plans, Lawrence would emerge as the undisputed political leader of Pittsburgh and, through the substantial media attention to Pittsburgh's "renaissance," a prominent national figure as well. At the same time, however, it put Lawrence in a subordinate position to Mellon since collective economic, rather than particularistic political, objectives formed the basis of the regime and ultimately of Lawrence's success.

Institutionalizing the Growth Machine: The Development of Pittsburgh's Civic Arena

The paramount position of elite-driven, collective economic objectives vis-à-vis party-driven, particularistic political concerns was reflected in the institution building that occurred during the late 1940s and early 1950s. Economic development was carried out within a corporatist decision-making structure that insulated development policy from party control. The shape of the new regime was almost immediately set with the establishment of the Urban Redevelopment Authority (URA) (1946), the institution with primary responsibility for Pittsburgh's renaissance. By formally joining the public and private sectors, the URA provided the institutional base for the growth machine. Following on its heels was the creation of the parking authority, the public auditorium authority, the Allegheny County Sanitation Authority, and the tunnel authority.[12]

The fact that the institution of the "public authority" was chosen as the primary linkage vehicle indicates the strong prevailing private-sector bias; a "public authority" is the body that most resembles private-sector organization, and it is the most insulated from public scrutiny and control. In Pittsburgh the bias was evident from the URA board's original composition; while Lawrence chaired the board, three of the five members were leading businessmen and Republicans.[13] Most important, however, was the precedent of insulating development policies from party politics. Key resources were being channeled away from the political party and into this rapidly developing civic arena. The institutional separation, which continues to be a defining characteristic and stands in sharp contrast to Chicago, was strengthened by several factors.

First, development issues have been, and continue to be, presented in technical rather than partisan terms. This pattern emerged largely because of the domination of development policy by businesspeople and the technical nature of Pittsburgh's early problems—smoke and flood control. Once developed, it becomes self-perpetuating, interacting with and reinforcing the "nonpartisan" institutions within the civic arena.

Second, Lawrence's governing style, which, in contrast to Daley's, drew a separation between party and government, further reinforced the pattern. Though not complete, certain areas of local government were kept free from party interference. Commenting on Lawrence's "dual hiring policy," Michael Weber, Lawrence's biographer, noted that policy-making positions and bureau, department, and authority leadership slots were filled on the basis of "education and experience," while "semi-independent authorities in Pittsburgh, such as the redevelopment and housing authorities in particular, enjoyed a remarkable freedom from politics."[14]

Finally, there has been remarkable stability among Pittsburgh's corporate, civic, and political leadership. Between 1945 and 1995, the ACCD has had only five executive directors and city hall has been home to only six mayors.[15] Moreover, Pittsburgh has benefited from the economic clout of its numerous corporate headquarters. The ACCD, as the civic embodiment of this power, has enjoyed enormous legitimacy as the city's visionary leader.

Pittsburgh's Renaissance

Pittsburgh's economic rebuilding, quite appropriately termed its renaissance, resulted in the redevelopment of more than one thousand acres of land as $632 million, more than $500 million of which were private funds, was invested over a fifteen-year period.[16] The city that had been likened to "Hell with the lid taken off,"[17] that Frank Lloyd Wright had recommended "abandoning,"[18] and that H. L. Mencken described as "so dreadfully hideous, so intolerably bleak and forlorn that it reduced the whole aspiration of man to a macabre and depressing joke"[19] had traded in its worn and tattered clothing for a suit of shining armor. With titles like "Pittsburgh, a New City,"[20] and "Pittsburgh Rebuilds,"[21] the nation's leading magazines—*Fortune, Business Week, Collier's, Newsweek, National Geographic, Time, Life, Atlantic Monthly,* and others—were loudly singing Pittsburgh's praises.

At the center of this attention was the partnership between business and government. The ACCD, which had gained international fame by the mid-1950s, was heralded as a "model of civic leadership," while Lawrence was transformed from political boss to "civic statesman." In the meantime, Pittsburgh's image went from one of a decaying industrial city to one of a corporate headquarters center.[22] It had become a model for the new American city. On the home front, the ACCD was rapidly becoming the city's unofficial leader.

While Pittsburgh's renaissance included sixteen separate projects, the key ones were flood and smoke control and the construction of Gateway Center, a

REGIME FORMATION   51

multibuilding office complex on the edge of the central business district. If these initial efforts had failed, the renaissance would not have taken place. Their success resulted from coordination among economic and political elites who secured legislative changes, created new institutions, and strong-armed key corporate actors. Pittsburgh's transition to a major corporate headquarters city was not an automatic, consensual development but a political success story in which individual actors figured prominently.

While flood control legislation was secured relatively smoothly, smoke control efforts were problematic. The Pittsburgh city council had actually passed a smoke abatement ordinance in 1941, requiring conversion from the highly polluting coal smoke to more efficient fuels. Implementation was halted, however, by World War II and the need for low-cost fuel. With the war's end, demands for smoke control resumed. The ACCD had been pushing hard for this legislation, and the new mayor, David Lawrence, had pledged full support in his electoral campaign.

The costs involved in fuel conversion stimulated significant opposition from residents, local coal interests, and the railroads. While the residents could use the ballot box to deal Lawrence a severe blow, the mayor stood firmly behind the bill, convinced that in the absence of smoke control no new investment would be made in Pittsburgh and that businesses would leave. Lawrence's gamble paid off; the state passed legislation, the city implemented its earlier ordinance, and residents, while balking at the increase in fuel costs, delighted in the increase in sunlight, cleanliness, and healthfulness.[23] Moreover, Lawrence passed the ultimate test for any politician—reelection—with flying colors.

Opposition from the coal interests and the railroads resulted in a showdown with Mellon. Both the coal interests and the railroads quickly learned, however, that they were outresourced. Mellon used his position as director of Consolidation Coal to dissuade local coal interests from boycotting Pittsburgh companies as they had threatened to do. The Pennsylvania Railroad, a powerhouse in state politics, was also humbled by Mellon's economic clout. When it demanded exemption from the smoke bill, Mellon, who was a director of the railroad and a principal stockholder, threatened to use other freight lines for his companies' business. The Pennsylvania Railroad acquiesced, and the state had a new smoke control bill.[24]

On the redevelopment front, for several years the ACCD had been seeking a developer for Gateway Center, a deteriorated area on the edge of Point State Park and the central business district. Equitable Life Assurance Society had expressed a keen interest in developing the land. While convinced by the passage of the smoke bill that Pittsburgh was serious, Equitable was finding the redevelopment process too cumbersome. The land in the redevelopment area belonged to numerous private owners, making acquisition a developer's nightmare.

State passage, in 1945, of the Housing and Redevelopment Act partially resolved the problem. A precursor to federal urban renewal legislation, the act granted local governments the power of eminent domain and the right to establish public authorities for land acquisition and clearance activities. The act had been passed in order to facilitate the Point State Park redevelopment, which was already under way. The following year, Lawrence, at the ACCD's prompting, successfully lobbied the city council to establish the Pittsburgh URA. The Gateway Center project and the entire Pittsburgh renaissance now had an institutional base backed by the full powers of the state.

By 1947 the institutional and legal components (the state passed a bill allowing insurance companies to invest in redevelopment activities) were firmly in place. The financial end, however, was proving a bit more elusive. Equitable demanded from the URA a guarantee of twenty-year leases for 60 percent of the proposed one million square feet of office space. To fully appreciate this dilemma, consider Robert Alberts's satirical but accurate depiction:

> He [Arthur Van Buskirk, Mellon aide and ACCD board member] asked them [corporations] to sign, as an act of "civic responsibility," twenty-year leases in office skyscrapers that had not yet been built, had not yet been designed, were to be erected in an area subject to floods at the far edge of the established business district, at rents 20 to 100 percent higher than those they had been paying in their older buildings, on land that had not yet been acquired, but would be acquired under a radical new proposition that had not been tested in the courts.[25]

Despite apparently overwhelming odds, the URA delivered. Once again, Richard King Mellon was the driving power, admonishing corporations that were planning to relocate that "the Mellon family is not going to redevelop this city . . . if companies like yours are not going to play a major role, it's just that simple."[26] With controlling interests in, and outright ownership of, some of Pittsburgh's major corporations, Mellon preempted the "exit" option. In 1950 the URA signed an agreement guaranteeing the leasing arrangements Equitable had demanded. By the end of the year, nine of the city's largest corporations had signed leases.

By 1953 Equitable had built three office towers, thus completing the first stage of Gateway Center. The next decade witnessed the construction of six additional office towers, a state office building, new headquarters buildings for U.S. Steel, Mellon, and Alcoa, luxury apartment complexes, hotels, a civic center, and parking garages. Pittsburgh's Golden Triangle, with its shimmering new skyscrapers, had been reborn.

Pittsburgh's renaissance was not limited to the central business district. The Jones and Laughlin (J & L) project, which followed the Gateway Center project, was the first industrial redevelopment of its kind in the country. J & L, one of Pittsburgh's and the country's leading steel producers and Pittsburgh's second-largest taxpayer, had run out of space in its South Side plant. It could either move out of the city or expand in its current location. The latter option, while certainly preferable to city leaders, required the displacement of 235 families. After gaining the support of the CIO president, Lawrence endorsed the project, appealing to the economic self-interest of the area's residents; they were steelworkers and the redevelopment was necessary to save their jobs.[27] The project proceeded, the families were reimbursed for their property and relocated, and J & L remained in the city.

Pittsburgh's Renaissance: A Political Analysis

Examining Pittsburgh's renaissance, Jeanne Lowe attributed the city's success to its "action formula": "first, bring together the top industrial–business leaders of the community in an organization to support a general program for overall community improvement; second, establish a cooperative working relationship between them and the political and governmental leaders to advance specific projects."[28] Implicit in this observation is the idea that business elites were the prime movers in Pittsburgh's economic rebuilding, a fact borne out by the cases. While Mellon clearly needed public support for his projects, it is equally clear that without his economic control the actual projects would not have been implemented. The key role played by Mellon further solidified the dominant position of economic elites in Pittsburgh's governing regime.

The way the renaissance was planned and implemented resulted in identifiable patterns of leadership and policy making that have characterized Pittsburgh ever since. The emergence of the ACCD as the city's unofficial leader was the most important development. For the next half century, the ACCD directly or indirectly set up almost all of the city's private, nonprofit institutions, creating a powerful corporatist decision-making structure that governed economic development in the central business district, in the neighborhoods, and in the region.

The fact that the ACCD is a civic body made up of CEOs is crucial; economic, as opposed to political, elites have dictated the path of leadership in Pittsburgh. Operating through public–private partnerships, a pattern for which Pittsburgh has become quite famous, decision making in many areas has been largely removed from party control. Corporatist institution building has furthered this insulation of issues as more resources are channeled through the civic arena.

The prominent and highly visible role played by economic elites in the renaissance also helped to shape a political culture centered around civic-mindedness, corporate participation in public affairs, and cooperative behavior. Although there clearly was significant strong-arming, especially by Mellon, the public hype surrounding the renaissance downplayed these aspects while emphasizing the "public good" component of the projects. These features were enhanced by the increasing separation between party and government, which in essence amounted to the weakening of the political machine. The newly developing institutional framework provided additional reinforcement as resource distribution appeared to reward civic actions rather than parochial behavior. Finally, the ACCD's early, and at the time quite spectacular, success added a strong dose of deference to the city's political culture.

ECONOMIC REBUILDING IN CHICAGO: MACHINE POLITICS AND THE PRO-GROWTH REGIME

Chicago's pro-growth regime was forged during the administration of Richard J. Daley (1955–1976). Allying himself with key members of the business community, Daley assembled a powerful pro-growth coalition centered around economic rebuilding. Like Lawrence, Daley had strong political motivations to support economic development. Unlike Lawrence, however, Daley maintained the upper hand, thus establishing early on the primacy of political objectives as the basis of the regime. This particular structuring of power resulted in a very different institutional framework than the one that developed in Pittsburgh.

Tying his political fortunes to the building of a powerful political machine, Daley established and maintained strong ties to the business community on a more informal basis than in Pittsburgh, where institutions formalized the relations. The lack of formal institution building, combined with the primacy of the political, left virtually no room for the party–government distinction that emerged during Pittsburgh's renaissance and that would envelop other policy areas. Although Daley shielded economic development from electoral politics, he did not relinquish control over it. No area of policy in Chicago was free from particularistic political concerns.

This arrangement was perfectly acceptable to the business community as long as Daley could deliver. And deliver he could. Thus, successful implementation of economic development projects became integrally tied to the survival of the political machine, the source of Daley's substantial power. In contrast to Pittsburgh, then, the accommodation process of Chicago's pro-growth regime strengthened the political machine and, consequently, the centrality of the electoral arena within the city's political system.

These distinctive patterns owe much to the divergent structures of the cities' economic and political systems. Chicago's economic base was much more diversified than Pittsburgh's. As the Midwest's industrial center, Chicago was home to the meatpacking industry; a leader in the production of agricultural machinery, men's clothing, and furniture; and a key player in the iron and steel industries. As a railroad hub, Chicago was the center of significant commercial trade. As a regional capital, Chicago housed many corporate headquarters (second only to New York) and the futures and commodities markets, and also provided financial, insurance, and real estate services. Consequently, Chicago's business community was more heterogeneous and fragmented than Pittsburgh's. While there were some powerful actors, there was no equivalent of a Richard King Mellon, who could "impose" a civic vision and then coerce powerful corporate actors into carrying it out. This fragmentation in the business community gave Daley more freedom than Lawrence, who was "stuck" with Mellon, to pick which business leaders he would work with. In turn, this element of choice enhanced Daley's power vis-à-vis the business community.

Politically, Chicago's strong council, weak mayor government has also meant more fragmentation. Historically, this plan was reinforced through a district-based system supported by powerful ward organizations. With fifty members, Chicago's city council could be a much greater challenge to a mayor than Pittsburgh's nine-member at-large body. Thus, where Pittsburgh's economic and political systems contained the seeds for centralization, Chicago's contained the seeds for decentralization.

Daley's strategy was one of centralizing his own power while allowing, indeed fostering, the fragmentation of city government. Daley's political machine gave him enough control over city government to support private sector development. Lacking the institutional structure found in Pittsburgh, Chicago found its economic development dependent on the survival of the political machine.

Finally, economic rebuilding in Chicago had different origins than those in Pittsburgh. Beginning prior to manufacturing's decline and lacking the crisis proportions of Pittsburgh's situation, economic rebuilding in Chicago was not characterized by the same sense of desperation and urgency that surrounded similar efforts in Pittsburgh. Thus, Daley was less compelled than Lawrence to support economic development.

Planning the Postindustrial City

Planning for the postindustrial city in Chicago can be divided into two stages— an early one characterized by a civic beautification campaign and a second by an emphasis on economic growth. The first period (1909–1930), in contrast to Pittsburgh, preceded the city's industrial decline. Rather than a desperate response to larger economic forces, it represented the visions of a small group of economic elites. The second period, which paralleled the Daley administration, focused on economic growth and included considerable residential redevelopment, characterized by significant displacement of African American families.

In 1893 Chicago took the world by storm when it hosted the World's Columbia Exposition. Importing ideas from European cities, Daniel Burnham, the fair's designer, used the event to promote his vision of the future city—a postindustrial, corporate-centered metropolis boasting wide boulevards, breathtaking lakefront parks, new office buildings, and upscale residences. Also taken by Burnham's visions was the Commercial Club, a group consisting of the city's top economic elites. Sponsoring the Burnham Plan of 1909, the club convinced the city to adopt it as the official planning document the following year.

While manufacturing employment continued to increase until the late 1940s, the adoption of the Burnham Plan signaled a new direction for the city's economy. Between 1909 and 1930, Chicago spent nearly three hundred million dollars on civic beautification.[29] The addition of new streets and expressways improved traffic flow, while the lakefront was transformed into the city's jewel. Grant Park, created out of landfill, became the city's cultural center with the building of the Field Museum of Natural History in 1919, the Shedd Aquarium in 1929, and the Adler Planetarium in 1930. North Michigan Avenue was transformed into the "Magnificent Mile" and was on its way to becoming one of the leading retail strips in the world.

This rapid flow of activities came to a sudden halt with the Great Depression. As in Pittsburgh, Chicago's downtown took a disproportionate hit; between 1939 and 1947, property values in the central business district decreased 13 percent, compared with 3 percent for the city as a whole.[30] In response, the Commercial Club replaced the civic beautification strategy with one that emphasized economic growth. Nevertheless, the Burnham Plan had set much of the tone for planning efforts in Chicago; subsequent plans were developed in the private sector, shared the corporate-centered city approach, and focused largely on the central business district and strategically located residential neighborhoods.

Spearheading the Commercial Club's efforts were Milton Mumford, assistant vice president of Marshall Field's, the retailing giant and publisher of the *Chicago Sun-Times,* and Holman Pettibone, president of Chicago Title and Trust Company. Operating through the private, nonprofit Metropolitan Housing and Planning Council (MHPC), headed by Fred Kramer, one of the city's largest real estate moguls, these men took the lead in getting state legislation passed, attracting private investment, orchestrating city bond campaigns, lobbying the city council, conducting studies, and assembling development plans. As Squires et al. observed, Mumford and Pettibone "established the redevelopment process in Chicago."[31]

Their key legislative successes included the passage of the Illinois Blighted Areas Act in 1947 and the Urban Community Conservation Act of 1953. The first act, a slum clearance measure that included eminent domain and public "write-down" provisions, became the model for federal urban renewal legislation two years later, while the Conservation Act, designed as a slum prevention measure, guided the federal Housing Act of 1954.[32]

These statutes were crucial to the implementation of the city's first master plan. Developed in 1943 by sociologist and demographer Homer Hoyt, the plan targeted twenty-two square miles of inner-city blight for residential redevelopment.[33] The pattern established by this plan—demolition of deteriorated housing, to be replaced by middle-income housing—would be repeated throughout the city. Thus, in contrast to Pittsburgh, where housing problems were acknowledged but initially given short shrift, from the beginning residential redevelopment was a key component of Chicago's economic rebuilding.

These distinctive trends can be traced to geographic and demographic factors. Chicago's Loop is surrounded on three sides by residential areas, whereas Pittsburgh's Golden Triangle is surrounded on three sides by water. In the one area that was residential—the Lower Hill—Pittsburgh's elites behaved quite similarly to their Chicago counterparts: they bulldozed the blight (see chapter 4). Additionally, Chicago's black population rapidly and significantly increased from 1910 to 1950, making race a central factor in redevelopment decisions. Thus, while Pittsburgh's renaissance began with smoke and flood control, two technological triumphs that did not involve any displacement and that gave the city's restructuring an early and quite significant honeymoon period, Chicago's efforts regarding residential development were born in controversy.

The first project executed under the Blighted Areas Act was Lake Meadows on the city's near South Side.[34] Begun in 1948 and completed roughly ten years later, Lake Meadows featured ten high-rise buildings containing 2,033 housing units on one hundred acres of land. In many ways Lake Meadows was a preview of Chicago's economic redevelopment program. It was the product of public and private activities: the newly created public Land Clearance Commission acquired the land through eminent domain, the city sold bonds to cover site acquisition and preparation costs, and New York Life Insurance Company developed the site. Second, it resulted in significant displacement. Finally, those displaced were overwhelmingly black. Although Lake Meadows was racially integrated, the new black tenants were not from the 3,416 families, mostly black, that had been displaced.

This pattern would be repeated many times and with similar consequences. The adjacent Prairie Shores, a development of five high-rise buildings with more than twelve hundred housing units and a shopping center, followed on its heels, also causing significant displacement. Sandburg Village, approved in 1957 and completed in 1963, displaced 3,871 persons, mostly black, on the city's near North Side. The Hyde Park Kenwood urban renewal, orchestrated by the University of Chicago, reduced that area's housing stock by 20 percent. While the overall population declined 26.4 percent, the African American population decreased by nearly 40 percent.[35]

While residential redevelopment was transforming select neighborhoods, the Loop was in decline; retail sales, property values, and employment had all exhibited a downward spiral, while construction of new office space ceased with the Great Depression. Concern over the fate of the downtown area among Chicago's economic elites, however, did not translate into a consensus on approach. In fact, as political scientist James Greer has observed, there was considerable conflict between those who favored a "growth" strategy and those who supported a "maintenance" approach.[36]

Even within the former group, there were bitter divisions. Edward Banfield's fine case study on the aborted Fort Dearborn development proposal documented the depth of the divisions among Chicago's economic elites.[37] The near-decade-long struggle over, and eventual derailment of, this major proposal, which called for a civic center and housing just north of the Loop, encouraged the formation of the Chicago Central Area Committee (CCAC).

The prime advocate for the growth strategy, the CCAC, headed by Holman Pettibone, drew its membership largely from major downtown businesses, particularly banks, real estate firms, insurance companies, architectural firms, and utilities. Establishing the CCAC did not eliminate opposition to development proposals from the business community. Rather, it weakened the effect of such opposition by organizationally concerting powerful forces behind its proposals. The Daley administration would provide a major boost as public power and private resources combined to reshape Chicago economically and spatially.

The Political Machine, the Business Community, and the Emergence of the Pro-Growth Regime

While private development plans were being generated and executed, the public end lagged. Chicago's governmental and political machinery, characterized by extreme fragmentation, were ill equipped to supply the wherewithal that major economic growth strategies require. Daley's election in 1955, however, changed all that. Reorganizing Chicago's political machine, Daley achieved a degree of centralized power unsurpassed in any other major U.S. city. In the process he redefined the relationship between the political system and the business community.

Chicago's Democratic machine, assembled by Mayor Anton Cermak (1931–1933) and continued by Mayor Edward Kelly (1933–1947) and party chairman Patrick Nash, was besieged by factional rivalries.[38] Routinely spilling over into the city council, itself dominated by the "gray wolves," these factional battles ensured that decentralization would continue to define Chicago politics. The situation was exacerbated by the administration of reform mayor Martin Kennelly (1947–1955). A businessman, Kennelly was no match for the "gray wolves." The ordinary stuff of politics—lobbying city council members and state legislators, addressing community and organizational opposition—quickly fell to the business elites. While obviously successful in their political maneuvering, this was not the most efficient division of labor between public and private sectors. The election of Richard J. Daley in 1955 altered that division.

Although promising to relinquish his position as party chair if he won the mayoralty, Daley abandoned the promise instead. Unquestionably, this was one of his most critical decisions. Simultaneously occupying the mayor's office and the chairmanship of the Cook County Democratic Central Committee, Daley acquired near-total control over jobs and money, the sum and substance of machine politics.

While civil service reforms decimated patronage reserves in most cities, Chicago proved the exception. Controlling between twenty and thirty thousand jobs, Daley established an impressive network of dependencies, many of which were unidirectional.[39] In 1955 Daley also usurped the council's budgetary power when he got the state legislature to give the mayor's office authority for formulating the budget. These two features enabled Daley to rearrange the balance of power between the executive and legislative branches of government. The "gray wolves" were silenced, the power of the mayor's office was greatly enhanced, and Daley was on his way to becoming one of the most influential political leaders in Illinois.

While the business community looked askance at Daley's election and the newspapers, seeing him as a political hack, refused to endorse him, Daley altered both of these relationships. Making it known, early on, that he shared the business community's concern over the fate of Chicago's downtown, Daley used his control over city government and the electorate to provide the certainty, deliver the resources, and manage the conflict that allowed an extraordinary amount of downtown development to occur. Given the fragmentation of Chicago's government, the divisions within the business community, and the absence of a Richard K. Mellon to coerce economic elites, Daley's role was pivotal in Chicago's economic development.

Recognizing the CCAC as the "official" spokesperson for the business community, Daley forged a growth coalition made up of key Loop interests, real estate developers, some top-level advisers, and several commissioners. This access in effect translated into a privatization of Chicago's planning function. The Development Plan of 1958, the first comprehensive plan for the city since the Burnham Plan, was essentially written by the CCAC even though it was issued by the planning department. Chicago 21, issued in 1973, made even less pretense; it was published by the CCAC. Further, the architectural plans in these documents were all designed by the private firm Skidmore, Owings and Merrill. Thus, the tradition established by Daniel Burnham, of private planning and physical development, was alive and well nearly half a century later.

In addition to access, Daley delivered the necessary land-use arrangements, zoning approvals, and infrastructure improvements that these plans required. A combination of transportation improvements and public construction made the Loop quite attractive to private investment. An expressway system was completed, compliments of generous federal subsidies, providing north, south, and westerly access in and out of the Loop.[40] O'Hare Airport, which by 1974 was the world's busiest, opened in 1955. The construction of two government buildings provided an anchor for downtown development. Between 1962 and 1977 the Loop gained thirty-two million square feet of new office space, capped off by the construction of the Sears Tower, the world's tallest building at that time.[41]

This downtown investment was accompanied by development activities on the south, north, and west sides of the Loop. McCormick Place, an exposition center containing three hundred thousand square feet of exhibit space, opened in 1960 along the lakefront on the near South Side.[42] Watertower Plaza, an eleven-story shopping and office complex, was developed on North Michigan Avenue, further cementing the fortunes of the Magnificent Mile. Several near North Side neighborhoods had been gentrified, while the University of Illinois (Chicago campus) was relocated to its current site on the near West Side, curbing blight and helping to gentrify the immediate environs (see chapter 4).

By the mid-1970s, most of the Development Plan of 1958 had been completed. The Loop and surrounding areas had been revitalized, thereby creating the buffer deemed necessary by the plan's architects.

Chicago's Growth Machine and the Primacy of the Political

Conspicuously absent from Chicago's early economic development is the type of institution building that characterized Pittsburgh's renaissance. Except where necessary, Daley avoided building institutions, particularly those that could compete with his political organization and perhaps rival his own power. In Chicago, fragmentation was the defining feature. In Pittsburgh, for example, responsibility for economic development was lodged primarily in the URA and secondarily in the planning department. In Chicago these responsibilities were distributed among numerous agencies, with Daley acting as chief coordinator. The Department of City Planning, for instance, was created by Daley to be the instrument for downtown revitalization, but zoning and land clearance activities were lodged in other agencies. As Squires et al. noted, "From the mid-1950s to the mid-1970s the hinge linking Chicago's mobilized business community and its fragmented public planning apparatus was Richard J. Daley."[43]

Daley's position at the center was not accidental, as his formation of numerous "advisory committees" illustrates. The Mayor's Committee for Economic and Cultural Development (MCECD), for instance, set up by Daley in 1961 to conduct economic and cultural planning, remained as a committee throughout Daley's entire administration. Ignoring the advice of the MCECD's executive director to establish it as a city department, Daley kept it solely under his control, thus ensuring that business elites came through the mayor's office.[44] Daley's role was thus twofold: to coordinate a fragmented bureaucracy to facilitate economic development plans and to provide insulation for economic development policy making. Relying on a powerful political machine that blended party and government (jobs were based on political performance), Daley accomplished both tasks. His control over city government enabled him to deliver the public-sector end of economic development. His control over substantial amounts of discretionary resources enabled him to practice a politics of divergence. By structuring the electoral arena around the distribution of material rewards and incentives, Daley kept electoral and neighborhood politics on an individual and issueless basis.[45] Securing mass support through material incentives in the electoral arena, Daley was then free to practice elite politics in the policy sector.

The other side of divergence strategy reveals a symbiotic relationship between electoral politics and policy politics. The greater the amount of downtown development, the more jobs and contracts that were generated. Thus, the largesse created by the policy focus fueled the machine. Conversely, the stronger the machine, the better able Daley was to deliver to business elites. Unlike in most cities, Chicago's business community did not push to reform the political system. In fact, the leading Republican businessmen took out a full-page ad endorsing Daley in the 1959 election.[46] With their interests well served, they had no need for "good government." The machine was doing just fine.

The primacy of political objectives also helped to shape a political culture unlike the one that was forming in Pittsburgh. With jobs tied to political performance, a market-oriented behavior fueled by strong parochialism permeated Chicago's institutional culture. While large portions of Pittsburgh's bureaucracy also remained under machine control and thus exhibited a similar culture, the increasing separation between party and government loosened the machine's hold while institutional expansion within the civic arena fueled the newly developing political culture. Chicago, by contrast, had only one game in town, with one set of rules. The civic-mindedness that was taking root in Pittsburgh's civic arena was truly alien to Chicago's bureaucracy.

It was equally alien to Chicago's electorate where cynicism about and mistrust of government were becoming growth industries. The pace of economic development, especially on the residential side, led many people to conclude that the political system did not represent their interests. Indeed, it could be their biggest enemy. This realization came early on to many in the black community as race and economic development formed an ugly nexus.

Race and Economic Development

That race guided Chicago's postwar redevelopment plans is no secret. Chicago's black population increased from 44,000 in 1910, to 233,000 in 1930, to 492,000 in 1950, and to 1.1 million in 1970.[47] Alarmed by the massive influx of African Americans in and around the city's "inner zone," Chicago's economic elites sought renewal through removal. Beginning with Hoyt's master plan in 1943, continuing in the Development Plan of 1958, its subsequent revisions in 1964 and 1966, and Chicago 21, one finds deliberate efforts to create a "white" buffer around the Loop.[48]

These efforts gained institutional protection early on when the Land Clearance Commission (LCC) was designated the primary urban renewal vehicle under the Illinois Blighted Areas Act. The establishment of the LCC was a direct attempt to bypass the already existing Chicago Housing Authority (CHA), which, under the stewardship of Elizabeth Wood, was a major proponent of integrated public housing.[49] With powers of eminent domain and the authority to resell the acquired land, the CHA seemed to many blacks and liberal white sympathizers the appropriate agency for a race-neutral redevelopment program. This was not the view, however, of the architects of the legislation. Commenting on Wood's views on integrated housing, Ira Bach, first head of the LCC, noted that they were "a little too far out to satisfy Pettibone, Mumford, and the others involved."[50]

Thus, the LCC became the redevelopment vehicle while the CHA was relegated to the supporting role of building replacement housing for African Americans displaced by LCC activities. Because the LCC sold the land to private developers, the land was not subject to the CHA's "nondiscrimination tenant selection policy."[51] Even the latter, however, would ultimately be rendered null and void by political pressures. Thus, from its very inception, Chicago's redevelopment program contained an unmistakably powerful racial dimension.

The massive concentration of blacks in only a few areas had been the result of fierce resistance by whites and the extensive use of restrictive housing covenants. The latter covered three-fourths of the city's housing stock by 1930 and was approaching 95 percent in some neighborhoods.[52] The CHA's open housing policy was a threat to this carefully crafted system. Even more threatening was the 1948 Supreme Court decision in *Shelley v. Kramer,* which declared such covenants unconstitutional.

While Chicago politicians had no control over the Supreme Court, in 1948 the city council wrested control over site selection from the CHA. Segregated housing in Chicago became the official policy as white aldermen vetoed the construction of public housing in their wards. The firing of Wood in 1954 constituted the de facto last rites for an integrated public housing policy. Daley's appointments to the CHA board further guaranteed that segregated housing would be the policy.[53]

With the CHA as the primary vehicle for replacement housing and the practice of segregating public housing the norm, redevelopment activities and racial segregation became locked in a vicious cycle. Between 1950 and 1954 more than 50 percent of new public housing units went to families displaced by urban renewal activities.[54] Under Daley, the pace of construction stepped up considerably. Between 1955 and 1970, the major period of urban renewal, 27,779 units were constructed, more than twice the number (12,460) for the prior sixteen years (1938–1954).[55]

With location decisions following the color line, African American neighborhoods on the South and West Sides absorbed more than 99 percent of the city's subsidized family units.[56] The South Side contains a nearly four-mile stretch of high-rise public housing within which the notorious Robert Taylor Homes, the largest public housing development in the country, is situated. Twenty-eight buildings, each sixteen stories high, occupy a two-mile stretch of abject poverty. Of the development's initial twenty-seven thousand residents, twenty thousand were children—all poor, all black.[57]

Politically, the cards seemed heavily stacked against any serious challenge to this system. Although the African American vote was critical in Daley's first and third elections, his fervent support of economic development and his CHA appointments sanctioned this segregated housing policy. A good student of Chicago political history, Daley seemed to have learned from Edward Kelly's mistakes. As mayor, Kelly supported integrated public housing; as payback, the party dumped him.[58]

Even federal intervention could not permeate the insidious interaction of race and politics. When a federal district court judge declared Chicago's public housing policy discriminatory (*Gautreaux v. CHA*, 1969) and ordered the provision of desegregated low-income housing, the CHA ceased production. Despite court injunctions and suspension of federal funds (twenty-six million dollars of Model Cities money in 1971 and twenty million dollars of urban renewal funds in 1972), the CHA between 1969 and 1980 built a meager 114 subsidized family units.[59] Meanwhile, the city was losing nearly 6,000 units a year, primarily in low-income neighborhoods, to arson and abandonment, while the CHA's waiting list jumped to 11,200 families.[60]

Perhaps even more telling was the relative quiescence of African American politicians. While there was some opposition from African American residents and local leaders to the early redevelopment and displacement activities, black machine politicians were conspicuously silent. In the material-based, issueless world of Chicago politics, loyalty, not causes, was the highest aspiration. Thus, from the beginning of the Daley administration, we can see a split between the incentives of black political elites and the interests of black voters.

REGIME FORMATION IN PITTSBURGH AND CHICAGO: AN ANALYSIS

For a variety of reasons, the formation of the pro-growth regimes in Pittsburgh and Chicago featured dissimilar accommodation processes. In Pittsburgh, collective economic objectives constituted the basis of the regime, whereas in Chicago particularistic and partisan political objectives were paramount. Thus, while both fall under the heading of "development" regimes, the political and institutional legacies vary substantially.

Guided by collective economic objectives, Pittsburgh's early institution building resulted in the development of a powerful civic sector. The subsequent channeling of resources away from party control shaped a political culture and a pattern of political behavior that emphasize civic participation, cooperative relations, and conflict avoidance. In Chicago the political machine emerged as the primary institution, weaving party and government in a tight web. As the primary mechanism for the distribution of resources, the machine heightened the significance of the electoral arena, an area that encourages conflict. It has also contributed to a political culture that encourages parochialism and a market-oriented behavior based on individual exchange.

The significance of these differences transcends individual policy areas. As Stephen Elkin has argued, "Once an institution is created, its effects carry over outside its specific domain in the form of habits and dispositions."[61] Institutions provide, or deny, options to citizens and influence the means by which they exercise those options. The role of institutions as gatekeepers and molders of political behavior will become quite apparent in the following chapter, which examines the opportunities for neighborhood mobilization.

Finally, as Elkin observed, there are "multiplier effects" of institutional development.[62] In Chicago, for example, the most significant ones would be administrative and political. The general underdevelopment of Chicago's governmental machinery would become an administrative nightmare for serious reform efforts. These would be further hampered by a political mentality characterized by deep mistrust and cynicism and poisoned by the irresponsible and opportunistic use of race by too many Chicago politicians.

4
Planting the Seeds of Discontent: Urban Renewal and the Neighborhoods

Make no little plans. They have no magic to stir men's blood....
—Daniel Burnham

The Prince *was written by Machiavelli for the Haves on how to hold power.* Rules for Radicals *is written for the Have-Nots on how to take it away.*
—Saul Alinsky

"Big plans," so characteristic of urban renewal, stirred many a person's blood, some favorably, some not so favorably. Resting on a physical definition of urban problems and the assumption of trickle-down benefits, these slum clearance and downtown development schemes selectively enhanced land values, usually around the central business district, in the hopes of making cities attractive to the middle class and to business. The view from the neighborhoods, however, was quite different. At this level urban renewal often meant displacement as lower-income housing was bulldozed to make way for more expensive housing, for institutional expansion, or for commercial development. For poor and working-class people, renewal meant removal; the benefits of development did not seem to trickle down to them.

Even more, many neighborhood residents were beginning to realize that their interests were totally expendable in larger urban development schemes. The political process through which these decisions were mediated, site selection in particular, favored those interests that had significant clout. Neighborhoods, especially older and poorer ones, were not among this privileged group.

The neighborhood consequences of urban renewal stimulated massive opposition. In numerous cities, growth machines encountered their first major challenge as neighborhood organizers opposed the policy orientation and top-down planning practices of the pro-growth regimes. In Chicago and Pittsburgh urban renewal set off similar protests among neighborhood groups. In both cities the governing regimes suffered a loss of legitimacy as their motives became highly suspect and their loyalty to all parts of the city was called into question. But, significantly, the two regimes, guided by dissimilar objectives and incentive structures, responded differently.

In Chicago the overriding response was one of resistance, whereas in Pittsburgh there were serious efforts at collaboration and cooperation with CBOs. These responses, combined with the institutional structures and the pattern of resource distribution in the two cities, influenced the character of urban renewal and the opportunities for neighborhood participation and mobilization. In Chicago, CBOs operated in a system that lacked the resources to support such participation and whose overall orientation ran counter to such developments. In short, Chicago's political and institutional structures allowed no room for CBOs. This posture of exclusion resulted in serious conflict when CBOs attempted to establish some presence in the neighborhood. Pittsburgh's institutional framework and its pattern of resource distribution actually encouraged organizational formation and inclusion. While there were tensions between the orientation of some of these organizations and the orientation of the governing regime, the space was there and the resources available to support organizational development in the neighborhoods.

CHICAGO: THE POLITICS OF CONTRADICTION

As indicated earlier, Chicago's early redevelopment programs contained a strong residential component. The amount of displacement, the lack of acceptable relocation practices, and the relative acquiescence of elected neighborhood officials (i.e., city councillors and ward committeemen) revealed early on the contradictions of machine politics; while portraying itself as the champion of the neighborhoods and the working class, when push came to shove, the political machine was really representing itself and therefore reflecting the interests of economic and political elites. This contradiction shook the foundation of the machine's legitimacy, introducing an element of instability into a system that thrived on social and political control and the suppression of issues. The case of the University of Illinois-Chicago campus, described in the following pages, reveals the beginnings of this uncoupling; longtime supporters of the Daley machine fought back when they realized they had been sacrificed in the larger game of economic development. Their protests signaled this new, and unsettling, development in Chicago politics: neighborhood challenges to the pro-growth regime.

Heavily influenced by the practices of Saul Alinsky, neighborhood organizing in Chicago assumed a highly confrontational character. While part of this orientation was directly attributable to the teachings of Alinsky, it was also conditioned by the overall orientation of Chicago's governing regime and its institutional framework. The primary political institutions in Chicago are the ward organizations whose overriding objective is to accumulate political power. Electorally driven, ward organizations operate in a system that practices an exchange politics at the level of the individual voter. Thus, the nature of the resources they distribute (jobs) is irrelevant to neighborhood organizations that seek benefits on a more collective basis. Moreover, when these community organizations needed collective representation in their battles against development, the ward organizations could not provide it since doing so would have required them to challenge the source of their own power. Not only were the ward organizations unable to represent neighborhood interests, but, with their power rooted in the neighborhoods, they saw CBOs as direct competitors, thus entering into a zero-sum game for neighborhood representation and control.

The particular structuring of power as reflected in Chicago's governing regime and the resulting institutional framework shaped very narrow opportunities for neighborhood organizations. The priorities of the governing regime and the nature of resource distribution helped to create sharp lines of division between CBOs and the political machine. The Alinsky approach to organizing, which took solid root in Chicago, further hardened the divisions, creating a legacy of cynicism and mistrust.

Educating the Community: The Location of the University of Illinois-Chicago Campus

"With the elections behind him, Daley returned to the task of making life better in his city, a city of neighborhoods, by plotting the elimination of one of the city's oldest and most colorful neighborhoods."[1] So began Mike Royko's vignette on the saga to plan and build a new campus for the University of Illinois (UIC). Though the campus project resulted in the direct displacement of more than eight thousand people and approximately 630 businesses, Daley's objective was not to destroy a neighborhood, but to get a state university campus built in the city of Chicago.[2] While this was in keeping with the Development Plan of 1958, the eventual site of the proposed campus was not. That plan, guided by visions of a postindustrial city, called for a downtown campus to replace the railroad terminals. The politics of decision making, which resembled a pluralist bargaining pattern among elites, forced a very different outcome, with devastating consequences for a neighborhood.

The case is instructive on several dimensions. First, it highlights the expendability of certain types of neighborhoods in urban redevelopment plans. Second, it underscores the political component of redevelopment decision making. The eventual site was no one's first choice; the two preferred sites, however, had powerful protectors and thus were eventually removed from consideration as development locations. Finally, it reveals the dubious representation provided by ward leaders for their neighborhoods and the fundamental contradiction of machine politics; it was not about the "little guy" after all but about a top-down decision-making process in which powerful elites rode roughshod over neighborhood residents because it was politically possible to do so.

Plans for a state university campus within the city had been on the drawing board since the early 1950s. Stalled for many years by state legislative and top-level university politics and conflicts over location, the project acquired new steam in 1959 when Mayor Richard J. Daley promised to match any suburban offer by paying the land cost differential between city and suburban locations. The financial resources came from federal urban renewal money, which, in another blow to housing objectives, could be spent on land acquisition and clearance costs for university and hospital expansion.

The site identification process ultimately produced three possibilities—the downtown railroad terminals; Garfield Park on the city's West Side; and the Harrison-Halstead corridor, a residential community that was 66 percent white, 20 percent Mexican, and 15 percent African American in 1960. Although the downtown location was the choice of Mayor Daley, Loop businessmen, the major newspapers, and civic leaders—all of whom viewed the campus as an institutional anchor for the downtown—the demands made by the railroads that owned the property proved to be insurmountable. The several railroads involved resisted any form of consolidation, demanded a high price for their land, and insisted that the city construct a new terminal. Lacking powers of eminent domain over the railroads, the city was politically outmuscled. Several years of negotiations resulted in a virtual deadlock since the financial costs of this site were far in excess of what the city was able or willing to pay. Under time pressures from the university to select a site, the city was forced to look elsewhere.

The proposal for the West Side site called for locating the campus in Garfield Park, which borders the residential communities of Austin and East Garfield. Although community residents pushed for the campus in the hope that it would stabilize property values, the site fell victim to powerful elite opposition.[3] The Chicago Park District, a formally independent agency and a gold mine of patronage, was opposed to breaking up large parks or ceding any of their land. Park district board member Jake Arvey, who was Daley's predecessor as party head and instrumental in Daley's rise to power, was also opposed to the site. Notable civic leaders objected to the perceived destruction of open park land, while downtown business elites still favored the railroad terminals. Finally, as in the case of the railroads, the city lacked eminent domain over park district properties. Thus, acquiring the land would have involved very high political costs.

By contrast, the site ultimately chosen, the Harrison-Halstead corridor, lacked any powerful protectors. Although alderman John D'Arco, the head of the first ward organization, did not favor the decision, Daley's firm hold over the city council ensured that there was a favorable majority vote. The major institution in the area—the famed Hull House—had a divided board and thus took no public position; it was ultimately relocated to a nearby site. Finally, since the city had previously declared the area an urban renewal site, it could exercise eminent domain, a power sorely lacking in the other two sites.

Opposition was forthcoming from neighborhood residents. Their late starting challenge, however, reveals much about the contradictions of machine politics. In contrast to the other two sites, where elites had greased the appropriate lines of opposition behind closed doors and far enough in advance of official action, the residents of Harrison-Halstead protested against what was virtually a done deal. Not privy to "inside information," they were victims of the city's closed-door planning process. While "public" discourse centered on the Loop and Garfield Park sites, Daley's top planners were researching the Harrison-Halstead site and were under strict orders not to reveal anything to the public or even to university officials. By the time Daley announced that the Harrison-Halstead corridor was an alternative site, it was in fact, the only site.

Even this announcement, however, did not stimulate immediate opposition. Designated by the city as an urban renewal area, the corridor had been slated for housing redevelopment. The residents, being loyal supporters of the machine, did not believe the city would violate its commitment. Moreover, they were under the protection of the powerful first ward organization. In the following description, George Rosen accurately portrays the sentiments of many of the area's residents: "In fact, the Italian, Greek and Spanish-speaking residents of the areas didn't believe it could happen. They knew the fabled power of the Italian political leaders, who were close to the Democratic city leaders, would never agree to such a proposal, which would change already committed plans for the area from residential renewal to institutional use."[4]

While the residents put their faith in their elected leaders, the city pursued its plans for a campus in the area. As the city's intentions became clearer, an opposition movement did eventually surface. Led by Florence Scala, a movement consisting largely of women conducted meetings, led protests, and picketed the mayor's office. The opposition did not stop the construction of the university campus, but it did educate a community, which learned that the "mayor of all neighborhoods" had just abandoned the city's oldest one in order to satisfy the preferences of political and economic elites.[5]

The painful lessons of the Harrison-Halstead corridor would be repeated in other areas throughout the city. Sharp lines of division would be drawn between neighborhoods and their elected leaders, whose legitimacy as local representatives had become highly suspect. In 1962, largely as the result of an organizing campaign by Florence Scala and some of her neighbors, Chicago voters sent the growth machine a message; they defeated six bond issues, including an urban renewal bond for $22.5 million.[6]

Grassroots Organizing: The Alinsky Tradition

The displacement caused by the University of Illinois campus was not new for Chicago; as noted previously, the city's early redevelopment contained significant residential redevelopment and displacement. What was new was that neighborhood opposition was becoming more organized. In the University of Illinois case it came late in the day and the residents were defeated. In other parts of the city, however, communities were organizing to fight the bulldozer. Enlisting the organizing skills of Saul Alinsky and the Industrial Areas Foundation (IAF), Alinsky's training school for organizers, Chicago's burgeoning neighborhood movement was developing a confrontational style that was ready and willing to do battle with political elites, economic elites, and city bureaucracy.

A University of Chicago–trained sociologist, Saul Alinsky abandoned his graduate studies in 1932 to devote himself full-time to what would become one of the greatest careers in community organizing history. A fervent believer in grassroots democracy, Alinsky was also a realist about power relations. The latter was reflected in his organizing strategy, which centered around the identification of an external target in order to unite neighborhood residents and the use of confrontational tactics against the opposition. Combining the passion and militancy of a radical with the careful attention to detail of an organizer, Alinsky was fully aware of the implications of his activities. He wrote, "The building of a People's Organization is the building of a new power group. The creation of any new power group automatically becomes an intrusion and a threat to the existing power arrangements. It carries with it the menacing implication of displacement and disorganization of the status quo."[7]

Clearly, there were many in Chicago who feared Alinsky and his IAF-trained organizers. The practice of "rubbing raw the sores of discontent" helped to create, and in some cases to reinforce, an "us versus them" mentality. This conflict could assume class dimensions, racial dimensions, and a neighborhood-versus-downtown tenor. Permeating all of these cleavages was the threat to the machine's system of social and political control in the neighborhoods.

Alinsky's organizing activities began in Back of the Yards, the residential neighborhood adjacent to the stockyards. The subject of Upton Sinclair's classic *The Jungle,* Back of the Yards was rife with ethnic hostility, poverty, disease, and, as a result of the Great Depression, staggeringly high unemployment. Working largely through the local Catholic churches and in conjunction with packinghouse organizers, Alinsky set up the Back of the Yards Neighborhood Council (BYNC) in 1939. Consisting of representatives from social, fraternal, business, labor, and religious organizations,[8] BYNC became involved in a wide range of areas, including child welfare, health care, a credit union, a free lunch program, juvenile delinquency, recreation, and housing. Positioning itself as the organizational representative for the community, the council quickly ran afoul of local political leaders, who saw BYNC as a rival to the power of the ward organization. The park district president, who was also the treasurer of the Cook County Democratic Party, killed the free lunch program and ordered BYNC out of its facility, and the head of BYNC out of Back of the Yards.[9]

The assault proved unsuccessful as BYNC's powerful supporters stepped forward. Prominent civic leaders, most notably Marshall Field III, publisher of the *Chicago Sun-Times,* saw BYNC as a fine example of local leadership and individual initiative. The Archdiocese of Chicago, BYNC's main institutional backer, also came to the council's defense. Reluctantly, the park district president backed down.

Alinsky's civic support, including that from the Field Foundation, which helped finance the establishment of the IAF, waned as Alinsky took on bigger entities and came out more forcefully for racial integration and equality. These factors came to a head in the black South Side neighborhood of Woodlawn, where Alinksy set up The Woodlawn Organization (TWO)—his second organization in Chicago and the first black community organization in the country. In contrast to Back of the Yards, the two major targets identified for organizing efforts by TWO—the University of Chicago and the board of education—enjoyed considerable support from civic and political leaders. Further, the confluence of these efforts with the civil rights movement pushed the race issue to center stage, a development with which Chicago's political leaders were not prepared to deal.

Alarmed by the University of Chicago's South Campus proposal, an urban renewal project that would cut a swath one block deep by one mile wide in Woodlawn, local ministers in 1958 called on Alinsky to organize the neighborhood. Protests by local leaders and residents against the imposition of plans from outside led to the formation of the Temporary Woodlawn Organization in 1961 and the permanent Woodlawn Organization in 1962. Basically, TWO wanted to be recognized as the official representative for Woodlawn; it also wanted the South Campus plan to be part of a much larger rehabilitation and conservation program for Woodlawn, and wanted replacement housing for those displaced by the campus extension.

After several years of demonstrations and negotiations, and a voter registration drive that, in a style akin to the freedom rides in the South, brought twenty-five hundred blacks on forty-six buses to city hall, TWO was granted "spokesperson" status. The city and the university also agreed to provide replacement housing. Although the latter was delayed significantly and was insufficient to deal with the displacement problem, Woodlawn Gardens, a 502-unit housing complex, was "planned, developed and built [by a] black community."[10]

While TWO was claiming victories, the IAF was suffering losses. Its relentless attacks, through TWO, on the University of Chicago offended some key supporters. Among the most important were Marshall Field III's widow and Dutch Smith, president of Marsh and McClennan, one of the largest insurance companies in Chicago. Smith resigned from the IAF board (he was also a trustee of the university), while Mrs. Field pulled the plug on IAF funding.[11] Alinsky, in their minds, had gone too far.

While TWO was battling with the university over the South Campus plan, many Chicago schools were deteriorating. Segregationist policies in housing and education, combined with white flight to the suburbs, created a tale of two school systems; many schools in white areas were underutilized, while African American schools were bursting at the seams. In some cases only a few blocks separated these schools, but the color line kept them worlds apart. Institutional sanction for this separation came from superintendent Benjamin Willis, who refused to open up white schools to black students in order to alleviate overcrowding.

Fired up by the civil rights movement, TWO met the school issue head-on, sending members to school board meetings, calling for Willis's resignation, successfully organizing a one-day boycott of an elementary school, and deploying "truth squads" to all-white schools on the Southwest Side to photograph empty classrooms. While TWO did not change school board practices, some of its tactics, like school boycotts and the "dump Willis" campaign, were successfully used by subsequent organizers to alter educational policy in Chicago.

In pursuing local self-determination, TWO had challenged the political machine and the practice of top-down planning. When it focused on education, it took on an even greater challenge: the racial policies of the city of Chicago. Underlying all its efforts was a fierce independence that unnerved many machine politicians and a militancy that unnerved many whites. The former contributed to a zero-sum mentality between neighborhood organizations and ward organizations. The militancy provided an incentive for the machine to play the race card (see chapters 2 and 5).

It is notable that Woodlawn, an all-black neighborhood, sought out the skills of white organizers (Saul Alinsky and Nicholas von Hoffman) rather than go to one of the numerous African American elected officials or to "Boss" Dawson, head of the alleged "black submachine."[12] Given the orientation of Chicago's black machine politicians, this is not at all surprising. As John Hall Fish notes in his exhaustive study of TWO: "In Chicago, most of the black aldermen and the black appointees on boards and agencies are oriented not to the group they represent but to that organization that effectively determines their political future. TWO was challenging such a process of representation in the black community."[13]

An alternative interpretation is that African Americans did not perceive their black leaders as having much power. If so, then they were rejecting an ineffective system of representation and leadership. In either case, the conclusion was the same: self-determination was seen as necessary for neighborhood preservation. This was the belief held by Alinsky and the one that was rapidly gaining ground in many Chicago communities, black and white.

A similar campaign, for example, was being waged in Humboldt Park, an area that was home to Poles, Ukrainians, Italians, and, increasingly, Puerto Ricans and African Americans. Situated near downtown, Humboldt Park in 1958 was designated a conservation area by the Department of Urban Renewal (DUR). While no immediate action followed, local pastors called in Saul Alinsky in 1961 to help stem the exodus of Catholic parishioners and reverse the tide of deterioration in the community.

Working with local organizations, Alinsky helped found the Northwest

Community Organization (NCO), an umbrella group representing 177 local groups. As in Woodlawn, the NCO sought to become the sole representative for the area, a move that put it at odds with ward politicians there. When Matthew Biesczat, ward committeeman and secretary of the Cook County Democratic Party, was invited to an NCO meeting, he told the organizer, "Look, sonny, I own this area. Just keep your two cents out of it. I decide what's going to happen."[14] This response, of course, came as no surprise. In fact, it was probably part of the Alinsky organizing strategy: find an issue around which to organize people.

The strategy paid off. The NCO did organize the community while its relations with ward leaders remained bitter. The issue of local control also put the NCO at odds with DUR and city officials. The NCO had issued an alternative to DUR's plan, the "People's Conservation Plan." After several years of battles between the NCO, the DUR, and the mayor's office over which plan would prevail, the DUR pulled out.

While primarily concerned with neighborhood self-determination, Alinsky organizers took on some citywide issues as well. This development resembled a pattern found in many cities. As the issues facing neighborhoods grew in scope from the bulldozer to disinvestment and economic restructuring, many organizers, perceiving the need to transcend local boundaries, began forming broader coalition groups.

Alinsky's first foray into citywide organizing came in 1969 when an air inversion wreaked havoc on Chicago. While Mayor Daley maintained that there was no pollution problem, the feisty *Daily News* columnist Mike Royko urged Alinsky to wage war. Alinsky responded by forming the Campaign Against Pollution (CAP), which succeeded in getting the city council to enact a strict air pollution measure and U.S. Steel's Southworks plant to install pollution controls.

In 1971 CAP changed its name and broadened its scope. It became the Citizen's Action Program and took on two monumental issues: the Crosstown Expressway and mortgage redlining. Proposed in 1968, the 22.5-mile, one-billion-dollar-plus Crosstown Expressway promised to be the "longest and costliest expressway in Chicago's history."[15] Running through the city's West and South Sides, the expressway would have eliminated 3,400 housing units with approximately 10,400 people and 1,462 commercial and industrial firms employing 18,475 people.[16] After four years of protracted battle in which CAP played a major organizing role, the expressway was defeated. A critical ally to CAP was Governor Dan Walker, the independent Democrat who beat the Daley machine (see chapter 2).

By the early 1970s, with a membership exceeding sixty organizations, CAP had made the issue of neighborhood reinvestment a central focus. Alarmed by the incidence of bank redlining in many older neighborhoods, CAP organized a highly effective "greenlining" campaign in which neighborhood residents deposited money only in banks that agreed to lend in their neighborhoods. The economic pressure was successful, as three banks signed reinvestment agreements.[17]

While CAP was changing individual bank behavior, the Metropolitan Area

Housing Alliance (MAHA), a Chicago coalition of housing groups, and National People's Action (NPA), a national coalition of CBOs established in the Alinsky tradition, waged successful battles at the city, state, and federal levels. In 1974 the city council passed the Chicago Municipal Depository Ordinance, requiring banks seeking city deposits to provide a geographic profile of their loans. In 1977 Illinois passed the Illinois Mortgage Banker Act, which mandated loan reporting requirements.[18] In 1975 the federal government passed the Home Mortgage Disclosure Act (HMDA), requiring banks to make mortgage lending data available for review, and then followed up with the Community Reinvestment Act (CRA) in 1977 to encourage bank lending in inner-city and minority neighborhoods.

What can be said of the record of these Alinsky-influenced CBOs in Chicago? Overall, their experiences represent a mixed bag of success and failure. BYNC did become the spokesperson for the community, providing key services to residents and winning its initial battle against local political leaders. Ultimately, it made peace with the political machine. Abandoning its militant posture of self-determination, BYNC became much more involved in economic development. The organization worked with the city on setting up an industrial park in the 1980s.

For CAP, the reinvestment campaign was its last hurrah, as internal dissension over goals and strategies consumed it. Nevertheless, its antiredlining campaigns did lead to the formation of the Community Reinvestment Alliance (1983). Consisting of thirty-five CBOs, the alliance negotiated lending agreements with three major Chicago banks in 1984, for a five-year commitment of $173 million.[19] The agreement was renewed for another five years in 1989 for $200 million.[20]

TWO and the NCO still exist. Having shed its militant origins, TWO is a mere shadow of its former self. Racked by internal disorganization, dealt a severe blow by the Daley administration (Richard J.) when it attempted to administer a major antipoverty program, and facing the seemingly unwinnable odds of increasing poverty, decay, and despair, TWO, in the 1990s, limps along.

The NCO stood its ground once again when the city and the corporate planners announced Chicago 21 (1973), "their" vision for Chicago's neighborhoods. This time, the NCO won its demands for a role in planning. The NCO has also spun off the Bickerdike Redevelopment Corporation, a private nonprofit housing CDC. Begun in 1967, Bickerdike has become an important producer of affordable housing in Chicago.

Beyond the specific cases, these groups, individually and collectively, contributed to an organizing legacy in Chicago forged by Alinsky and built around the belief that local self-determination is the key to neighborhood survival. Following this path, however, put these groups in direct conflict with political, business, and institutional leaders. Alinsky's organizers were often red-baited, while all of these organizations were infiltrated by the Chicago police department's spy unit. The acrimonious context in which community organizing often took place hammered home some powerful lessons. Among the most important were that politicians and the political system could not be trusted to represent neighborhood interests, and that big institutions (banks, universities, the media) were the enemy. These lessons reinforced a political culture already steeped in cynicism and mistrust. Politically, they contributed to shaping an "us versus them" or "powerless versus powerful" mentality.

Finally, there remains a strong element of bitterness. For blacks seeking a measure of respectability in a city that for too long had denied it, there was the bitterness of knowing it still hadn't come. For neighborhoods seeking to wrest control from the political machine and corporate planners, there was the bitterness that comes from being on the wrong end of a raw deal. This legacy of local self-determination, conflict, division, and bitterness would bear down hard on subsequent mayors who tried to forge alternative coalitions and more progressive administrations.

PITTSBURGH: THE GROWTH MACHINE, CORPORATISM, AND THE NEIGHBORHOODS

The Allegheny Conference, Pittsburgh's "unofficial leader," emerged from its early development successes a hero. Despite seemingly overwhelming odds, the ACCD solved the city's smoke and flood problems, making Pittsburgh an attractive location for business. The physical transformation of the Golden Triangle and the commitment of corporations to stay in Pittsburgh proved the city was indeed viable, an image that was reinforced by the favorable national media attention the city received. The ACCD was truly ensconced in its honeymoon phase.

When the ACCD turned its attention to other areas of development, however, its image began to tarnish. The Lower Hill urban renewal project, which was characterized by significant residential displacement, called into question the ACCD's legitimacy. Lacking the crisis proportions of the earlier initiatives, it was hard to justify the human costs of the project. As in Chicago, urban renewal set off alarm bells in many neighborhoods, stimulating organized opposition to the bulldozer. Unlike in Chicago, though, these efforts were not resisted by an institutional structure driven by political objectives.

The primary institutional presence in Pittsburgh's neighborhoods was the Allegheny Council for the Improvement of Our Neighborhoods (ACTION-Housing, Inc.), a private, nonprofit organization set up by the ACCD to function as its housing arm. The establishment of ACTION represented an institutional expansion of Pittsburgh's civic sector to the neighborhoods. It also continued the practice of channeling resources through nonpartisan mechanisms. Unlike Chicago's ward organizations, or even Pittsburgh's for that matter, ACTION had resources to give to CBOs. Moreover, with its power rooted in the business community (its funding and board members were from the corporate community) as opposed to the neighborhoods, ACTION did not perceive CBOs as threatening. Continuing the pattern of behavior established in the renaissance, ACTION sought collaborative and cooperative relationships with neighborhood organizations and city government. While ACTION did face problems achieving its objectives in the neighborhood, they did not stem from or lead to a zero-sum situation. Rather, ACTION's neighborhood experience was very much one in which, through cooperation, all participants could gain.

The ACCD Goes Residential: Pittsburgh's Lower Hill Redevelopment

Redevelopment of the Lower Hill constituted the largest urban renewal project in the country at the time and the URA's first residential venture. It also had the dubious distinction of being the most controversial component of the city's redevelopment program, calling into serious question the ACCD's legitimacy. Bordering the eastern end of the central business district, the Lower Hill contained the city's largest concentration of blacks; almost all of its eight thousand residents were African American. It was also home to the city's poorest residents.[21] By 1961 all this had changed; the original residents were gone, replaced by a civic auditorium, high-rise apartments, and a highway.

As with the University of Illinois case, the Lower Hill was not the original choice for locating a civic auditorium but the path of least political resistance. The proposal for the auditorium came from Edgar Kaufmann, owner of Kaufmann's, the city's major department store. In 1949 Kaufmann pledged five hundred thousand dollars to the city to construct an auditorium for light opera. The Kaufmann Foundation, in concert with the ACCD, also agreed to fund any studies necessary for the project's execution. The city, in turn, would have to match the contribution.

With approval from Mayor Lawrence and the city council, the ACCD and the Pittsburgh Regional Planning Association (PRPA) carried out a site selection study. After considering fifteen sites, they chose the estate of Robert King, uncle of Richard K. Mellon. Located within the residential East End, the proposed site was surrounded by middle- and upper-middle-class housing. While Lawrence and the city council approved the site, residents launched a major opposition drive. Initially unmoved, Lawrence changed his position when the opponents obtained a court injunction against any activity. According to Michael Weber, Lawrence feared judicial intervention since the city had applied a very liberal interpretation in exercising condemnation powers. Rather than risk a court-imposed narrower definition that could jeopardize the city's entire redevelopment program, Lawrence sacrificed the site.[22]

A second site, Schenley Park, was picked. Since this was city-owned land, there would be no problems with condemnation. But this site became problematic as well when opponents secured a court injunction on the grounds that the project violated the terms on which the land was given to the city.[23]

In 1951 the city came to focus on the Lower Hill area. Given its proximity to the Golden Triangle and its designation as the city's worst slum, the Lower Hill had already been under the URA's watchful eye. The URA developed a proposal for slum clearance, residential development, and construction of a highway system, civic auditorium, sports arena, and parking complex. After a four-year hiatus, Lawrence pushed the project through the city council, and in 1956 demolition began. The delay, partly the result of difficulties in obtaining federal monies, halted all activities but one; fearing the handwriting on the wall, many residents left the area, moving into other densely populated black neighborhoods.

By the time the civic auditorium opened in 1961, a total of 1,551 families and 413 businesses, almost all black, had been displaced. Not only were these numbers nearly seven times greater than those in the Jones and Laughlin (J & L) redevelopment, but the Hill project lacked any occupational quid pro quo (see chapter 3). Moreover, whereas the J & L families were compensated for their homes, Hill residents, who were predominantly tenants, received virtually no relocation assistance. In part this resulted from the large numbers leaving the area prior to the city's approval of the project, but even those who lingered did not fare much better; urban renewal's early record on relocation assistance was abysmal. Finally, Pittsburgh's public housing stock, which was expected to fill the gap, was woefully inadequate; less than one-third of the families displaced from the Lower Hill moved into public housing even though more than 70 percent were eligible.[24]

The Lower Hill also differed from the J & L redevelopment on the racial dimension. In the former project the residents were white; in the latter they were almost entirely black. "Bulldozer" and "Negro Removal" were becoming the new metaphors for Pittsburgh's economic revitalization as the city's renaissance took a new and ugly turn.

Institutional Expansion: ACTION-Housing, Inc., and the Neighborhoods

The scope of displacement in the Lower Hill stimulated opposition in other neighborhoods that felt equally vulnerable. Protests against the bulldozer forced the city to abandon its renewal plans for the Upper Hill District. In Manchester, a middle-class black neighborhood, the Manchester Community Corporation headed off the bulldozer when it secured federal designation as a historic area. In Oakland, also known as "Pennsylvania's third largest downtown,"[25] community groups battled for years the expansion plans of the University of Pittsburgh.

Simultaneous with these efforts, and partly in response to the debacle in the Lower Hill and to the city's acute housing problems, the ACCD in 1957 established ACTION-Housing, Inc., a private, nonprofit corporation. Like its institutional brethren, ACTION adopted an approach that emphasized collaboration with city government and cooperative relations in the neighborhood.

Described as "briskly businesslike" in its orientation by historian Roy Lubove,[26] ACTION was motivated by a wholly different set of incentives than the ward organizations in Chicago. Whereas the latter pursued political objectives, tied primarily to electoral politics, ACTION and its corporate backers were motivated by a desire to demonstrate how civic involvement and commitment could address urban social problems. Thus, while its initial foray was in housing, ACTION responded to neighborhood protests against urban renewal by soliciting citizen involvement in its neighborhood activities. While largely perfunctory at first, these organizing activities quickly expanded, taking on a whole new dimension. Ultimately, however, the housing and community organizing initiatives demonstrated to ACTION and the civic community that addressing urban social problems was much more complex than engaging in downtown revitalization efforts. The corporate model that worked so well in the renaissance was problematic in this other domain.

ACTION's primary responsibilities were to increase the supply of moderate-income housing, revitalize old neighborhoods, and implement the citizen participation requirements of federal urban renewal legislation. With a board composed of the mayor (Lawrence, then Barr), Richard King Mellon, and seven ACCD members, ACTION was clearly the neighborhood extension of the ACCD. Its modus operandi, not surprisingly, closely resembled that of the ACCD: initiate an idea, mobilize corporate support and resources, develop a workable plan, and execute it.

In the housing area the idea was that mass production and rational administration would reduce the cost of building moderate-income housing. The argument was made that if the private sector did not address the housing problem, the public sector would be forced to—not a palatable idea to Pittsburgh's economic elites. Finally, the case was made for the establishment of a development fund within ACTION that would provide loans to private builders, guarantee loans secured from financial institutions, and provide money for land purchase.

Persuaded by this logic, local corporations and foundations gave $1.5 million in grants and loan commitments in 1959 to establish the Development Fund.[27] With the pieces coming together, Pittsburgh's corporate community would demonstrate yet again the power of private enterprise to address urban problems. East Hills, which bordered the racially changing neighborhood of Homewood-Brushton[28] and the all-white suburb of Penn Hills, would be its newest showcase.

The plans called for a predominantly moderate-income, racially mixed community that would combine apartments, townhouses, and detached homes. The 1,680 units would yield a mix of rental and owner-occupied housing. Innovative design techniques—planned unit development and cluster housing strategies—

were used to reduce development costs. The project was divided into four stages, with completion of the first scheduled for spring 1963.

Unlike the revitalization of the Golden Triangle, the housing initiative encountered bureaucratic obstacles and social and racial upheaval, all of which significantly delayed the project, increased the costs, and forced ACTION to take advantage of newly created federal housing subsidy programs. The idea of privately financed housing gave way to heavily subsidized housing, while the projected racial and economic mixes also fell by the wayside.

ACTION's plans for mixed owner and rental units and its active promotion of a racially integrated community hit a stone wall with the Federal Housing Administration (FHA). As federal insurer of mortgages, the FHA had a strong bias against rental housing and an overwhelming preference for white borrowers. Pulling in the other direction were the changing demographics of the adjacent Homewood-Brushton. The recipient of many displaced Lower Hill blacks, Homewood-Brushton went from 22 percent black in 1950 to 66 percent black in 1960.[29] Replacing the Lower Hill as the area with the highest concentration of African Americans in Pittsburgh, Homewood-Brushton became a deterrent for many whites to move into East Hills.

Foot-dragging by the FHA led to delays and difficulties in obtaining financing. This factor, combined with developer turnover and problems in selling units, created severe financial strains for the project and its sponsor, ACTION. Strapped for cash, ACTION-Housing turned to the federal government, taking advantage of the newly created 236 rental subsidy program.[30] The infusion of public money allowed ACTION to halve the rents at East Hills. In the process, the community's economic composition was dramatically altered as numerous low-income and welfare families moved in.

Changes in the economic mix were further aggravated by the larger racial climate. The riots that followed Martin Luther King's assassination accelerated white flight from the city, making communities like East Hills even less attractive. Within two years East Hills went from 50 percent to 95 percent African American.[31] Thus, the original plans for a privately financed, racially mixed, moderate-income community, with some high- and low-end units, ended up as a heavily subsidized, mostly black, moderate- and low-income community.

In summary, then, ACTION's record regarding housing is a mixed bag. Numerically, the results are impressive. Between 1960 and 1971, ACTION was responsible for 14 percent of the city's total new housing starts and a whopping 56 percent of Pittsburgh's FHA housing.[32] Nevertheless, ACTION did not accomplish its goals of producing privately financed housing or racially and economically integrated housing. This shortcoming reveals more about the limits to the corporate model than any specific deficiencies on ACTION's part.

ACTION's other major initiative, organizing neighborhoods, also had mixed results. On the one hand, it was a major force for organizing neighborhoods in the fifties and early sixties, first through citizen renewal councils, as required by federal urban renewal legislation, and then through its urban extension program. The latter, in combining community organizing and self-help, sought to bring neighborhoods into the larger decision-making process. On the other hand, top-down neighborhood organizing embodied a series of tensions that were realized when ACTION's urban extension program merged with the federal antipoverty program.[33]

Responding to neighborhood protests against urban renewal, in 1958 ACTION's executive committee authorized its director to "take the necessary steps leading to the organization of citizens neighborhood councils or associations in specific areas marked for urban renewal activities."[34] The first organizations set up by ACTION—the East Liberty Citizen's Renewal Council (1958) and the Bluff Area Citizen Renewal Council (1959)—performed the largely perfunctory role of counseling residents on relocation-related matters. Becoming more ambitious, in 1963 ACTION fashioned an urban extension program that incorporated the principles of democracy, self-help, and human development. With Ford Foundation and local foundation funding, ACTION sent "urban experts" into three neighborhoods (Homewood-Brushton, Hazelwood-Glenwood, and Perry Hilltop) to organize residents, groups, and local institutions around physical and social planning and neighborhood improvements. The ultimate goal was to bring neighborhood planning efforts into the "mainline comprehensive city planning and urban renewal process."[35]

The community organizing effort proved more successful on the process end than on the outcomes end. In Homewood-Brushton, for example, approximately five hundred persons participated in the efforts of the Homewood-Brushton Citizen's Renewal Council, the local organization set up by ACTION. Over a two-year period, the council developed a physical plan and a social plan for wholesale neighborhood improvement. While the area did see some material improvements (housing code compliance, employment counseling, preschool classes, removal of abandoned cars, better street maintenance, liquor license limitations), the city's response in terms of resources fell far short of what the plan called for and of local expectations. Apparently, Homewood-Brushton had not been slated by the city for official redevelopment activities and therefore could not be given priority status in terms of municipal services.[36] Thus, while ACTION did help to channel resources into the neighborhood and did train many residents, albeit largely middle-class ones, in community planning, the end result left many residents with a sense of deep frustration.

The Urban Extension Program was plagued by an even more fundamental problem; ACTION's philosophy, as embodied in urban extension, was essentially contradictory. ACTION's director, Bernard Loshbough, and the board of directors were guided by middle-class reform values of efficiency, managerial expertise, and top-down organizing. Elitist in nature and based on the corporate model, these were the principles that guided ACTION's housing efforts and its establishment of citizen renewal councils. But the urban extension program, which was fashioned around populist visions of local planning and self-help, directly challenged those principles.

The showdown came when the newly created antipoverty program was merged with Urban Extension in 1964. The federal government's emphasis on "maximum feasible participation" of poor people clashed with the middle-class reformism of ACTION and its supporters, the business community. This clash occurred in the context of a growing civil rights movement in Pittsburgh, which lent a racial dimension to the contradiction. One local civil rights leader criticized ACTION for its close association with the "city's white power structure."[37]

This external conflict between centralization and decentralization had a parallel within ACTION. James Cunningham, a community organizer from Chicago, brought some fairly radical principles with him when he became director of ACTION's neighborhood programs. His populist leanings and strong commitment to participatory democracy were far from the managerialism of his boss, Bernard Loshbough. As historian Roy Lubove has observed:

> Cunningham's zealous pursuit of the city of God . . . contributed to tensions in the ACTION-Housing community organization program. In one sense, ACTION-Housing was the most improbable agency to initiate and direct a movement for neighborhood self-assertion. It had been established in large degree to facilitate the civic coalition's renewal program. The community organization function placed ACTION-Housing in the awkward position of mediating between the neighborhood interests it helped arouse, on the one hand, and the political and business leadership upon whom it depended for support, on the other. The conflict was resolved, in part, by ACTION-Housing's tendency to work with a middle-class neighborhood clientele committed to stabilization rather than upheaval, and by a strong emphasis upon "self-help" rather than direct action.[38]

After passage of the Green Amendment in 1967, which allowed local governments to directly run the antipoverty program, ACTION bowed out of the program. One year earlier, James Cunningham had bowed out of ACTION.

ACTION's experiences in community organizing clearly indicate that it was an inappropriate vehicle for such activities. But unlike Chicago's ward organizations, ACTION was not on a collision course with CBOs. This is largely attributable to an even more fundamental difference; ACTION's power was rooted not in the neighborhoods but in the corporate and civic sectors. Further, achieving its overriding objective—demonstrating the superiority of the corporate model—did not require ACTION to have a neighborhood base. ACTION could go elsewhere.

ACTION remained the premier housing entity in Pittsburgh, becoming more involved in rehabilitation than in new construction. In part this reflected changes in federal urban renewal policy, which replaced the earlier emphasis on slum clearance with neighborhood "conservation and preservation." It was also responsive to changes in FHA practices, which began to encourage private investment in central cities. Finally, ACTION's director, Bernard Loshbough, sought to demonstrate yet again how the private sector could, through a more efficient and rational organization of production, excel in the rehabilitation field and even turn a profit.

The mode of production—large volume and top-down practice—preempted the type of neighborhood participation sought by the Urban Extension Program. While ACTION did consult with neighborhood leaders on its rehab projects, it was usually in response to demands to do so rather than the result of self-initiated processes. When ACTION established the Allegheny Housing Rehabilitation Corporation (AHRCO), a private, for-profit corporation, in 1968, it was clear that production and top-down planning had taken precedence over organizing and grassroots development. ACTION was going with its strengths.

Although ACTION ultimately distanced itself from the neighborhoods, its initial role reinforced certain patterns and set some precedents. The prominent role of civic leadership in the city's affairs was once again demonstrated. With ACTION playing the main role in housing and neighborhood organizing, Pittsburgh's civic sector was expanded; government was important but, as in the renaissance, it was not the lead actor.

The use of a private, nonprofit entity also helped to reinforce the party–government distinction that began under Lawrence. The relationship between ACTION, the antipoverty program, and the neighborhood councils, on the one hand, and the ward organizations, on the other, is best characterized as one of mutual noninterference. Unlike Chicago, many of the ward organizations in Pittsburgh were perceived as weak by neighborhood organizations.

Finally, ACTION helped to set a precedent for bringing neighborhoods into the planning process. Organizing efforts, rather than being discouraged, as in Chicago, were encouraged. Nevertheless, ACTION's top-down approach embodied fundamental tensions between centralist and populist tendencies. Moreover, the racial, social, and class dynamics of neighborhood development revealed the limits to the ACCD's corporate model. The conflicts that occurred in Homewood-Brushton and in the antipoverty program were real; the contradictions were real. But the precedent that was set would influence the eventual accommodation worked out between the ACCD, the city, and the neighborhoods, an accommodation centered around a unidimensional progressivism.

This characterization of Pittsburgh and Chicago is not meant to be all-inclusive. The purpose here is to identify larger political patterns and predominant types of behavior in the two cities. Not all organizing in Pittsburgh was top-down in structure and cooperative in approach. Similarly, not all groups in Chicago were cut from the Alinsky cloth.

PLANTING THE SEEDS OF DISCONTENT: URBAN RENEWAL AND THE NEIGHBORHOODS

In arguing for a more dynamic view of development policy than is offered by either regime theory or growth machine theory, Cynthia Horan suggests that we need to "do more than assert that development policymaking serves the political objectives of local governing coalitions."[39] Emphasizing the role that local political interests play in redefining economic imperatives, Horan calls our attention to the critical variation among cities, particularly "the composition and agenda of the governing coalition, the local economic structure, and the institutional resources of the local state."[40] The cases in this chapter support these contentions.

First, they illustrate the prominent role of the political process in mediating policy decisions. Even where economic objectives appear to be paramount, as in urban renewal projects, and even regarding initiatives that enjoy broad and powerful support (e.g., obtaining a university campus within the city), political maneuvering ultimately dictates key decisions, including which projects get executed, how they are carried out, and where they are located. These decisions affect who gets removed or, in political science parlance, who benefits and who bears the costs. Moreover, there is a ripple effect as the decisions and their consequences bear directly on issues of race and neighborhood growth and decline.

Second, the cases point to critical variation within political processes across cities. The way in which power is structured within a city influences institutional development, resource distribution, and ultimately the behavior of regimes. This variation is particularly critical to the ability of CBOs to gain access to the system and influence decision making. In Pittsburgh, the establishment of an institutional presence within the neighborhoods that could work with CBOs was consistent with the underlying logic of the regime: institutional expansion of the civic-sector arena around planning objectives. Unlike Chicago's ward organizations, ACTION had resources sought by CBOs. Moreover, since Pittsburgh's corporatist regime's and ACTION's power were not rooted in the neighborhoods, CBO formation was not a threat to the power of the regime or central to its agenda. Collaboration between ACTION and CBOs on housing and other neighborhood initiatives constituted a relationship within which all parts could gain (though not necessarily to the same extent).

Ultimately, the collaboration failed as the tensions between populist tendencies and corporatist logic proved insurmountable. ACTION's response to these tensions is yet again indicative of the fundamental differences between Pittsburgh and Chicago. In Pittsburgh these tensions resulted in a retreat by ACTION from community organizing initiatives. As part of an institutional framework with citywide power rooted in the business and civic sectors, ACTION had no necessary stake in the neighborhoods.

In Chicago, when tensions arose between the ward organizations and the

CBOs, the former sought to eliminate the latter. With its power base in the neighborhoods, the ward organizations could not retreat. And, unlike the institutions in Pittsburgh's civic arena, Chicago's ward organizations were unable to distribute the type of resources that the CBOs were seeking. There was no place for CBOs within the structure of Chicago's political and institutional frameworks. As chapter 5 will show, for CBOs to gain access to political influence would require the overthrow of the political elites who dominated the regime.

Another significant difference between the two cities was the treatment of race by elites. In Pittsburgh, civic elites were more prone to support racial integration efforts than their counterparts in Chicago. This is probably explained in large part by the demographics of the two cities; Chicago's African American population constituted a much larger proportion of the total population and it increased much faster than in Pittsburgh. Even more significant is the behavior of political elites in Chicago. Extremely sensitive to electoral pressures, most white politicians publicly opposed racial integration, with some even openly courting antiblack sentiment. The racial dimension in Chicago, as chapter 5 will show, enormously complicated efforts to build a progressive movement that would empower communities in their struggle against the political machine.

5
Challenge and Response: The Politics of Cooperation Versus the Politics of Confrontation

> *While the economic space for redistributive reforms exists, the political space is much more restrictive.*
> —Todd Swanstrom

The analysis thus far clearly indicates the emergence of two distinct patterns of political and institutional development in Pittsburgh and Chicago. These patterns are important in shaping the opportunities for neighborhood participation and for political leadership. When neighborhood discontent spilled over into electoral politics, the experience in the two cities varied markedly. In Pittsburgh the process of accommodation that began during urban renewal continued, with neighborhoods gaining formal recognition in the corporatist structure. In Chicago the underlying logic of the political system derailed one mayor from a pro-neighborhood course and nearly succeeded in sabotaging the efforts of a second.

In addition to political and institutional factors, political behavior in Chicago has been strongly shaped by race. In fact, Chicago's experience with race qualifies, both conceptually and empirically, Logan and Molotch's thesis on the centrality of land-use conflict and their division of the urban populace into two groups: rentiers and nonrentiers.[1] In Chicago, racial conflict is often the primary factor in local politics, heavily influencing elections and the coalition assembly process. Inextricably and negatively tied to machine politics—the machine was increasingly seen as antiblack—the race issue became cautiously, and often uncomfortably, allied with reform issues. With different and often competing agendas, coalition building among challengers is extremely difficult. These factors significantly affect the process of challenge and response.

THE RISE OF THE NEIGHBORHOOD MAYORS

Although elected ten years apart, Peter Flaherty (1969) and Jane Byrne (1979) both capitalized on the growing neighborhood discontent, waging successful antimachine, pro-neighborhood mayoral campaigns. Both were outspoken, controversial figures who declared all-out war on existing practices of governance. While both were highly politicized elections, Flaherty's actions, once he was elected, helped depoliticize neighborhood issues whereas Byrne's actions as mayor enhanced the politicization and conflictual environment of neighborhood and racial issues. The difference is directly attributable to Byrne's retreat from her promising reform beginnings. Flaherty, by contrast, stayed the course, weathering the opposition but avoiding the backlash that capsized Byrne's reelection hopes. Examining the two administrations will show how the political and institutional differences between the two cities helped to shape very distinct mayoral strategies.

Peter Flaherty: "Nobody's Boy," 1969–1977

Although a product of Pittsburgh's Democratic Party and political machine, Peter Flaherty broke with the machine in 1969, challenging the party's candidate in the Democratic mayoral primary. Adopting the slogan "Nobody's Boy," Flaherty declared his independence from the machine, charging it with waste and inefficiency. Using traditional urban reform rhetoric, Flaherty appealed to the middle-class voter on tax issues.[2] Flaherty also attacked the business community, declaring his independence from the ACCD. Promising to halt public subsidies for downtown development and to redirect resources to the neighborhoods, Flaherty endeared himself to the neighborhood movement, which had become highly critical of the city's famed "public–private partnership." This stance also reinforced his fiscal position, and hence his appeals to the middle class and to property owners.

The anti-machine, pro-neighborhood strategy proved successful. Flaherty beat the machine candidate in the primary by seventeen thousand votes out of a total of approximately one hundred thousand votes cast. He then went on to trounce his Republican opponent by a nearly 2–1 margin.[3]

Once in office, Flaherty continued his double-barreled assault. His war on the machine included major cutbacks in city employment (10 percent in the first year alone and 27 percent over the entire administration);[4] the replacement of all department heads, bureau superintendents, and supervisors, most of whom were connected to ward bosses;[5] a restructuring of key parts of city government; and a rechanneling of resources. The net effect was to purge city government of many of its loyal machine troops.

Carrying out his pledge to be "Nobody's Boy," Flaherty appointed management types who lacked machine or business community connections. As described by Clark and Ferguson, Flaherty's appointments were "young, aggressive department heads who looked for more efficient procedures."[6] The administration's wrapping was truly of the "good government" variety.

Not only was Flaherty winning the political battle in city government; he was winning the popular battle among the public at large. True to what Clark and Ferguson termed his "New Fiscal Populism" rhetoric, Flaherty returned annual budget surpluses,[7] thus allowing him to commit one of the most popular acts in local politics: he decreased the property tax three times and abolished the city's wage tax.[8] At the same time, New York City was teetering on the edge of bankruptcy, Cleveland was heading toward default, and many older cities were staring into an abyss of fiscal disaster.

Flaherty's aloofness from the political machine was matched by his distancing from the business community. Rejecting informal gestures from the ACCD to work together, Flaherty gave notice that the days of "business as usual" were over. This message was reinforced through a series of structural and personnel changes in the URA and the Department of City Planning, which suspended the institutional ties to the business community. The URA, the engine of development activities during Pittsburgh's renaissance, was forced to cede its city planning functions to the Department of City Planning, which reported directly to the mayor. Thus, a key tie with the business community was broken.

Changes within the planning department further distanced city government from the political and growth machines. For openers, nearly 75 percent of the planning staff were removed or had left during the first year of the administration.[9] Given the importance of the informal system of personal longevity to the more formal public–private partnership, this was undoubtedly a significant blow to existing arrangements.

Replacing these links were formal ties to the neighborhoods. In 1971 the planning department set up the Community Planning Program to help neighborhood organizations work with the bureaucracy and with developers.[10] These activities opened up the planning process and gave official recognition to neighborhoods. Interestingly, ACTION Housing, Inc., the private, nonprofit corporation set up by the ACCD to organize neighborhoods during urban renewal, was bypassed by Flaherty. Viewing ACTION as a tool of the ACCD and the business community, Flaherty chose to omit it from the process.

In sum, Flaherty's reorganizations altered formal channels of communication within the city. Ties with the business community were weakened as planning became more of a public as opposed to a private function. As part of this transition, neighborhood groups were seeing the first signs of incorporation. Indirectly, this weakened the machine since neighborhood groups could go directly to the administration.

This last feature is consistent with Flaherty's machine predecessor. In general Barr's treatment of federal programs and social programs revealed a strong programmatic, as opposed to political, strain. Thus, in contrast to Chicago, Pittsburgh's machine and nonmachine mayors reinforced the party–government distinction. Flaherty's "outright assault" on the machine was in some senses a continuation of Barr's "silent transfer of power." Flaherty's flamboyant style, however, articulated the process in a way that was uncharacteristic of the Barr administration.

Stylistic differences notwithstanding, Flaherty's administration maintained the bifurcated nature of Pittsburgh's political system; planning activities and resources had never been under the control of the machine, nor had they been subject to electoral review. Thus, opening up a channel in city government for neighborhoods was not a direct attack on the ward organizations. However, the incorporation of these groups into the civic arena further decreased the significance of the ward organizations.

Flaherty's actions also helped to shift the city's policy orientation from a near-total preoccupation with downtown development to a focus on neighborhood concerns. One immediate result was an increase in resources for neighborhoods. Neighborhood loan programs, administered through the city, and the arrival of Community Development Block Grant (CDBG) funds, with their neighborhood spending requirements, altered distribution patterns; 50 percent of federal money went to neighborhoods, replacing the practice of allocating all federal dollars to the central business district.[11]

Despite Flaherty's commitment to the neighborhoods, he did alienate some neighborhood organizations. While he redirected federal resources to neighborhoods, his fiscal austerity measures resulted in service cutbacks. Moreover, Flaherty's aloofness apparently extended to neighborhood groups as well; Flaherty truly was "Nobody's Boy." Disgruntled neighborhood groups notwithstanding, the level of disaffection did not prove to be fatal; Flaherty won both the Democratic and Republican Party endorsements in 1973, thus securing the mayor's office for another four years.

Jane Byrne: The Politics of Rising Expectations, 1979–1983

In 1979 Jane Byrne did the "undoable": she beat the infamous Chicago machine. The long years of urban renewal, the machine's continued insensitivity to the black community, and the overall neglect of neighborhoods had created distinct pockets of resistance. Jane Byrne was among the first to recognize the new electoral possibilities; she was also among the first class of casualties. The growing contradiction between political elites and masses contributed to Byrne's victory in 1979. The growing contradiction within Chicago politics, which substituted race for class, contributed to Byrne's defeat four years later.

Byrne seized upon the growing discontent with machine rule by appealing directly to those who had been left out. Charging that Chicago had been taken over by a "cabal of evil men," Byrne promised to restore government to the people.[12] For the neighborhoods, Byrne promised to open up the decision-making process, establish neighborhood planning councils, and allocate more resources for neighborhood development. For African Americans, Byrne promised to end the machine's monopoly on city hiring and contract processes that had frozen blacks out. Appealing to white liberal reformers, she promised to end corruption in city government and dismantle the patronage system.[13]

The campaign appeals were successful; with a coalition of African Americans, white lakefront liberals, and disaffected white ethnics,[14] Byrne defeated Bilandic, the machine incumbent, in the primary by more than fifteen thousand votes and sailed into the mayor's office with more than 82 percent of the vote in the general election, a record for Chicago mayoral elections.[15]

The euphoria surrounding the election followed Byrne into city hall. Making good on her neighborhood appeals, Byrne created a Department of Housing and a Department of Neighborhoods and hired a leading consulting firm to conduct a neighborhood needs assessment and make recommendations for increasing community participation. For African Americans, there were top-level appointments to the school board, the housing and transit authorities, and the police department. Capping it off was the appointment of Renault Robinson, a black activist, as a top-level adviser.[16] For the reformers there was the attraction of Byrne's transition team, headed by a Northwestern University professor and charged with recommending improvements in municipal administration. There was also the promise of a nationwide search to bring "the best and the brightest" to Chicago government.[17]

The excitement surrounding the new administration was short-lived, however, as Byrne changed course, leaving her campaign pledges and promising administrative starts far behind. Unlike Flaherty, who went on to dismantle the machine, Byrne made peace with the "evil cabal" she had run against. That treaty spelled the end of any substantive neighborhood policies, the end of her appeals to the African American community, and certainly the end of even a pretense of "good government."

The offices that Byrne set up to represent neighborhood needs became funnels for patronage and the distribution of campaign literature. Commenting on the Department of Neighborhoods, Greg Hinz of Lerner Papers said it was "the center for one of the most blatant uses ever of public money for private politics."[18] Not surprisingly, its contact with community organizations was quite limited.

The neighborhood needs assessment suffered a similar fate; its contents were suppressed and its recommendations for substantive neighborhood input watered down to an advisory role.[19] Even this watered-down version was further diluted; the Community Development Advisory Committee (CDAC), set up by Bilandic to satisfy federal requirements for citizen input in CDBG decisions, was virtually ignored by Byrne. The promise of open government was quickly replaced by the reality of top-down decision making.

Not only the process but also the content of neighborhood and city planning resembled business as usual. Byrne's Comprehensive Plan was a major reversal of her campaign promises to balance the needs of neighborhoods with those of the downtown area. In calling for increased attention to the central business district, the plan represented a continuation of the old corporate-centered strategy of economic development. Heeding the words of Daniel Burnham to "make no little plans," Byrne proposed one megaproject after another, topping it all off with a proposed one-billion-dollar world's fair for 1992.[20] Through her reversals, Chicago's first reform mayor reinforced the neighborhood–downtown cleavage, fanning the fires of activism and opposition in the process.

Byrne's reversal of promises to the African American community came a little later but with an equal vengeance. Her promise to overhaul the city's patronage system and thus give blacks their fair share was dashed by a city council ordinance, supported by Byrne, that restored twenty-five thousand jobs to the patronage system. Equally infuriating were her top-level personnel policies, which included the replacement of blacks by whites on the Chicago Housing Authority and the school boards and the appointment of a white police superintendent over a black; these institutions were pivotal in the battle for racial equality.[21] But the most devastating act of betrayal came in the ward remap when Byrne presided over the conscious effort to dilute the political power of African Americans and Hispanics by decreasing the number of majority wards for the two groups.

Finally, the lakefront liberals, who saw in Byrne an end to machine governance, were equally disillusioned. The transition team's report went the way of many a government report—unopened, left on a dusty shelf.[22] The restoration of patronage, the peace treaty with the "evil cabal," and the continuation of closed-door, top-down decision making convinced many starry-eyed reformers that under the Byrne administration Paddy Bauler's words still rung true—"Chicago ain't ready for reform."

Flaherty and Byrne: A Study in Contrasts

Flaherty and Byrne clearly pursued diverse governing strategies. Byrne's retreat was due largely to the strength of Chicago's machine, the dissonance of her electoral coalition, and the deep-seated electoral divisions. Flaherty, by contrast, faced a much weaker political machine, governed in a city with a strong civic sector and well-developed institutions, and one with fewer cleavages.

The existence in Pittsburgh of a powerful business-backed civic arena that controlled key institutions and resources contributed to the bifurcated nature of the political system; the machine was not the only game in town. Indeed, for neighborhood groups the machine was often irrelevant since development politics was contained in the civic arena; the URA and the planning department were, after all, instruments of the ACCD. Thus, a pro-neighborhood stance in Pittsburgh did not signal an attack on the ward organizations.[23]

In Chicago, the machine was the preeminent game in town, with the ward organizations controlling neighborhood resources. The legacy of the Daley years was one of individual, not collective, politics. Organizing efforts outside of the political machine were staunchly resisted, creating a zero-sum relationship between neighborhood organizations and ward organizations. In this context, appeals to the neighborhoods constituted a prelude to war. From the neighborhood side, the absence of a well-developed civic sector to tap into for resources and the machine's stranglehold on city government pointed to one conclusion: neighborhood incorporation required the overthrow of the political machine. Jane Byrne could not deliver to the neighborhoods without directly attacking the ward organizations, something she was ultimately unwilling to do.

Although internal conflict plagued Chicago's machine in 1979, it was much stronger than Pittsburgh's machine when Flaherty leveled his attack. Hence, dismantling the machine would be a more formidable task in Chicago than in Pittsburgh. Moreover, Byrne had good reason to reconsider her relationship to the machine; Richard M. Daley, the late mayor's eldest son, had his eye on the mayor's office. Byrne hoped her alliance with Vrdolyak, leader of the "evil cabal," could provide the organizational wherewithal to counter the challenge.

But what about her electoral coalition? After all, Byrne did defeat the machine incumbent and take the general election in a landslide even by Chicago standards. A closer look, however, shows a less favorable picture. First, much of Byrne's electoral support was an antimachine vote; Byrne lacked a committed base of voters. This was especially problematic given the dissonance of her electoral coalition of African Americans, lakefront liberals, and disaffected white ethnics—groups that represented distinct and competing agendas. Finally, it was a weak coalition; the first two groups had no influence in the machine, which held a majority in the city council, or in city government, while the third group—Northwest Side Poles—had always played second fiddle to the Irish in Chicago politics.

These dilemmas were aptly summed up by the new mayor: "I can't govern this city unless I cut a deal with them [Vrdolyak and Burke, the leaders of the "evil cabal"]. I have no constituency in the council. I don't have anything in the bureaucracy. I bark orders from the fifth floor and nobody listens. If I don't have these people with me, government won't operate."[24] Given the uncertainty of Chicago's political landscape, Byrne opted for familiarity; after all, she did come out of the machine.

Byrne's deal with the Vrdolyak faction of the machine solved some problems, created others, and definitely influenced her course as mayor. The problems solved, as well as the ones created, reveal much about post-Daley Chicago politics and point to key differences from Pittsburgh's political landscape. The alliance with Vrdolyak solved the city council problem; Chicago's legislative body resumed the rubber-stamp role it had perfected during the Daley years. Consequently, this deterred Byrne from battling the ward organizations, suggesting yet another fundamental difference between the two cities. Chicago has a district-based council directly tied to the ward organizations.[25] Under Flaherty, Pittsburgh had an at-large council whose members were less concerned about neighborhood-specific resources and were not as closely tied to the ward organizations as their Chicago counterparts. Finally, Pittsburgh's city council has nine members, compared with Chicago's fifty. Consequently, Flaherty could buy off council opposition without sacrificing the neighborhoods to the ward bosses; Byrne could not.

Supplementing Chicago's community–ward organization cleavage was the racial divide. Although African Americans were the most loyal supporters of Richard J. Daley in his early administration, they never achieved full citizenship in Chicago's political system; black politicians had second-class status within the machine, while the interests of blacks as a group had been largely ignored. Thus, for African Americans, political liberation required either machine appropriation or machine overthrow.

The latter course would create a natural alliance between neighborhoods and African Americans. However, this was torn asunder by the other side of the racial cleavage, a division in which the machine played a pivotal role. Since the mid-1960s, race had been the foundation of Chicago politics, with the machine increasingly becoming the defender of white interests. While blacks and neighborhood groups could assemble around a common rejection of machine politics, staying together over the formation of a new agenda was quite another matter. Early in her administration, for instance, Byrne did appoint blacks to the school board and housing authority, but she replaced them with whites when Richard M. Daley became a rival for white electoral support.

Flaherty, by contrast, did not face a sharp racial divide. As discussed in chapter 2, Pittsburgh's African American community was not politically organized, the machine never portrayed itself as the "great white hope," and there was a lack of effective mechanisms for articulating racial issues. Finally, African Americans constituted a much smaller portion of the electorate than in Chicago (17 percent vs. 38.7 percent), thus making appeals to the white community less risky.[26] Flaherty did, for instance, publicly oppose busing even though it meant losing black support. Nevertheless, the drop-off he suffered in black wards did not effect his reelection bid.[27]

Chicago's African American community had become highly mobilized. Their greater numbers, their geographic concentration, and the machine's insensitivity led to major organizing efforts. Jane Byrne's victory, which owed much to the black vote, served as a valuable lesson in electoral politics. After her offensive actions toward the African American community, blacks turned the lesson on the instructor, carrying out massive voter registration drives that added over 125,000 new black voters. These efforts were instrumental in defeating many Byrne-backed candidates and ultimately in smashing Byrne's reelection bid in 1983.

The respective position of the two machines, their relative strength, and their command of resources shaped very different types of politics in Chicago and Pittsburgh. In Chicago the electoral arena is central to resource distribution questions, whereas in Pittsburgh the institutions of the corporatist system have been the key players, with their control over resources increasing. This difference shapes the opportunities for coalition building, political leadership, and governance.

In an insightful analysis of Pittsburgh's public–private partnership, Louise Jezierski called the Flaherty years a "grassroots rejection of the partnership through elections."[28] The irony of Flaherty's administration is that his institutional response removed neighborhood issues from electoral politics; planning mechanisms formalized the linkage between neighborhoods and resources. Neighborhood issues were placed in the sphere of elite politics, where they would not come into conflict with racial politics or even ward politics. This is very much in keeping with the logic of corporatism, which seeks the transformation of competitive politics into "noncompetitive and rational politics by putting decision making above mobilization of demand."[29] In essence, then, Flaherty did not dismantle Pittsburgh's governing structure; he merely altered its direction somewhat and in doing so laid the foundation for an expansion of elite politics.

Byrne, however, could not escape the rough-and-tumble of the electoral arena. Like Flaherty, Byrne failed to alter the city's governing arrangements. She reshuffled the deck among machine players, but in style and substance reinforced machine rule in Chicago. This meant, however, turning on an electoral coalition that had been energized by the politics of rising expectations. It also meant reinforcing rivalries within the machine. When Byrne made her fateful decision to go with the "evil cabal" out of her belief that she could not turn that electoral coalition into a governing coalition, she merely hardened the already deep cleavages in Chicago's political system.

PICKING UP THE PIECES: HEALING IN PITTSBURGH, REVOLUTION IN CHICAGO

Proceeding on very different paths, Flaherty and Byrne left their successors two very dissimilar legacies. Flaherty's approach to the neighborhoods provided the beginnings of incorporation, institution building, and the removal of neighborhood issues from electoral politics. Caliguiri took these modest beginnings and expanded on them dramatically. Byrne, on the other hand, politicized an already volatile neighborhood–downtown and neighborhood–machine conflict and fanned the fires of the race issue. Harold Washington, Chicago's first African American mayor, was left to grapple with both of these seething conflicts. His administration, by refusing to deal with the "evil cabal," brought the conflicts center stage as the alleged "City That Works" was transformed into "Beirut on the Lake."

Caliguiri and the Expansion of the Corporatist State, 1977–1988

Richard Caliguiri was city council president when Flaherty left the mayor's office in 1977 to work in the Carter administration. Caliguiri served the remainder of Flaherty's term, promising the Democratic organization that he would not seek election to the office. Changing his plans, Caliguiri skipped the Democratic primary but ran in the general election on the Pittsburgh-for-Caliguiri ticket, defeating the Democratic candidate (Thomas Foerster) by approximately 5,300 votes out of a total of roughly 147,000 votes.[30]

An independent in partisan terms, Caliguiri avoided Flaherty's highly individualistic style. Eager to work with the downtown business interests and the ACCD, Caliguiri invoked the city's famous symbol of public–private cooperation; his campaign theme was "It's Another Renaissance." This renaissance, however, included the neighborhoods as well as business.

In both cases Caliguiri had a solid institutional base from which to expand. Work with the business community was facilitated by the institutions that had emerged from Renaissance I (ACCD, URA, the Regional Industrial Development Corporation, and Penn Southwest), while formal ties to the neighborhoods had been established by Flaherty.[31] Capitalizing on these beginnings, the new administration engaged in extensive institution building to address neighborhood development needs. The ties between CBOs and city government, particularly the URA and the Department of City Planning, were strengthened, while more resources were channeled to the neighborhoods. Thus, Caliguiri was empowering the newest component of Pittsburgh's corporatist system—the neighborhood interests.

Almost immediately, the administration created a Department of Housing, which under the leadership of Paul Brophy initiated two innovative neighborhood housing programs: the Housing Improvement Loan Program (HILP), a citywide housing assistance program begun in 1978, and the North Side Revitalization Program (NSRP), implemented the following year, which targeted six neighborhoods. The novel feature of these programs was that they brought together neighborhood organizations, which marketed and monitored the programs; private lending institutions, which originated and serviced the loans; and the URA, which used its bonding capacity to leverage funding for the program. The latter, in fact, represented one of the first uses of tax-exempt financing for such a program in the country.[32]

The city, responding to recommendations made at the 1979 Citizen Participation Conference, also helped to set up numerous programs and offices.[33] The Community Technical Assistance Center, set up in 1980 with partial funding from the city, provides a range of services to CBOs. The city also began funding the private, nonprofit Pittsburgh Architects Workshop, founded in 1968 to provide planning and design assistance in moderate- and low-income neighborhoods. In 1979 the city set up the Neighborhoods for Living Center to serve as a marketing tool for Pittsburgh neighborhoods. The first director of the NLC, Mary Lou Daniels, had headed the Pittsburgh Neighborhood Alliance, the advocacy group formed in 1970 to lobby for more responsive leadership.

While neighborhood organizations gained a greater role in community development and a greater share of resources under Caliguiri (75 percent of federal money went to the neighborhoods, compared with 50 percent under Flaherty),[34] his neighborhood policies did not engender opposition like that found in Chicago. There the opposition influenced Byrne's retreat and pushed conflict to the center of Washington's administration after he refused to retreat.

The dissimilar outcomes are traceable to political and institutional factors. First, Pittsburgh's ward organizations were considerably weaker than those in Chicago and did not have a zero-sum relationship with CBOs as in Chicago. Moreover, Pittsburgh's at-large system weakened the connection between ward organizations and the city council. Caliguiri's neighborhood policies did not threaten the political base of city councillors. When there was council opposition, it was issue-specific rather than generated by the opposition bloc as it was in Chicago. Consequently, Caliguiri was more successful with the council than was Washington.

Second, Caliguiri's neighborhood focus, unlike Byrne's initial focus and Washington's platform, did not pit neighborhoods against the downtown; Caliguiri sought to renew contacts with the ACCD. Moreover, much of the neighborhood activity supported by the administration was real estate–based in a city where the private sector had virtually abandoned the neighborhoods. Thus, at best, CBO activities were seen as complementary to those of the business community; at worst, they were considered benign.

Finally, the method of incorporation extended the institutional logic of downtown economic development activities to the neighborhoods. It was an approach that ACCD members and URA people understood. Commenting on community development corporations, John Robins, Caliguiri's URA chairman, stated, "If they didn't exist, we'd have to create them."[35] A similar theme was echoed by Evan Stoddard, Caliguiri's URA director, when he referred to CDCs as "development outlets," saying they "were geographically based and take care of all aspects of their neighborhood. [We] do not attempt to work directly in neighborhoods, we work through them [CDCs]."[36] Caliguiri's approach to neighborhood incorporation further removed neighborhood issues from electoral politics.

Harold Washington: Renewing the Revolution, 1983–1987

In Chicago in the early 1980s, just the opposite was happening; the electoral arena had become the battle place for control of the city. The underlying cleavages of class (neighborhoods vs. downtown), race (white vs. African American), and political orientation (machine vs. progressive), combined with the battles for control within the machine, dominated the city's electoral politics. The 1983 mayoral election was perhaps the most volatile and bitter in the city's history.

As it became clear that the Democratic primary battle between the machine titans—Byrne and Daley—was dividing the white vote to the advantage of black candidate Harold Washington, the race card was played with a vengeance. Ed Vrdolyak, former leader of the "evil cabal" and since turned Byrne confidant and party chairman, told Democratic precinct captains, "Don't kid yourself, it's a racial thing. I'm calling on you to save your city, to save your precinct."[37] With more than a slight touch of poetic justice, Vrdolyak's last-minute appeal to one of the baser instincts in American politics backfired; the white vote remained divided, while the black vote was further energized.[38] Harold Washington, an African American U.S. congressman from the city's South Side who had broken with the machine in 1977, won the primary with 36 percent of the vote. Jane Byrne received 34 percent, followed by Richard M. Daley with 30 percent.

Although Washington was the Democratic candidate for mayor in a city where outcomes are decided in primary elections, 1983 was different. The strong two-party competition, which almost resulted in Chicago electing its first Republican mayor in fifty-six years, reflected the depth of the city's political and racial divisions. In one of the closest elections and highest turnouts (82 percent) in the city's history, Washington won with 51.4 percent of the vote. Many Democratic ward committeemen, fearing Washington's reform credentials, worked for the Republican challenger, Bernard Epton, a foreshadowing of the governing difficulties Washington would face. Many white voters, fearing the color of Washington's skin, voted for Epton, a signal of the political difficulties in store for the new mayor. Running on the slogan "Epton, Before It's Too Late," the Republican challenger received 79.3 percent of the white Democratic vote.[39]

While the bulk of Washington's electoral support was in the black community, his coalition also included Hispanics, white progressives along the city's lakefront, and some of the more progressive white community activists. Running on a reform platform that emphasized fairness and open government, Washington, like Byrne before him, offered a message that resonated among the city's disenfranchised. Unlike Byrne, however, Washington stuck with his electoral coalition; he had a committed bloc of voters in his black base, while his electoral coalition—African Americans, Hispanics, white progressives—had an ideological consistency (a liberal coalition) that Byrne's lacked. Hence, Washington had a greater margin of electoral security.[40]

Nevertheless, Washington shared two important handicaps with his predecessor. First, his electoral coalition, coming from the ranks of Chicago's disenfranchised, was ill matched for the elites who had dominated Chicago politics for so long. Second, Washington's election, which underscored the city's new demographic realities (whites were a minority) put the race issue center stage. The first handicap would lead to significant conflict within city government, while the race issue would plague Washington's progressive policy efforts.

Carrying the electoral revolution into office, Washington declared war on some long-standing practices. The new directions were unveiled in the administration's first major policy document, "Chicago Works Together." In contrast to Byrne's Comprehensive Plan, which directed resources to the central business district, the Washington document emphasized neighborhood and minority empowerment through mechanisms of balanced development, job creation, industry retention, affirmative action, and citizen participation (see chapter 6).[41]

While the shift in policy direction appealed to Washington's electoral constituency, it had its strong detractors. Chicago's business community had been weaned on machine politics, closed-door processes, and insider privileges. Unlike Pittsburgh, Chicago lacked a strong independent civic or business sector. With the latter's fortunes tied to the strength of the machine, Washington's attack on it threatened the very relationship that had bestowed special status. The calls for balanced development signaled a shift in public investment from downtown to the neighborhoods. Citizen participation and neighborhood planning, from which Byrne had retreated, challenged the ward organizations. Open and fair government threatened the very lucrative contract process, while affirmative action was yet another assault on that beleaguered Chicago industry—patronage.[42]

Washington's efforts to expand the scope of policy benefits were, like Byrne's before him, strained by the realities of machine power and racial conflict. The white machine aldermen, who held a majority on the city council, resisted Washington's reforms, perceiving them as threats to their power base. Black machine aldermen, who by virtue of their political training understood "fairness" to mean, "it's our turn," were baffled and indeed angered by many of Washington's policies and appointments. Many black voters felt the same way. Finally, many white ethnic neighborhoods reacted to the election of a black mayor with resistance and fear.

Despite compelling opposition, Washington stuck with his electoral coalition and his campaign platform. Rather than compromise with the "evil cabal" as Byrne had done, Washington stood firm, setting off the city's famous "council wars," which pitted the "Vrdolyak 29" (the white machine bloc) against the mayor's twenty-one (all the black aldermen and the white reform aldermen). Council opposition had little to do with substantive disagreement and much to do with embarrassing the mayor and gaining bargaining chips in the battle for political power. Major economic development projects, which were approved during the Byrne administration, were defeated or put on hold by the city council when Washington tried to forward them.[43] Approvals of mayoral appointments and budgets were consistently delayed in efforts to stall the administration completely.

Although the machine was internally divided and electorally weakened, it was still a formidable obstacle to Washington. Lacking a majority on the city council, Washington used his neighborhood base as a counterweight to the machine. The election was over, but the campaign had just begun. Citizen involvement and conflict strategy were the principal tools in the campaign, as political logic and reform goals coalesced to challenge the machine in the city council and in the wards.[44]

NEIGHBORHOOD DEVELOPMENT IN PITTSBURGH AND CHICAGO: ECONOMIC LOGIC VERSUS POLITICAL LOGIC

Since the latter half of the 1970s, funds for neighborhood development have come primarily from the CDBG program. Passed in 1974 as part of Richard Nixon's "new federalism,"[45] the legislation for this program contained several broad objectives: the "prevention or elimination of slums or blight"; maximum feasible priority to activities which will benefit low- or moderate-income families"; and "other community development needs having a particular urgency."[46] Intended to give wide discretion to local policy makers, the CDBG program was ultimately reshaped by local political and institutional factors. The experiences in Pittsburgh and Chicago underscore the significance of local factors; from the very inception of the programs, there were marked differences.

In Pittsburgh the block grant program began during the antimachine, proneighborhood administration of Peter Flaherty. He was in his second term in office, had already restructured the URA and the Department of City Planning to focus on neighborhoods, and had removed a substantial amount of patronage from city government. CDBG money was thus an additional resource with which to strengthen his commitment to the neighborhoods. Moreover, the institutional machinery was in place to execute the commitment.

In Chicago the CDBG program began at the end of Richard J. Daley's administration. Absorbed by the machine, CDBG funding under Daley and his caretaker successor, Michael Bilandic, was spread primarily among three agencies: Urban Renewal, Model Cities, and the Parks Department. The latter two were notorious patronage operations, while Urban Renewal often served as an appendage of the growth machine. Finally, funding decisions were made without citizen participation and usually over the objections of neighborhood groups.

From these divergent beginnings, two unique stories would unfold. Largely insulated from electoral pressures, Pittsburgh's CDBG program has been guided primarily by an economic logic; resources are targeted and concentrated, CDBG funds are used to leverage additional resources, decision making is centralized and hierarchical, and the substantive focus is economic development. Finally, the program has been characterized by a remarkable amount of stability. Conceptually, this particular channeling of resources represented an expansion of the growth paradigm; organizationally, it represented an extension of the corporatist system.

In Chicago, the CDBG program became embedded in machine politics. Implementation of the program has been guided largely by political logic; resources are dispersed, either for patronage/electoral purposes or equity concerns; the overall program lacks a clear focus; and more often than not it has been viewed as a tool to reward friends and punish enemies. Consequently, the program has been marred by significant conflict and instability. Conceptually, the channeling of CDBG resources represented an extension of the electoral model; organizationally, it fortified the ward system.

Before examining the experience in the two cities, a word on size is in order. One can easily say that following an economic logic is much easier in a smaller city since there are fewer groups vying for a piece of the pie. While valid, this point should not cloud the significance of political and institutional difference.

Swanstrom's examination of Cleveland, a city not much bigger than Pittsburgh, showed the CDBG experience to be highly conflictual, more like that of Chicago.[47] Louise Jezierski's comparison of Cleveland and Pittsburgh, which reiterated Swanstrom's findings on the former, highlighted the diverse political and institutional factors as explanatory variables.[48]

Pittsburgh: Corporatism and the Neighborhoods

In Pittsburgh, CDBG money was instrumental in establishing the Pittsburgh Partnership for Neighborhood Development (PPND), a centralized funding mechanism that brings together the city's leading community development corporations (CDCs), foundations, city government, and the business community. Formed during the Caliguiri administration (1988) and supported by his two successors (Masloff and Murphy), the PPND is engaged in the formulation of community development strategies, resource network management, grant making, and resource leveraging.[49]

Operating on an informal basis since 1983, the PPND reflects the city's evolution away from electoral politics through a conscious process of institution building. Consequently, neighborhood development, as a policy priority, enjoys a high level of stability. Between 1978 and 1987, 80 percent of the city's capital budget went to neighborhoods.[50] At the height of Chicago's capital spending in neighborhoods (1986), a mere 20 percent of the total went to neighborhoods.[51] Additionally, operating support for CDCs and other CBOs was given line-item status in Pittsburgh's capital budget.

Neighborhoods acquired official priority with Flaherty's establishment of the Community Planning Division, which gave them information on, and input into, the city's capital budget. Additional practices, initiated by Caliguiri and still in operation, significantly increased information flow to the neighborhoods. Each year the city's planning department circulates a draft of the six-year capital budget, an accompanying policy narrative, the final capital plan, and "Progress in the Neighborhoods," a detailed breakdown of all city investments by neighborhood and project. The department and the city council also conduct public hearings on the capital budget draft. This is in sharp contrast to Chicago, where capital spending remains a mystery to neighborhood organizations.[52]

Central to neighborhood incorporation was the recognition of CDCs as intermediaries between city government and the neighborhoods. In Oakland the Department of City Planning funded Oakland Directions, Inc., in 1970 to participate in planning efforts. In 1979 the URA worked with the Manchester Citizen's Corporation on a local redevelopment project. And on the city's North Side, the North Side Civic Development Corporation was funded to carry out a development study for the area.

The concept of CDCs as intermediaries for neighborhood development gained ground rapidly; where there were no CDCs, the city funded their establishment. In the Homewood and East Liberty neighborhoods, CDCs were set up to work with the city in planning and implementing development policies.

These activities were funded with federal dollars, primarily CDBG funds. Under Flaherty, CDBG administration, which included allocation decisions and evaluations, was placed in the planning department, thus shielding it from electoral politics.[53] Under Caliguiri, the shielding was increased as CDBG monies were folded into the capital budget process in the planning department.

This allocation process also helped to build key constituencies centered around planning and capital budgeting activities. Composed of Department of City Planning and URA personnel and CDCs, these constituencies were strengthened by the continuity of personnel. Caliguiri's planning director held the position for twelve years. His successor was the former assistant director for community planning and capital programs within the planning department. Leadership in the CDCs has also exhibited remarkable stability.[54]

The constituency and resource base were expanded with the arrival of the Local Initiatives Support Corporation (LISC), a national program begun by the Ford Foundation. Invited by the ACCD in 1982, LISC's task was to raise money for neighborhood development from the corporate community. Physically housed within the ACCD offices, LISC was the link between the business community and neighborhood development. Thus, by the early 1980s neighborhood development was high on the city's agenda and CDCs were key players in that arena.

When in 1983 the Ford Foundation sought to initiate a program that would provide operating funds for CDCs, it found Pittsburgh's nonprofit sector very receptive and well organized. Pulling together representatives from local foundations (Howard Heinz and Mellon Bank), the URA and the DCP, and neighborhood organizations, the Partnership for Neighborhood Development was inaugurated. Five CDCs (Manchester Citizens Corporation, Oakland Planning and Development Corporation, East Liberty Development, Inc., North Side Civic Development Council, and Homewood-Brushton Revitalization and Development Corporation) received a commitment of one hundred thousand dollars a year each in operating funds for a three-year period. Initially located in the ACCD and then in the Pittsburgh Foundation, the PPND aggregates public (CDBG), private (through LISC), and foundation monies for the community development effort.

The generous funding led to resentment among other groups, which along with the local press, referred to these CDCs as the "Fortunate Five."[55] Taking their protests to the planning department, these groups persuaded the city to set up two additional funding pools: the Neighborhood Fund, Inc. (1984), which provides grants under $10,000, and the CBO Fund (1985), which provides grants up to $35,000. Between 1983 and 1989, forty-six groups received funding through this three-tier system with the lion's share of money going to the large CDCs; the PPND allocated $5 million in operating funds,[56] the CBO Fund allocated $1.2 million in project funds, and the Neighborhood Fund allocated $301,000.[57]

By the mid-eighties, the city had a hierarchical funding system centered around neighborhood development objectives. CDCs that receive PPND funding execute multiple economic development projects and function as the organizational ambassadors for their neighborhood or region.[58] Organizations supported by the CBO Fund do smaller-scale economic development projects, while those supported by the Neighborhood Fund do feasibility studies for economic development projects. Organizations in the latter pools are encouraged to move into the next grouping.

Decision-making power mirrors the funding hierarchies. The PPND is governed by a board composed of foundation and bank representatives and the executive directors of the ACCD, the URA, and the planning department. The two smaller funds—CBO Fund and Neighborhood Fund—are overseen by the Advisory Committee on Community-Based Organizations (ACCBO), a fifteen-member committee with representatives from city planning, foundations, banks, neighborhood organizations, the city council, and the academic community.[59] ACCBO monitors the performance of its grantees and makes funding recommendations to the Department of City Planning, including recommendations for groups to be admitted to the prized partnership. Since the PPND's inception in 1983, six new groups have received funding.

The city council has been conspicuously absent from this funding system. Although the CDBG funding was merged with the capital budget within the Department of City Planning, the city council did control 5 percent of the grant, representing half of the city's "discretionary," or unspecified local option money with which the council funded CBOs. However, complaints of arbitrariness from these organizations and the demand for a funding system comparable to the PPND resulted in the formation of a separate organization (ACCBO) to make funding recommendations.[60]

This transfer of control over CDBG monies was not challenged by the city council, which as an at-large elected body was not giving up much in the way of resources. Indeed, it has even been suggested that the council welcomed the move since it "relieve[d] the Council of political backfire."[61] This may be an exaggeration, but there was definitely strong precedent for the council to avoid control since the bulk of CDBG monies had been folded into the capital budget process.

Finally, another precedent was operative—the seemingly apolitical nature of neighborhood development in Pittsburgh. I say "seemingly" because politics is by no means absent from funding decisions. However, it is confined to the foundations, the bureaucracy, and the CDC movement as opposed to the more visible and volatile electoral arena. This is not the politics that we associate with political machines, patronage, or vote getting, any and all of which would stigmatize council attempts to control the CDBG allocation process. Thus, the larger political ethos was yet another deterrent to council control.

The relationship between politics in the electoral and civic arenas is indeed an interesting one. In Pittsburgh the balance has clearly swung toward the latter, a factor brought home by the city's introduction of district elections in 1989. After the first district council was elected, the battle was on to regain control over CDBG monies. With district constituencies, councillors now had to bring home the bacon, and the CDBG was an attractive meal. On the other side were the CDCs and planning department officials, the solid constituency seeking to protect its resource base. As of 1996, council efforts to wrest control over portions of the CDBG money have been unsuccessful.

The battle over the CDBG monies raises an interesting dilemma for neighborhood representation. In 1987, Pittsburgh voters passed a referendum to institute district elections for city council. The referendum was carried out under the pressure of a lawsuit charging the city with racial discrimination. In 1989 the city elected its first district-based council since 1911.

Writing on this development, Louise Jezierski called it yet another victory for the neighborhoods, lumping it together with the increased role of the CDCs.[62] I would challenge this assertion, arguing that the CDC movement has produced strong leaders in the neighborhoods who are zealously guarding their resources. If the city council meetings suggested anything, it was that CDCs and the district councillors are on a collision course over the control of neighborhood resources. In their own right, both are neighborhood leaders, but their constituencies differ. While CDCs bring many resources to the neighborhood, their constituency has increasingly become the foundations, the banks, and city planning and redevelopment authority personnel. The constituencies of the councillors are the voters in their district.

In the battle over CDBG monies, the CDCs appear to have the advantage. Their track record in neighborhood development has gained them strong credibility among funders and the civic sector in general. The institutionalization of ties with the civic and business sectors has strengthened their legitimacy. Finally, the prevailing logic in Pittsburgh has been one of planning, which can be loosely defined as that which takes place outside of electoral politics. Once again, the points go to the CDCs.

The strength of this logic is evident in the comments of many CDC staffers about the city council. Their objections to council control over CDBG include charges of parochialism, "small-p" politics, and lack of qualifications. These sentiments are strikingly similar to those expressed by turn-of-the-century businessmen who supported reforms in urban government. Within this context, council attempts to regain control over the CDBG program are tantamount to swimming against a strong tide.

The insulation of the CDBG program from electoral pressures has permitted a high degree of stability: programmatically, housing continues to be the top priority;[63] organizationally, all of the original five CDCs are still funded by the PPND. This stability has allowed CDBG money to be used as a lever for additional resources. The PPND began with that goal and has continued to operate on that basis. In 1989 the PPND set up the Development Fund to provide grants and to issue loans to CDCs at below-market rates. Capitalized with nearly eight hundred thousand dollars from local foundations, the PPND leveraged nearly six million dollars more by 1993 from public and private funders.[64] In one sense, then, CDBG has been treated more like an Urban Development Action Grant (UDAG), which uses public money to attract private money, than as a distributive policy tool.[65] Hence, economic, as opposed to political, logic seemed to be the main driving force.

In March 1988 the PPND was incorporated and a full-time director hired. This development was consistent with corporatist logic; the big CDCs had come into their own, thus earning the right to be represented by a peak association. The newly hired director, Sandra Philips, came from the Oakland Planning and Development Corporation, where she was executive director since its inception in 1980. While lacking the resource base of the ACCD,[66] the PPND is in many ways its neighborhood analogue. The creation of a private, nonprofit entity that mixes public and private funds and is subject to review by the business, foundation, and government sectors has strengthened the prevailing logic of institution building and planning over organizing and electoral politics. And, as the three-tier funding system demonstrates, it tilted the balance toward centralist as opposed to populist tendencies.

Chicago: Conflict Strategy and the Neighborhoods

"Look-it, here's what I would've done if I was mayor. There's $126 million; so each alderman gets a million a piece and I get $76 million. So I tell them, 'Take $1 million for your ward, use it the way you have to, and let's pass this thing . . . forget all this principle stuff.' I miss the days of Daley when there wasn't all this talk of principle, and the city actually got things done."[67] Alderman Mell's commentary on the 1983 CDBG application echoes the sentiment of many Chicago politicians: resources are political; you use them to gain support and keep people happy; you don't bother with policy. Jane Byrne, despite her reform beginnings, did nothing to dissuade this line of thinking. But Harold Washington was not subscribing to this philosophy. His attempts to change the underlying logic of resource distribution encountered an entrenched political system and mentality that were quite formidable in their opposition.

While "council wars" permeated every aspect of the Washington administration, neighborhood issues were particularly contentious. It was here that the machine guys stood to lose the most. It was also an area in which they could embarrass the mayor as well as play the race card. Finally, in seeking to convert resources from patronage usage to policy usage, Washington's approach to the neighborhoods threatened an existing system of resource allocation.

In contrast to Caliguiri, whose neighborhood policies expanded a system, Washington's neighborhood initiatives directly attacked the power base of aldermen and ward bosses and the system of governance from which they derived their power. Neighborhood policies thus reflected the larger battle over who would control the city and to what and whose ends. The CDBG program and the city's bonding authority, two key sources of neighborhood funding, were major stakes in what was increasingly becoming a zero-sum game. Mayor–council conflict characterized both of these programs as the politicization of neighborhood issues reached an all-time high.

Washington restructured the decision-making process and funding priorities of the CDBG program along the lines of open and fair government. Citizen participation workshops were conducted, public hearings were held, and the funding recommendations of the CDAC were listened to for the first time. Not surprisingly, the funding recommendations differed from those of the Byrne administration; $13.5 million (approximately 15 percent of the total allocation of $147 million) was moved out of the administration, where it was supporting patronage jobs, and into neighborhood improvements. Allocations for housing, health care, and senior citizen programs were also increased.[68] Finally, the administration froze any spending that involved housing demolition and residential displacement, something community groups had advocated for years.[69]

Washington's first CDBG application received high praise from community activists but hit a stone wall in the city council; the Vrdolyak 29 had discovered the principle of checks and balances. The majority bloc passed an ordinance requiring council approval for all reprogramming decisions and all contracts in excess of fifty thousand dolllars. A similar measure dealing with reprogramming decisions, proposed by independent alderman Larry Bloom in 1982, died in committee. The majority bloc also demanded project information on a ward-by-ward basis. This was the first time such a request was made of a mayor.

While the administration balked at these requests, it did reach a compromise with the council just days before HUD's filing deadline. The council was given approval power for contracts over fifty thousand dollars and for 90 percent of reprogramming decisions; the mayor could reprogram 10 percent of the original CDBG application without council approval.

Commenting on the CDBG fight, a *Chicago Tribune* editorial stated, "The aldermen simply were not ready for Mayor Washington's radical CD budget outline.... They could not understand a budget that actually adhered to the federal intent in granting funds."[70] This is not surprising since Chicago was notorious for violating federal guidelines.[71] Under Byrne, CDBG money was reprogrammed so often and for so many questionable uses that it was referred to as "Jane Byrne's Fix-it-Fund."[72] Byrne's funding decisions—both initial and amended—were made over the objections of the CDAC, which, in the words of one reporter, functioned "largely as window dressing."[73]

While local oversight was lax, the feds were singing a different tune. Granted the legislation was broad, but spending millions on snow removal, TV ads promoting the city, a school bailout, and a jobs program (ten million dollars for 3,800 jobs), which just happened to occur during the mayoral campaign, gave new meaning to the term "local discretion."[74] HUD wasn't buying it. Charging the city with exceeding the limit for "public service" expenditures, HUD demanded a repayment of twenty-six million dollars.[75] Despite Byrne's erratic approach to CDBG funds, the council was silent. Even Alderman Bloom's proposed ordinance died a quiet death.

Under Washington, the silent approvals of the past gave way to acrimonious debate, council changes, mayoral vetoes, and program-threatening delays. The year 1983 was merely a taste of what was to come as the CDBG program became the latest hostage in the ongoing saga called "council wars."

Between 1983 and 1986, the CDBG application process resembled a political football.[76] The scenario was the same: Washington submitted his CDBG application to the council, whereupon the council demanded more control and revised his funding recommendations. In 1984 the city just met an extended deadline. In 1985, executive–legislative conflict nearly sabotaged the entire CDBG grant as the city missed HUD's deadline. The two-month delay resulted in thirteen hundred layoffs, stalled contracts for two hundred CBOs, and the temporary paralysis of the Departments of Housing and Economic Development, both of which relied heavily on CDBG-funded staff.[77]

The council came under fire from community activists and the media, but it was not deterred. The CDBG was a weapon with which to derail the Washington administration, and the council was going to exploit it. For many in the majority bloc, the funding controversies were no-lose situations. The council's funding revisions shifted monies from wards allied with the mayor, which were predominantly poor and African American, to white, middle-class machine wards. Thus, Washington's objections to council revisions allowed the council to play the race card; Washington was the mayor of "Black Chicago."[78] The situation also allowed for a swipe at his reform credentials; like any other "boss," Washington was rewarding his friends and punishing his enemies.

At the same time Washington was operating under new federal guidelines that tightened eligibility requirements.[79] Interestingly, these guidelines were instituted in response to local abuses like those in the Byrne administration. Moreover, Washington, with the help of Congressman Daniel Rostenkowski, had negotiated Chicago's way out of the Byrne debacle in 1983; HUD forgave the money that Byrne misspent on the condition that Chicago strictly adhere to the guidelines.

Despite assurances to HUD, as part of the 1984 compromise, Washington submitted the council's recommendations. The following year, HUD demanded that the city repay $422,000 in misspent funds. Of the seven agencies that HUD declared ineligible, five were council recommendations. While Washington promptly removed the other two from the 1985 application, the Vrdolyak 29 stood pat. True to Chicago tradition, they were unimpressed with federal regulations; money should be used for *all* neighborhoods.[80]

The problems with the council's recommendations went beyond eligibility.

Of the thirteen organizations recommended, six had never submitted a proposal, several were tied to precinct captains, and one was run by a lawyer in Vrdolyak's law firm.[81] These recommendations were clearly inserted to put Washington in the politically sensitive spot of having to defund white agencies.

Washington was thus caught between a rock and a hard place in 1985. Given HUD's ruling, he could not submit the council's recommendations. The council, however, would not approve any application that deleted those agencies. And, while the logjam continued, thirteen hundred people were temporarily unemployed, two agencies decimated, and countless projects on hold. Many of those laid off staged protests at city hall, demanding an end to the political wars that were jeopardizing their communities and their lives. While the majority bloc was the target of the protest activity, they felt it aided their cause; it proved that Harold Washington could not manage the city. It also fueled the myths about the chaos and disorder that would result from the election of a black mayor.[82]

The logjam was finally broken in July with a compromise agreement. The ineligible agencies were removed from the CDBG application and given city funds ($300,000), while state and motor fuel tax funds ($1.3 million) were committed for street paving on the city's white, middle-class Northwest and Southwest Sides.[83] In essence, Washington used local resources to buy off political opposition.

If the real issue in the mayor–council battles was funding for neighborhood improvements, the conflicts, time, and diversion of resources that characterized the CDBG experience could have been easily avoided. Early in his administration, Washington proposed a $94-million general obligation bond for neighborhood capital improvements. Unencumbered by CDBG restrictions, the bond would cover repairs in *all* neighborhoods.

While the administration was battling with the Vrdolyak 29 over CDBG funds, the bond proposal languished in Ed Burke's finance committee.[84] Once again, machine aldermen were willing to sacrifice constituent interests in the larger quest for political power. Their priorities were aptly summed up by Alderman Richard Mell: "I will sacrifice a vote that probably won't be popular in my community for the good of the coalition [the Vrdolyak 29]."[85] Washington's effective use of community pressure, however, forced machine alderman to go with popular demands over the "good of the coalition."

Washington's bond proposal was the largest neighborhood improvement program in the city's history. For the neighborhoods it was a significant and welcomed departure from the typical practice of issuing general obligation bonds for downtown improvements. It also departed from the "friends and enemies tradition" of machine politics; according to the original proposal, 63 percent of the bond would go to the twenty-nine opposition wards, even though they represented only 58 percent of the wards. And, Vrdolyak's ward was to receive more than thirty-nine other wards.[86] Some allies of the mayor thought that Washington had gone too far in appeasing the opposition.[87]

Although the money was to be distributed equitably among the fifty wards, the finance committee tabled the proposal. Defending his actions, Burke said the bond would force an increase in taxes. The evidence, however, was not in Burke's favor. A comptroller's office study showed taxes increasing by only $3.20 on a sixty-thousand-dollar home to pay for a $110-million bond.[88] Moreover, the city council approved three bonds totaling $213 million under Byrne, five million dollars of which went for construction of luxury boxes at Comiskey Park, without raising the tax specter.[89] As one alderman anonymously confessed, the real reason was the unwillingness to assist the mayor in getting "credit for neighborhood improvements."[90]

It was not the flimsy economic argument, however, that doomed the opposition, but a well-orchestrated public relations campaign by the mayor's office. Elaborate bus tours, for press and aldermen, of some of the city's neighborhoods highlighted the problem; these neighborhoods, many of which were in machine wards, still had their original WPA streets, absent gutters or curbs, and crumbling in abundance. The media blitz and the mobilization of community support were effective; in 1985 the aldermen capitulated, passing a $185-million general obligation bond.

The Politics of Contradiction: Race Versus the Neighborhoods

While the administration won some key resource battles, neighborhood and minority incorporation would remain elusive as long as the opposition had a legislative majority. A court-ordered remap and special ward elections, however, changed that. In March 1986, Washington had twenty-five votes on the council. With his vote as the tiebreaker, Washington finally had a majority, which would make governing easier.

On the electoral front, Washington also seemed to be making progress. The bond campaign was a good sign; using collective policy benefits, Washington mobilized white ethnic support to defeat his machine enemies. On one hand, this would seem natural given the machine's history of neighborhood neglect. In Chicago's racially charged environment, however, it was anything but natural. The city's racial divisions threatened to drive a wedge through Washington's progressive coalition.

Washington's attempts to bridge the city's racial divide through a "fairness" platform met an early challenge. In response to the 1983 election, two major coalition groups—the Northwest Neighborhood Federation and the Southwest Federation of Neighborhood Parishes—merged, forming a powerful alliance known as Save Our Neighborhoods, Save Our City (SONSOC), which brought together white ethnic organizations from numerous neighborhoods. Although many of these organizations had battled the machine, they were not comforted by the election of an African American mayor. Indeed, many had supported Washington's Republican opponent.

In April 1984, SONSOC held a convention that revealed the fundamental contradictions between black empowerment and neighborhood empowerment agendas. Attended by 750 delegates armed with fifteen thousand signatures, the convention centered around the "Declaration of Neighborhood Independence." Nicknamed the "White Ethnic Agenda," the declaration included a series of demands for neighborhood preservation.[91] It also portrayed Washington as the enemy and accused him of playing racial politics.

In a bold move, Washington supported a study of one of the declaration's more controversial components—a home equity insurance program designed to protect property values against decreases resulting from racial change. Although two Chicago suburbs had used similar plans to protect integration, it was a highly controversial proposal. In fact, a similar proposal by the Southwest Federation was supported by candidate Jane Byrne in 1979 and then abandoned by Mayor Jane Byrne.[92] Given the city's history of racial discrimination, particularly in housing, the plan's insidious assumption that black movement into a neighborhood destroys the neighborhood and the racist reputation of some of the sponsoring organizations, Washington's endorsement was met with consternation in the African American community.[93] Even the traditionally conservative Chicago Urban League refused to back the mayor.

Despite the controversy, Washington saw the program as a tool for bridging the city's racial divide. The researchers conducting the study concluded that the program should be used to promote peaceful integration.[94] Finally, Washington saw this as a way to expand his electoral base within the white ethnic community.

For SONSOC, home equity was both a policy goal and an organizing tool. Since many SONSOC members had been trained in Alinsky's style, they were highly combative, using fear to mobilize support and painting politicians and government as the enemy. Their concerns for neighborhood stability, which in Chicago parlance meant all-white, made the city's first African American mayor a particularly good target. While some members of SONSOC supported peaceful integration, they were drowned out by the more vocal opponents of integration.[95]

The proposal ultimately became mired in symbolic and racial politics. As misunderstandings, constituent pressures, and feelings of betrayal on both sides came to dominate, distance, rather than bridges, characterized the relations between Washington and the sponsoring organizations. In the 1987 election, opposition to Washington decreased significantly in these wards (primarily among renters), but there was no noticeable increase in support.[96] While the causal connection remains a matter of speculation, Washington withdrew his support for home equity after his reelection. According to some accounts, he was reconsidering his position before he died.[97]

The home equity campaign took a particularly ugly turn after Washington's death as racial accusations were hurled on both sides. Marlene Carter, the black alderperson whose ward included part of the affected area on the Southwest Side, called it "an insult to blacks" and a "racist move."[98] In a very close city council vote, the measure was passed, only to be vetoed by Eugene Sawyer, Harold Washington's black successor. SONSOC took its campaign to the state level, where Democratic Speaker of the House Michael Madigan, whose district includes the Southwest Side, secured passage of the measure.[99] A home equity district, encompassing five neighborhoods on the Southwest Side, was subsequently set up.

In retrospect, the battle seems more symbolic than substantive. The program attracted few participants, as "flight" remained the preferred option of many white homeowners. This course, combined with the ugly and contentious battles over the home equity proposal, revealed once again the difficulties of building a progressive coalition in a city torn by racial and class cleavages.

CHALLENGE AND RESPONSE

The preceding examples highlight the interaction of political and institutional factors in shaping the opportunities for coalition building and leadership. Most important, they illustrate how patterns of resource distribution become embedded in larger political and institutional frameworks. In Pittsburgh, for instance, even though Flaherty's election was seen as a coup for the neighborhoods, in the larger institutional scheme his administration did not depart from established patterns of behavior. The route that neighborhood incorporation took under both Flaherty and Caliguiri represented an extension of the institutional logic of corporatism to the neighborhoods. Institutions were set up to give representation to peak associations, thus placing neighborhood issues in the sphere of elite politics. This segmentation was reinforced through the hierarchical structure that placed the big CDCs at the top and the more grassroots organizations at the bottom of the funding ladder. The PPND thus continued the tilt toward centralism over populism that began with ACTION-Housing's foray into the neighborhoods.

In addition to conformity to larger institutional patterns, neighborhood incorporation in Pittsburgh was aided by political factors. The relative weakness of the city's ward organizations and the at-large structure and small size of the city council removed potential sources of opposition. The domination of resource distribution channels by civic associations and the paucity of resources in the electoral arena dampened the possibility for mobilization on a racial basis. Had such mobilization occurred, it could have added a sharp divisiveness to the city's political system, making it more difficult to define issues strictly in neighborhood terms.

In Chicago, the realities of machine power and racial strife led the Byrne and Washington administrations in very different directions from the Pittsburgh mayors. Neighborhood demands were perceived as direct threats by the ward organizations, while demands by African Americans were threatening to large segments of Chicago's white electorate. Both of these factors contributed to shaping patterns of behavior and resource distribution that hampered reform efforts. Jane Byrne, for instance, did set up new institutions (the Departments of Housing and Neighborhoods) to address neighborhood concerns, but these quickly fell prey to the same political logic that dictated all of Chicago's bureaucracy: resource distribution patterns reflected electoral concerns. By contrast, the agencies set up by Caliguiri reflected the underlying logic and orientation of Pittsburgh's civic sector. The Department of Housing, for example, was driven by programmatic concerns of experimentation, expertise, and efficiency.

Perhaps even more emblematic of the embeddedness of resource distribution patterns and political behavior are Harold Washington's efforts to reform the system. His attempts to alter the underlying basis for CDBG allocation helped to mobilize neighborhood groups while at the same time putting the administration on a collision course with the political machine. A similar pattern obtained in Washington's approach to the general obligation bond controversy.

Although the differences between the two cities can be viewed in structural terms, the stark contrast between Washington's and Byrne's use of resources requires another explanation. Despite her auspicious beginnings, Byrne essentially used the resources at her disposal to fortify the existing political system. Conversely, Washington used resources to mobilize a resistance movement. These divergences point to the role of agency: the two mayors had different coalitions, made different political calculations, and consequently fashioned different strategies. Thus, governance, as well as its consequences for neighborhood and minority inclusion, results from the interaction of agency and structure. Chapter 6 will take a closer look at this interaction by focusing on Washington's efforts to implement a progressive agenda within the confines of Chicago's underdeveloped policy-making structure.

6
Chicago: The Barriers to Multidimensional Progressivism

> *Regime transition is constrained, then, not only by the larger political economy but also by the recalcitrance of the public organizational field through which it must be accomplished.*
>
> —Johnston and Holt, 1995

Although this conclusion was drawn from an examination of the experiences of New Haven's first black mayor, John Daniels, it could just as easily have been based on the Washington administration. The term "public organizational field," as used by Johnston and Holt, refers to the city's political process and its public administration (institutions).[1] Shaped by past practices and agreements that have created a set of vested interests and habits, both of these domains become extremely resistant to change.[2] Washington's attempts to change the basis of resource distribution clashed head-on with an entrenched political system that operated according to very different rules and reward structures. Beneficiaries of the existing system, who perceived these initiatives as a threat to their interests, vigorously fought back. While this is to be expected, the political system also operates in more subtle and less explored ways. To paraphrase Johnston and Holt, one of the legacies of the prior regime is that it traps "would-be governing coalition" members between the past and the future.[3]

In examining Chicago Works Together, Harold Washington's wholesale effort to change the form and content of Chicago government, we will see this more subtle aspect of the political system at work. Washington's coalition was caught between a past in which electoral victory was identified with a disproportionate share of the spoils and an intended future where more equitable rules of distribution would apply. The multidimensional focus of Washington's reform efforts set off conflicts between coalition members, thus adding internal political problems to the already existing external opposition.

Washington's efforts also ran afoul of an institutional structure and culture that were antithetical to much of what he was trying to achieve through his reforms. As stated in chapter 3, the absence of a "public" policy focus and the underdevelopment of the governmental machinery, which were the legacy of the Daley regime, would be a nightmare for reform efforts geared toward enduring change. The picture of urban politics painted in chapter 1 illustrates the problem. Washington altered some components of the regime (its composition, overall orientation, and ordering of priorities), but the institutional framework and larger political culture, and their influence on political behavior, remained unchanged. Thus, there was significant turmoil within the political system as its major components (how power is structured, institutional framework, and political culture) were severely out of sync.

REDEFINING LOCAL GOVERNMENT: CHICAGO WORKS TOGETHER

"The Chicago Development Plan 1984 [Chicago Works Together] is the strongest indication thus far that American cities are willing to try to harness economic development for their disadvantaged residents."[4] This observation made by three planners, one of whom, Norman Krumholz, is regarded as among the most progressive city planners in the country, attests to the radical nature of the document. Chicago Works Together (CWT) formed the basis of the Washington administration's policy agenda. Based on significant input from the neighborhoods and emphasizing balanced growth, neighborhood development, job creation, affirmative action, and public participation, CWT embodied a multidimensional progressivism in both content and procedure. The latter was evident from the numerous task forces used by the administration to advise on and assist in policy formulation.

In practical terms, CWT sought a complete redefinition of local government. Implementing CWT, however, required much more than definitional change. The thrust of CWT challenged some long-standing beliefs and practices, both of which can be summed up by the old adage that in politics you reward your friends and punish your enemies. Local government in Chicago was organized around a conception of government as a reward system for individual behavior. Notions of "public" policy and collective benefits were, for the most part, absent from the institutional culture. Washington's efforts to change this were often seen as merely shifting the spoils of victory from one group to another as current actions were interpreted through old lenses.

Examining efforts to reform the contracting and hiring procedures, to make government accessible, and to balance development reveals the struggles of a progressive administration seeking to change the rules of the game. Resistance, accusations, and conflict became the new order. These difficulties were compounded by Washington's own administration (composed largely of outsiders, many of whom were political neophytes), in which conflicts over the means and ends of policy were not uncommon. Representing disenfranchised and poor populations, there was also conflict over the distribution of reform. External resistance prevented Washington from institutionalizing his reforms, making it imperative that the progressive coalition stay together. The internal rumblings, however, did not look promising.

Opening Up City Government: Contracts and Hiring

When scholars cite local government's dependence on business for economic growth as a limit on redistributive capacities, they ignore the vast economic resources of local government; city governments are major economic players. Between 1981 and 1986, the Chicago city government awarded $2.7 billion in contracts, for an annual average of just over $450 million. The single largest recipient of contracts was the construction industry, with yearly averages of $192,737,226 and a six-year total of nearly $1.2 billion.[5] In a twist on the dependence angle, city contracts accounted for 27 percent of construction firms' sales.[6]

Chicago mayors have long been aware of the purchasing power of local government expenditures; contracts topped the list of insider privileges. Prior to Washington, for instance, 50 percent of the city's purchasing dollars, on average, went to only 3.5 percent of the vendors who received city contracts.[7] Only rarely was a minority-owned firm among this exclusive club. But this was not the case in all cities. Minority business enterprise (MBE) programs were well established in numerous cities, including Birmingham since 1974, Houston (1975), Cincinnati (1978), Portland, Oregon (1979–1980), Oakland, California (1980), and Atlanta (1982).[8] When Maynard Jackson, former Atlanta mayor and informal adviser to Harold Washington on the mechanics of set-aside programs, suggested that Chicago was "far behind," it was indeed an understatement.[9]

Mayor Washington took heed. Viewing city government's purchasing power as a way to expand job opportunities within the city and among groups that had been locked out in the past, the administration sought to reform Chicago's contracting practices.[10] Internal struggles, however, slowed the process. Bill Ware, Washington's chief of staff, who sought a reform and apolitical image for the administration, was constantly urging caution. His overzealousness in protecting the mayor from charges of political cronyism earned him the nickname "Bottleneck Bill." Other top aides, most notably Washington's corporation counsel and former civil rights attorney James Montgomery, wanted quicker action. The result was a compromise; a major study of the city's contracting and purchasing practices was conducted, which provided the basis for subsequent reforms.

When the study, the Lowry Report, was made public in March 1985, it documented enough past discrimination to justify overhauling the city's contracting practices.[11] Prior to 1984, less than 10 percent of the city's prime contracts went to minority or women business enterprises, even though minorities made up nearly 60 percent of the city's population.[12] Between 1982 and 1984, when African Americans represented nearly 40 percent of Chicago's population, black-owned firms received only 7.4 percent of the city's contract dollars. For Hispanics the numbers were even worse; they represented 14 percent of the population, but Hispanic-owned firms received only 1.5 percent of the city's purchase dollars.[13] The Lowry Report also uncovered gross inefficiencies in the city's purchasing process; clear policies, procedures, and monitoring activities were characteristically absent.

With "council wars" raging, however, the main issue was power. Unable to get council approval for his reforms, in April 1985 Washington issued Executive Order 85-2, requiring city agencies to award 25 percent of their contracts to minority business enterprises and 5 percent to women business enterprises.[14] Within ten months, 29.1 percent of city contracts had gone to minority or women business enterprises.[15] By 1987, minority business enterprises received 33 percent of the city's contract dollars, while women business enterprises received 5.6 percent.[16]

Washington extended the set-aside provisions to commercial development as well. Private developers who benefited from low-interest revenue bonds or from the purchase of city-owned land were expected to adhere to the 30 percent contract provision. These good-faith agreements were reached with developers on a major North Loop redevelopment project that was expected to yield $166 million in MBE contracts for the construction stage alone.[17] The good-faith agreements applied to the postconstruction stage as well.

Although the contract set-aside program ultimately increased the proportion of city work going to minority- and women-owned businesses, the early stages of the program were marked by controversy. A weak certification process (the city had to certify that firms were minority- or women-owned) and weak to nonexistent monitoring of contracts resulted in the awarding of approximately one-third of the contracts to front companies.[18] The Department of Purchasing, the implementing department, was part of the old bureaucracy over which Washington lacked any control. Washington's initial efforts to overhaul the department were defeated in council. The administration's 1985 budget request, for instance, contained funding for twenty-one contract compliance personnel specifically to monitor the affirmative action program. The city council approved seven positions, four of which were filled by existing personnel from the Department of Public Works.[19] In response to a federal investigation of the city's contract set-aside program, Washington was able to secure more positions for the purchasing department. A new director was hired, and the certification and enforcement processes were significantly improved. As a result, most of the "shell" companies were eliminated.

The difficulties that plagued the program in its beginning stages are not unique to Chicago. Front companies have haunted contract set-aside programs in other locales, including the city of Philadelphia and the state of Maryland. While it is beyond the scope of this analysis to determine whether some portion of the difficulty is endemic to contract set-asides (i.e., the incentives for businesses to act fraudulently), it is clear that Chicago's institutional structure and culture were impediments to effective implementation. Prior to Washington's executive order, the city did engage in minority contracting, although on a very limited scale and in a highly informal fashion, usually for electoral purposes. Thus, the existence of very weak certification and enforcement processes comes as no surprise. Unfortunately, Washington's attempts to change the institutional structure were hampered by political opposition (city council) and the Shakman decrees. A more cautious type, à la Bill Ware, would have urged the administration to wait until all the necessary pieces were in place. However, in a climate of rising expectations, such caution can be politically costly as coalition members become disenchanted with the slow pace of change.

Washington's other major affirmative action initiative, city hiring, did result in some disgruntled coalition members. The grumblings were not the result of inaction by the administration, but rather of what was perceived by some as too much action for one part of the coalition and not enough for another part.

The administration's approach to hiring was similar to its approach to contract set-asides: internal debate and analysis of past practice followed by an executive order. In August 1985 the Task Force on Affirmative Action was established. Directed by the commissioner of personnel, the task force concluded, after an exhaustive study of the city's hiring practices, that historically minorities and women had been subjected to discrimination. Moreover, it found that "minorities and women were even more seriously underrepresented in the City workforce in 1983 than they were ten years earlier in 1973."[20] The overall findings of racial bias in hiring are not unique to Chicago. What is significant is the latter finding, which showed minorities and women losing ground. If anything, most cities were making up ground for minorities and women during this period.

The somewhat unusual pattern in Chicago owes much to the underlying logic of the political system: the perception of city government as a resource base for electoral purposes rather than as a policy tool for economic development within communities or among minorities. The data on new hires for blacks during the Byrne administration are illustrative of this logic:[21]

	1980	1981	1982	1983
Percent	47.44	46.74	28.42	30.52

The most interesting feature is the roller coaster pattern. The percentage of Byrne hires that went to blacks is quite high in her first two years when she was delivering on her promise to "open up" city government. With the challenge from

Table 6.1. New Hires by Race and Gender, Chicago

Year ending June 30	White	Black	Hispanic	Women	Total
1980	2,091 44%	2,279 47%	380 8%	1,311 27%	4,804
1981	2,731 44%	2,922 47%	511 8%	2,364 38%	6,252
1982	1,579 64%	706 28%	156 6%	634 26%	2,484
1983	1,662 58%	875 31%	173 10%	911 32%	2,867
1984	321 32%	533 56%	96 10%	376 38%	989
1985	700 24%	1,831 64%	287 10%	848 30%	2,858
1986	707 30%	1,297 55%	278 12%	914 41%	2,351

Source: *Chicago Sun-Times,* September 7, 1986.

Richard M. Daley in 1982, however, we see a precipitous decline, as Byrne furiously went after the white ethnic vote. In typical Chicago fashion, blacks were the sacrificial lamb of racial politics.

With markedly different views of city government, hiring practices under Washington changed dramatically as African Americans, Hispanics, and females were hired in record numbers. Unable to obtain city council support, Washington relied on an executive order for an affirmative action plan. Tables 6.1 and 6.2, comparing hiring practices of the Byrne and Washington administrations, indicate the magnitude of the change across the board.

Particularly significant were the gains made by women. The city that proudly identified with such metaphors as "broad shoulders" and "hog butcher to the world" watched women assume positions that traditionally had gone to men: commissioners of housing, planning, and purchasing, deputy chief of staff, budget director. In all, 39 percent of Washington's top-level staff were women; under Byrne, the proportion was 12 percent.[22]

While Washington's hiring practices were much more racially and gender representative than past practices, many Hispanics felt shortchanged in the mayor's fairness agenda. Like African Americans and women, they bore the scars of a history of discrimination. In 1983 Hispanics represented 14 percent of the population but only 3.9 percent of the municipal workforce.[23] Blacks, by contrast, made up approximately 40 percent of the population and accounted for 27.6 percent of city government jobs. While not holding Washington responsible for the sins of past mayors, Hispanics, as part of the electoral coalition, expected their fair share. Given their tiny representation in the city workforce, however, anything but a painfully slow move toward parity would require vastly greater efforts than the administration had produced. In a report critical of Washington's efforts, the Mayor's Advisory Committee on Latino Affairs (MACLA) issued its own affirmative action plan that demonstrated that the city could reach parity in twenty-one years if 34 percent of new hires each year were Hispanic.[24]

Twenty-one years was still a long time, and 34 percent was a very high figure; it was 3.5 times the percentage (10 percent) for 1985. Reaching this goal would have meant fewer white and black hires and steep political costs. Washington would have risked losing his white support, meager though it was, would have confirmed charges that he was antiwhite, and would have angered his African American constituents, many of whom did believe that "their turn" came before that of Hispanics. With the administration already under such attacks, affirmative action hiring was yet another reminder of the difficulties of implementing redistributive policies in racially tense environments.

Washington did not follow MACLA's recommendations; the following year, Hispanics accounted for 10 percent of new hires. The hiring situation, as well as ill feelings between some African American and Latino administration members, was a continual strain on the coalition. Many Latinos felt that although they were part of the electoral coalition, they were being excluded from decision-making processes.[25] Although Washington's Latino vote increased in 1987, the coalition remained tenuous and died shortly after Washington's death.

An equally controversial program was the First Source Agreement. Designed to "target employment opportunities to Chicago residents,"[26] the program, like affirmative action and contract set-asides, was entangled in internal battles. Administration staff who were concerned with the mayor's "reform" image argued against a program that critics could easily label as patronage. Indeed, key spokespeople in the business community, including the director of the Chicago Association of Commerce and Industry, expressed strong opposition to the program.[27] Those less concerned, or perhaps more pragmatic, argued that no matter what Washington did, his detractors would cast it in a negative light. Thus, why not go for broke, so to speak. Finally, some in the administration worried about the legality of a mandatory hiring program.

Chicago First was thus born of compromise. In 1987 Washington signed an

Table 6.2. Mayoral Appointments by Race, Chicago

	White	Black	Hispanic
Department heads			
Byrne[a]	83%	17%	0%
Washington[a]	55	42	3
Mayor's office			
Byrne	90%	6%	4%
Washington	45	43	11

[a] Figures are for the last year of the Byrne administration and the first year of the Washington administration.
Source. *Chicago Sun-Times,* April 1, 1984.

executive order requiring contractors who received public subsidies to first consider city residents for job openings. The Chicago First Office, under the jurisdiction of the Mayor's Office of Employment and Training (MET), coordinated the contracts, screened applicants, and made referrals to contractors who were obliged to make good-faith efforts to hire city residents. This watered-down version was further diluted during implementation by poor communication and a lack of coordination within the bureaucracy. City departments issued contracts without informing the Chicago First Office, thus diminishing its ability to execute first source agreements.

Opening Up City Government: Access and Neighborhood Resources

Bureaucratic inertia also proved problematic to another administration goal: accessibility. Washington's first executive order established a Freedom of Information Act, thus removing Chicago's dubious distinction as the only big city without one.[28] While important symbolically, the order was no match for the veil of secrecy that had for so long shrouded city government.

The magnitude of the problem was not lost on the new mayor. In its comprehensive study of city agencies, his transition team concluded the following:

> One of the most obvious and pervasive facts about Chicago city government that has repeatedly been evident in our research is that basic information needed to understand how the City works, to assess how well services are provided and to determine who is responsible for various city programs is incredibly difficult to obtain. Simple questions like what an agency actually does, the total amount of money an agency spends, and the names of people who run the agency are difficult to answer. Getting even this simple descriptive information requires consulting several different sources, many of which are hard to decipher.[29]

The report was directed by Dick Simpson, a political science professor and former Chicago alderman.[30]

Compounding the typical problems of bureaucracy, Chicago departments operated under what Kretzman termed a "machine politics of secrecy."[31] Information was zealously guarded by political operatives and transmitted, if at all, through an informal word-of-mouth system. Even machine aldermen were kept in the dark, as the veil of secrecy protected that powerful resource, information.[32]

Washington's predecessor, Jane Byrne, though promising to open up city government, elevated the politics of secrecy to new heights. The report of her transition team, which cited enormous amounts of waste and corruption in city government, was buried for fourteen months. When it was exhumed, through a leak to the *Chicago Tribune*, Mayor Byrne was furious. Apparently forgetting the role of the press in a free society, the mayor barred all reporters from city hall.

CHICAGO 119

Clearly, more than a Freedom of Information Act was needed. With Executive Order 83-1 as a base, the administration launched the Affirmative Neighborhood Information Program. Under this program, the Department of Neighborhoods would gather information from various city departments, organize it in user-friendly fashion, and then distribute it to CBOs. Numerous meetings with community groups, local foundations, and academics produced a consensus that housing data was the top priority. In response, the city assembled a housing data catalog to enable CBOs to "monitor ownership of problem buildings, monitor the conditions of buildings, and track the progress of buildings in housing court."[33]

Contrary to initial assumptions, assembling the catalog took nearly one and a half years, as the seemingly simple task of collecting and disseminating information in usable form became a bureaucratic nightmare. Many of Washington's appointees were political neophytes who had not previously served in Chicago city government; thus, a certain learning period was unavoidable. Their task was further complicated by recalcitrant bureaucrats, some of whom actively sought to sabotage administration programs. To many other bureaucrats, these requests were viewed with suspicion (information is power) or confusion since government was not known for its accessibility to neighborhood organizations. Political opposition supplemented the institutional side of the nightmare. As part of its continuing battle with the mayor, the city council defunded the Department of Neighborhoods.

Not all efforts to reach out to neighborhoods were as cumbersome as the Affirmative Neighborhood Information Program. The administration, for instance, disseminated information through workshops and public hearings. The city conducted annual workshops on the CDBG application process. Budgetary reforms resulted in expanded financial disclosure by the city and in the holding of public hearings on the corporate budget (Executive Order 83-4). In 1987 the city held its first workshop on the capital improvement plan.

The mayor also made visibility a top priority, attending many neighborhood functions, even those at which he was the target of attack (see chapter 5). Likewise, department heads were expected to appear at community forums to provide information on their activities and to explain resource allocation practices.

The administration also provided various mechanisms for neighborhood input into city decision making. The Community Development Advisory Committee (CDAC), though in existence since the Bilandic administration, was given real decision-making power for the first time (see chapter 5). Task forces, totaling more than fifty and with members from all sectors of the city, were assembled by Washington to address numerous policy issues, including industrial retention, neighborhood development, jobs, energy, crime, infant mortality, and solid waste disposal. Chicago Works Together II, the city's revised development plan (1987), was the product of extensive community input; a nearly two-year process by a fifty-nine-member task force representing business, labor, government, neighborhood, education, civic, and cultural interests, and a public forum attended by several hundred people. Finally, many of Washington's appointments came out of the community-based movement and were committed to open and participatory government.[34]

The partnership with the neighborhoods was fortified with resources as the administration pursued its complementary objectives of balanced growth and neighborhood development. Subsidies for downtown development were decreased; when they were provided, they were linked to neighborhood development. Several of the major North Loop developers, for instance, provided free technical assistance to CBOs. Chicago First was also a linkage program, tying commercial development to job creation for city residents. The most ambitious linkage program, however, was the one with the developers of Presidential Towers.

Presidential Towers, a $200-million upscale housing development just west of the downtown, received generous federal and local subsidies. Completed in 1985, the deals for these four high-rise buildings had been orchestrated by former mayor Byrne. With the help of Congressman Dan Rostenkowski, who provided the long arm of government, the developers secured a $158-million FHA loan and avoided the requirement that 20 percent of federally subsidized units be kept for low-income tenants. The city, through the sale of tax-exempt bonds, provided the developers with a $180-million low-interest construction loan. It also sold the land at bargain-basement prices.[35]

When interest rates dropped in 1986, the developers of Presidential Towers sought to renegotiate their loan with the city. Washington agreed to float a bond, which would allow them to retire their first loan if they would fund affordable housing with the fees paid on the bond. The developers agreed, and the city established an affordable housing trust fund.

Finally, the city increased its own allocation of resources to neighborhoods. The restructuring of the CDBG program directed resources out of government patronage and into neighborhood development. The capital budget and five-year Capital Improvement Plan (CIP) were reorganized, creating a separate category entitled "Neighborhood Infrastructure."[36] The general obligation bond in 1985, the first such bond for neighborhood improvements, ensured that this would not be an empty category; 20 percent of the city's capital spending went for neighborhood infrastructure in 1986, up from 13 percent in 1985.[37] Passing a $130-million general obligation bond in 1987, the city protected its commitment to the neighborhoods; the 1987–1991 CIP called for 20 percent of capital funding for the neighborhoods. During the Washington administration, the city spent $300 million on neighborhood infrastructure improvements.[38]

CHICAGO WORKS TOGETHER: A POLITICAL ANALYSIS

Chicago Works Together was a radical planning document. Its attempts to redistribute economic resources and political power required a substantial overhaul of

Chicago's governmental machinery. Washington faced the problem, cited by Clavel in his study of five progressive city governments, of "doctrinal coherence" outstripping existing administrative capacity.[39] The institutional framework that Washington inherited was incapable of implementing the administration's policy agenda. Changing the structure and substance of policy making is a long-term endeavor requiring behavioral change as well. Thus, at the most fundamental level, the Washington administration had to change how ordinary citizens, politicians, and bureaucrats viewed government, politics, and race relations. While there was some progress along these lines, in his five short years in office Harold Washington did not achieve this. What would have been accomplished had he lived is a matter of speculation. Nevertheless, there are several lessons to be drawn from those five years.

Perhaps the starkest lesson is the difficulties of achieving multidimensional progressive reforms. The institutional impediments to, and the long-term nature of, such change make it imperative that the supporting coalition stay together. Minimally, this requires that diverse groups be able to stand in each other's shoes, so to speak. Under the best of circumstances, this is extremely difficult, and Chicago in the 1980s did not represent ideal circumstances. Battles over affirmative action revealed the lingering effects of the city's political culture. Many African American members of Washington's coalition felt that their time had come, not an unreasonable expectation in Chicago's political system. Many Hispanics sensed this and resented what they perceived as African Americans behaving in the manner of white machine politicians. Between the past of machine politics and the future of progressive politics lay conflict among coalition members.

Chicago Works Together also suffered from the strains of trying to implement a redistributive agenda in a context of shrinking resources. While Washington was carrying out an affirmative action hiring plan, he was cutting the city's workforce to close a $150-million budget deficit left by Mayor Byrne.[40] While Washington was increasing resources to neighborhoods, President Reagan was starving the source of those resources; CDBG funds decreased by 22 percent between 1983 and 1986, while total federal aid to Chicago dropped 45 percent from 1982 to 1986.[41]

The decline in resources and the institutional obstacles also created strains in the community organization sector. Some organizers who came from an Alinsky background of confrontation with government were lukewarm toward Washington; others, for whom race was a factor, were downright hostile (see chapter 5 on SONSOC). Among those who strongly supported Washington there was an element of disappointment; Washington's election and Chicago Works Together promised sweeping reforms, while bureaucratic, political, and economic realities were shaping an incrementalist strategy.[42]

A second lesson centers around the complexities of institutional change. Washington was much more successful in mobilizing constituencies for political battles, for instance, than he was in trying to alter institutional behavior. The latter was especially difficult in Chicago as a result of the Shakman decrees, which sharply limited Washington's power to hire and fire city workers, and by the political culture, which hung like an albatross around the neck of reform. To many white bureaucrats, for example, affirmative action and contract set-asides were not part of a redistributive policy agenda designed to correct past injustices. Rather, these measures were seen as attempts by a "black Boss" to reward his African American constituents. Such interpretations do not create the supportive institutional climate necessary for reform policies.

A third lesson centers around the distinction between personalized and institutionalized reforms. For the most part, Washington's reforms fell under the former heading. The most obvious reason is council opposition. Prior to having a majority on the city council, Washington was forced to rely on executive orders, which are not binding on subsequent mayors. A second and less obvious reason has to do with divisions within Washington's own coalition, which to some extent undermined the future of the progressive movement. Grimshaw has persuasively argued that Washington's reluctance to purge the black machine loyalists from the city council was motivated partly by pragmatic concerns; Washington believed that he had enough support in the African American community to make these aldermen toe the line.[43] In the short term the strategy worked, but in the long term it was counterproductive; these aldermen were the first to defect upon hearing the news of Washington's death.

Perhaps more instructive, though, is the case of MACLA. Although Washington was pressured into approving this commission's formation,[44] he did not try to silence or dismantle it when it issued reports that were highly critical of the administration. Even its practice of issuing "report cards" for various department heads on their affirmative action hiring records, while distasteful to the department heads, did not inspire Washington to undermine MACLA's efforts. Part of the explanation is political; Washington did not want to lose Hispanic support. But part was also ideological; Washington was committed to open and participatory government. Consequently, he felt compelled to support MACLA's continuation. This last point suggests a fundamental dilemma for progressive administrations. The commitment to open and participatory government may in fact be its undoing if it leads to enough conflict.

Despite overwhelming odds, Washington did make city government more open, more representative, and more responsive. In so doing, he made a powerful contribution to Chicago's "social learning"—that is "understand[ing] and act[ing] on behalf of the community in its entirety."[45] Social learning results from inclusionary, not exclusionary, regimes. Washington's broad-based coalition and his inclusionary policy agenda made minorities, women, and neighborhoods visible and legitimate parts of the governing and policy-making communities.

Social learning is not easily turned back. And, as the policy literature informs us, programs develop clienteles, making their termination difficult. However, when the gains are not institutionalized there is much less protection. Under Washington, neighborhood and minority gains came through individual decisions and executive orders, neither of which are binding on subsequent mayors. Unlike Pittsburgh, for instance, Chicago has no partnership for neighborhoods with a dedicated funding stream. Rather, neighborhoods, African Americans, and Hispanics must renegotiate a political settlement in a system that retains much of its "friends and enemies" character. Within this context, social learning becomes a source of tension between open and closed government, as well as between inclusionary policy and insider privileges.

In Chicago these tensions play out in the process of coalition building. Whether Washington would have been able to maintain his progressive coalition through the sheer force of his leadership is a matter of speculation. One thing that is clear is that no candidate since Washington's death has been able to reassemble his coalition. This inability constitutes the biggest political limit to progressive government in Chicago.

7
Pittsburgh: The Limits of Consensus

Our steel communities must not be discarded like so many strip mines.
—John Barbero

The examination thus far suggests that neighborhood organizations in Pittsburgh have been relatively successful in terms of acquiring resources, legitimacy, and some status within the governing regime. Their success is especially evident when juxtaposed with the experience of community organizations in Chicago. But the analysis has also revealed that the progressivism in Pittsburgh is essentially unidimensional; it is organized around economic development activities in the neighborhoods. Such a progressivism could take root because it basically extended the logic of the larger corporatist system to the neighborhoods. It is therefore not surprising that CDCs have been the primary organizational beneficiaries of neighborhood incorporation; they receive the lion's share of resources from the PPND, the URA, and the planning department.

The collaboration required by the economic development activities of CDCs encourages consensual relations. Here again, Pittsburgh's neighborhood organizations were extending the logic of the system. However, consensual approaches preempt any serious questioning of the larger political economy within which these organizations operate. Herein lies the contradiction. These organizations have not changed the larger relations of power within the city, and their consensual approach prevents that. Thus, while Pittsburgh's CDCs, to date, have directly benefited from the corporate community, they are in a vulnerable position, dependent on the continued goodwill of those corporate actors. In a critical examination of the CDC movement, Robert Fisher offers the following caution:

The new partnerships between the community, voluntary, public, and business sectors will remain problematic as long as the latter are the chief causes of the problems communities face. Business may help communities when it makes good business sense. Corporate leaders and neoconservatives might even think that community-based approaches are the strategy of the future. But the profit motive and investment demands destroy low-income communities much more often than they help them. Businesses often overcharge for products, especially in poor areas; they oppose higher corporate or wealth taxes, which could fund social programs; they flee communities when wages rise or other communities offer better "sweetheart" deals that lower taxes and startup costs; they depress wages rather than limit profits; they lay off workers because of "restructuring"; and they support urban policies that channel money away from neighborhoods and into downtown development or economic growth councils set up to attract new businesses with tax-subsidized deals.[1]

Fisher's observations highlight the contradictions within the CDC movement; some organizations may benefit while entire areas may lose as disinvestment becomes the dominant theme. This has been the case for the Lower Mon Valley outside of Pittsburgh, where disinvestment by U.S. Steel tore the economic life out of the municipalities there. Unlike Pittsburgh, where economic elites in 1943 had a vested interest in saving the city, the private interests of U.S. Steel were antithetical to those of the community; profit enhancement meant major disinvestment. In 1978, 73 percent of U.S. Steel's revenue came from steel; by 1985 it had dropped to 33 percent.[2]

The ACCD, following its typical pattern, funded the establishment of CDCs in the Mon Valley.[3] While this approach had been effective in Pittsburgh, the situation in the Mon Valley was markedly different. Pittsburgh had gone through economic hard times, but the city still maintained an economic base. Home to fifteen corporate headquarters and two major universities (University of Pittsburgh and Carnegie Mellon University),[4] Pittsburgh generated enough white-collar jobs to provide somewhat of a buffer against deindustrialization. For many municipalities in the Mon Valley, there was no buffer; their economic base was gone. In 1986, for example, Pittsburgh's unemployment rate was 7.4 percent, while Duquesne's had risen to 21.3 percent.[5]

The level of economic dislocation suggested to some that a more radical approach was necessary. One such group was the Tri State Conference on Steel, a coalition of political and religious activists founded in Youngstown, Ohio, in 1979 to prevent mill closings in Ohio, West Virginia, and western Pennsylvania. Working with local union officials, community organizers, and progressive Catholic clergy in the Mon Valley, Tri-State set up the Steel Valley Authority (SVA) to take over, through eminent domain, and reopen closed steel mills, thus directly challenging the legitimacy of corporate decision making. Adopting a combative approach, the SVA defied the logic of the corporatist system and the existing structure of power relations.

This chapter examines the efforts of the Tri-State Conference and the Steel Valley Authority to go outside of the established system of relations that characterize Pittsburgh's unidimensional progressivism. The activities and experiences of the SVA reveal both the limits to, and the limits imposed by, consensual politics. Because the major disinvestors, U.S. Steel and secondarily Mellon Bank,[6] were represented on the ACCD's executive committee, the ACCD could not take positions that would appear to be critical of their actions. Thus, it too declared the steel industry dead, indicating that it was time for the Mon Valley to shift economic gears.[7] The unwillingness of Tri-State and SVA organizers to accept this position put them in direct opposition to the ACCD and the civic community. Once outside the bounds of consensual politics, however, they could not gain access to the selective incentives that were available to CDCs.

DEINDUSTRIALIZATION IN THE MON VALLEY

The Lower Mon Valley, an area that encompasses thirty-eight municipalities and three Pittsburgh neighborhoods (South Side, the 15th ward, and the 31st ward), was home to approximately 279,000 people in 1990.[8] Together with Pittsburgh, this area constituted the steel capital of the United States; 40 percent of the country's steel was produced in those mills in 1900.[9] Naming their football team (Steelers) and their beer (Iron City) for their local industry, Pittsburghers obviously wore this distinction with pride. Though hard work, jobs in the steel mills paid good wages and provided good benefits; the basic hourly rate for a steelworker in 1983 was $13.43.[10]

Restructuring in the steel industry changed all that as corporate disinvestment severed the economic lifeline of cities and towns in the Mon Valley. Plant shutdowns by U.S. Steel and LTV (formerly Jones and Laughlin, Pittsburgh's biggest employer in the 1970s)[11] obliterated entire workforces; 75,000 steel jobs were lost between 1950 and 1987.[12] Between 1979 and 1984 alone, U.S. Steel cut its employment in the Mon Valley from 28,000 to 6,000.[13] Devastating as they are, these numbers reveal only a partial picture. It has been estimated that "for every 1000 jobs lost in the primary metals, an additional 130 manufacturing jobs were lost by those who directly supply the industry."[14]

The dramatic decline in employment opportunities triggered massive outmigration; between 1960 and 1980, twelve mill towns averaged population losses of 32.4 percent.[15] With the incidence of migration highest among younger, more marketable persons, unemployment remained high, exceeding more than 20 percent in many mill towns by 1986. Boarded-up main streets and sharp increases in crime, divorce, alcoholism, and suicide became the new hallmarks of these once proud towns.

These individual tragedies were magnified manyfold at the community level. As one-company towns, these areas relied heavily on taxes paid by the steel companies; in some cities as much as 60 percent of the municipal budget came from the steel industry. When this source of revenue dried up, local governments dramatically reduced their services; by 1990 two municipalities had declared bankruptcy while another three lingered in its shadows.

Organizing the Valley: The Tri-State Conference on Steel

For steelworkers, layoffs were not uncommon; the cyclical nature of the industry had immunized them to temporary joblessness while union-won unemployment benefits carried them until the next upswing restored their jobs. Thus, when layoffs began in the early 1980s, the initial reaction lacked any element of surprise. However, when the upswing failed to materialize and benefits were exhausted, frustration took hold. This soon turned to anger and resentment as a result of key decisions by U.S. Steel.

In 1982 U.S. Steel purchased Marathon Oil for $5.9 billion. The following year, it announced that large portions of the Duquesne mill would be closed and its blast furnace (Dorothy Six) demolished. In its place, U.S. Steel had proposed developing an industrial park. The money spent to acquire Marathon Oil, it was estimated, was sufficient to "modernize and update every U.S. Steel facility in the country."[16] But U.S. Steel had other plans; it was getting out of the steel business.[17]

The disinvestment activities created strong anticorporate sentiments among many in the Mon Valley. The most extreme expression came from the Denomination Ministry Strategy (DMS), a group of Episcopal and Lutheran ministers. Adopting a highly confrontational approach, the DMS engaged in activities such as depositing dead fish in the Mellon Bank and throwing skunk water on the children of corporate executives while they were in church.[18] Although most people repudiated the actions of the DMS, anticorporate feelings ran deep. The Tri-State Conference on Steel capitalized on these feelings to mobilize support for reopening the steel mills under worker/community ownership arrangements. Tri-State's calls for democratic decision making ran counter to the ACCD's top-down approach, while its proposals for worker/community ownership were a direct assault on the hegemony of capital.

The radical nature of these proposals is fairly obvious. Nevertheless, politically conservative residents gave their support, while elected officials, including Pittsburgh's mayor Richard Caliguiri, and Pennsylvania's two Republican Senators—the late John Heinz and Arlen Specter—endorsed these ideas. This seemingly odd fit is traceable to the level of economic devastation in the Mon

Valley, which destroyed the corporate sector's legitimacy, making many people receptive to, indeed desperate for, alternative ideas. Building on these frustrations, Tri-State organized local support for proposals that rejected the inevitability of manufacturing's decline and challenged the legitimacy of corporate control.

Providing an analytical framework for what was happening in the Mon Valley, Tri-State presented several arguments. First, it argued that plant closings were neither isolated events nor simply responses to external market forces but part of larger corporate restructuring schemes. Second, the well-being of communities did not figure in these schemes. Nevertheless, these "private decisions" had major public consequences. Therefore, they could not be treated as private decisions. Third, the magnitude of the problem combined with the resources of U.S. Steel called for a regional response. The individual municipalities in the Mon Valley were too weak to go it alone.

For Mon Valley residents, many of whom were third-generation steel employees, the decisions of U.S. Steel were the ultimate acts of betrayal. With corporate legitimacy hanging by a mere thread, if at all, Tri-State's portrayal of corporate planning as self-serving and antithetical to community needs struck a sensitive, and indeed bitter, chord.

While the plan to demolish Dorothy Six was just one of many decisions detrimental to the area, it became a cause célèbre for Mon Valley resistance efforts. Built in 1964, Dorothy Six was the region's most modern blast furnace. Tri-State organizers argued that it could be run on a profitable basis and commissioned a set of feasibility studies to explore the options available to them. U.S. Steel argued the opposite. The battle was on.

Bringing together labor, community, and religious leaders and elected officials, the campaign organizers held meetings and demonstrations, culminating in a January rally with Jesse Jackson as the keynote speaker. The heightened media attention was important, but the organizers pinned their real hopes on the feasibility studies. As it turned out, they were not disappointed. Locker/Albrecht Associates, the firm conducting the study, concluded that the furnace and the Duquesne mill could be profitably operated and that its closing would eliminate 7,400 jobs and $1.2 million in local tax revenues.[19] Unmoved, U.S. Steel dismissed the findings of the study.

As the battle continued, another study was conducted by Lazard Freres. Although the preliminary report supported the earlier feasibility study, by the time of the final report in January 1986, market conditions had changed substantially and the conclusion was that the mill could not be operated profitably. The battle was over.

Dorothy Six was given its last rites, but the SVA was about to be christened. Though unsuccessful, the campaign to save Dorothy Six seriously blackened U.S. Steel's reputation in the Mon Valley. It also highlighted the need for a permanent mechanism that would be powerful enough to develop and implement alternatives to corporate disinvestment.

Challenging Big Steel: The Founding of the Steel Valley Authority

Trained in Youngstown, Ohio's school of hard knocks, Tri-State organizers knew well the systemic obstacles to battling "Big Steel."[20] After several unsuccessful attempts to keep plants open, Tri-State seized on the very tool the ACCD had used to engineer the Pittsburgh renaissance: a public authority with power of eminent domain. Using the Municipalities Authorities Act of 1945, as the ACCD had done forty years earlier, the SVA promoted an alternative to passive acceptance of plant closings and their devastating consequences: community ownership of abandoned steel plants. In contrast to the ACCD, which used the public authority to promote the interests of capital, Tri-State sought to use the device to protect the interests of workers. In the case of the Mon Valley, this meant regulating capital. This difference put Tri-State and the SVA outside of the well-established system of public–private partnerships that developed during the Renaissance and that continues to characterize Pittsburgh's corporatist system of governance. The SVA's "outsider" status, combined with its fundamental challenge to capital, sharply curtailed its abilities.

While to date the SVA has failed to keep any steel mills open through eminent domain, the very fact of its existence is a strong reminder that economic decisions represent choices from a set of alternatives. The establishment of the SVA, which involved overcoming some powerful myths, as well as its defeats and successes, reveal much about the prospects for alternative strategies of economic development.

On January 31, 1986, the SVA, representing nine municipalities in the Mon and Turtle Valleys, including the city of Pittsburgh, was incorporated.[21] This only came, however, after many debates about municipal sovereignty, financial liability, and the decision-making authority of the SVA. In short, local governments feared creating a powerful mechanism that would usurp their own authority. To allay these fears, each municipality was given veto power over SVA decisions. Thus, in contrast to the public authority of Robert Moses, which was synonymous with unlimited power, from the beginning the SVA had a built-in weakness.[22] For some municipalities, even this check was insufficient. Duquesne was among this group; fearing that U.S. Steel would drop its plans for the industrial park, Duquesne did not join the SVA.[23]

There were ideological disagreements as well. The SVA's promotion of public ownership appeared too close to socialism for some local actors. While total public ownership was only one of the alternatives promoted by the SVA, its approach was indeed radical. In his excellent analysis of the politics of plant closings, John Portz suggested that the SVA "represented the beginnings of a populist player role in which government authority would challenge decisions made by private economic actors and would play a major role in guiding the investment and disinvestment process."[24]

This role was based on the belief that private decisions that have major public consequences cannot be treated as private decisions. As Monsignor Charles Owen Rice, known as Pittsburgh's "labor priest," bluntly stated, "Capital is too powerful to be left to the care of capitalists and their compulsive search for instant, maximum profit."[25] It was this notion of public consequences that provided the justification for seeking powers of eminent domain. According to one of the SVA's planning documents, "Eminent domain is the legal power to condemn, acquire and hold private property for a public purpose, upon payment of 'just compensation.' In this case [SVA], the public purpose would be to save steelmaking jobs and the communities and other businesses which depend upon them."[26]

Organizationally, the SVA was committed to active grassroots participation. Since this ran counter to the traditional hierarchy in the Mon Valley (U.S Steel and the United Steel Workers Association [USWA] were top-down operations with very little rank-and-file participation) the SVA and Tri-State had to mobilize individuals who had not been politically active. Labor and religious leaders were instrumental in mobilizing support. The ecumenical community, which had worked with Tri-State from the beginning, couched the consequences of plant closings in collective rather than individual fashion, thereby establishing a moral basis for examining corporate social responsibility. Its position was articulated in a pastoral letter entitled "A Religious Response to the Mahoning Valley Steel Crisis," which stated "Economic institutions, although they have their own purposes and methods, still must serve the common good and are subject to moral judgement. . . . We believe that industrial investment decisions ought to take into account the needs and desires of employees and the community at large. . . . Human beings and community life are higher values than corporate profits."[27]

The first battle undertaken by the SVA was against American Standard Corporation, which in the summer of 1985 announced its intentions to close the Union Switch and Signal plant in Swissvale and sharply reduce its Westinghouse Airbrake plant in Wilmerding. Between 1981 and 1985, twelve hundred jobs, one-third of the total at these two plants, had been eliminated. This new plan would completely eliminate Union Switch's workforce and pare employment at Airbrake to five hundred over an eighteen-month period.[28] After a study by the Philadelphia Area Cooperatives Association (PACE) revealed that the plants could be operated profitably, SVA filed suit to prevent dismantlement of the Swissvale plant. While the case was shifted between state and federal courts, American Standard removed much of its equipment from the plant. The SVA was compensated for its court fees, but the plant was lost.

The SVA's biggest battle began in 1986 when the LTV Corporation filed for bankruptcy. This action threatened the future of LTV's steel plant on Pittsburgh's South Side, which closed in 1985. Embarking on what turned into a five-year (1986–1991) eminent domain battle, the SVA devised a plan in which it would own the steel mill and lease it to an operating company funded by private investment and, through a partial employee stock ownership plan, workers. A combination of delays, market changes, and ultimately costs, however, prevented this.

With state funding, the SVA conducted a metal retentions study. The findings, which showed a shortage of domestic semifinished steel slabs (60 percent of which was being met by imports),[29] encouraged the SVA to commission marketing and environmental studies and to begin negotiations with potential investors as well as with LTV. Although LTV at first did not take the SVA seriously, it shifted gears when investors expressed interest. Using residential rates as a basis for calculations, which were four to five times higher than industrial rates, LTV increased the assessment on its property. It did agree to lower the assessment if the SVA would get the state to forgive any liability that LTV would incur for environmental problems on the site.[30]

The negotiations continued, but the market for slab took a nosedive while the market for scrap increased substantially. Both the ACCD and LTV pressured the community to abandon efforts to reopen the mill. Supporting their case were the new market conditions and the absence of any site activity; the mill was still closed. The community acquiesced, and the site was put up for sale in 1991.[31]

The SVA's visions are bold; its promotion of worker and community ownership, of democratic decision making in the workplace, and of reviving industrial plants challenges conventional thinking. More than any other group in Pittsburgh, the SVA has its work cut out for it; by attempting to use a quite traditional tool—eminent domain—for nontraditional purposes, it has challenged the very bedrock of American capitalism, private property. In so doing, it confronted not only the entrenched powers of the corporations and economic elites but an ideology and mythology that are as old as the Republic itself. The power of this mythology was evident in the concerns, by municipalities, over the potential authority of the SVA. These same towns, however, watched U.S. Steel, a private corporation motivated not by community concerns but by internal factors, exercise substantial powers. In a free enterprise system, business decisions are the purview of the private sector, a view reinforced by the political culture of liberal democratic capitalism. What this fails to capture is the enormous impact that corporate decisions have on public life, an impact that is magnified manyfold in one-industry towns such as those in the Mon Valley.

This was the message of the SVA—that eminent domain was to be the tool through which economic and social responsibility to the community would be enforced. Whether or not it succeeds in reopening steel mills, the SVA is a powerful reminder that there are alternative visions for economic development.

THE STEEL VALLEY AUTHORITY: AN ANALYSIS

The SVA represents both a departure from and a continuation of established patterns in Pittsburgh. The less obvious of the two, continuation, can be seen in the SVA's institutional approach to economic problem solving. A major component of Pittsburgh's renaissance was the institutionalization of the growth machine through the establishment of a corporatist system of decision making (see chapter 3). Thus, in the same way that the ACCD took an institutional approach to the economic crisis in the city of Pittsburgh, the Tri-State Conference was following a similar route a half century later. Moreover, the Tri-State Conference used the same institutional device: the public authority.

The actions of Tri-State and the SVA also represent a departure from "business as usual" in Pittsburgh. While Tri-State and the ACCD both invoked the power of the state through the establishment of public authorities, there was a fundamental difference in terms of intended beneficiaries. The ACCD used state power to promote corporate interests that were believed to trickle down to the general community, whereas the SVA was designed to use public policy to directly protect worker interests. The latter, employing a bottom-up strategy, however, would pit state authority against several powerful corporate interests. In essence, then, the SVA threatened to alter existing power relations. In so doing, it went beyond the limits of consensus that more or less bound the CDCs in Pittsburgh and the Mon Valley. The SVA's unsuccessful attempts to reopen steel mills illustrate the power of that consensus.

Although prominent elected officials supported the formation of the SVA, their position appears to be more of a cautious compromise than an actual commitment to the radical potential of the SVA. The level of dissatisfaction among constituents in the Mon Valley made inaction politically costly. Supporting the establishment of a public authority that would be hamstrung by economic, political, and structural constraints, however, seemed relatively safe.

While the legislature granted the SVA power of eminent domain, for instance, it did not appropriate any funds for taking over properties. This lack of economic resources limited the SVA's ability to use its main vehicle—eminent domain. In the Swissvale plant case, for instance, a federal court judge denied the SVA an injunction on the grounds that the SVA lacked "the resources to condemn the plant."[32] Although the SVA successfully got the case remanded to state court, the absence of financial resources and the time factor doomed their efforts. Reiterating the sad irony of the story, the SVA director lamented, "We won on the merits but lost on the fair market price."[33]

As a public authority, of course, the SVA had the power to issue bonds, but issuing bonds against a closed manufacturing plant is next to impossible. Another potential source of funding, the development community, was virtually closed to the SVA; the former had given the steel industry its last rites while the SVA was administering CPR. In several reports issued by the ACCD, for instance, the message was clear that the areas in the Mon Valley needed to focus their economic energies away from steel.[34] Reinforcing this message with resources, the ACCD and foundation community assisted in setting up CDCs in the Mon Valley, which they then funded to undertake housing and commercial activities.[35] Hence, the resources of the civic community were used to replicate the cooperative system of relations that supported economic development in Pittsburgh's central business district and in its neighborhoods. Civic leaders and funders were not interested in supporting challenges to corporate decision making or efforts to reopen steel mills.

The SVA was also politically hamstrung. Internally, the veto power of each municipality served as a powerful check. Externally, it is unclear how much political support the SVA enjoyed. U.S. Steel is a powerful economic and political actor in Pittsburgh and the region. A member of the ACCD's executive committee, the company enjoys important civic status as well. Consequently, political figures are reluctant to openly criticize the corporation for its disinvestment activities. The town of Duquesne, for instance, refused to join the SVA for fear that U.S. Steel would abandon its plans to convert the old mill to an industrial park.

Structurally, the SVA's strategy was entangled in a contradiction; it was using a legal tool (eminent domain) to challenge private ownership in a legal system set up to protect private property. Further, it was using a system that moves very slowly. In his study of protest politics, Michael Lipsky showed how inaction by local governments can derail a challenge to their activities.[36] A similar analogy can be applied here. As the LTV and Dorothy Six cases illustrate, the market does not wait for the legal system. Moreover, as the director of the SVA commented, "If a plant is closed long enough, you lose your customers."[37]

The limits faced by the SVA raise serious questions about the capacity for building and sustaining broad-based movements. Tri-State and the SVA, by bringing together labor and community activists, sought to obliterate the urban trenches that impede the development of class-based movements. In a sense, the SVA represents the "trans-enclave" consciousness that Plotkin suggests is necessary to build broad-based movements.[38] Nine municipalities were able to come together in an area that historically was characterized by extreme fragmentation. The level of economic devastation in the Mon Valley undoubtedly boosted the organizing efforts of Tri-State and the SVA. The ability to maintain this momentum over the long haul, however, will be challenged on numerous fronts.

First, the power of enclave consciousness, which contributed to weakening the structure of the SVA, will remain a centrifugal force. Second, the power of the larger political culture, which paints efforts like the SVA's as "deviant," may also dampen loyalty to the SVA's cause. From the very beginning, in fact, there was strong doubt among many in the Mon Valley about the wisdom of community ownership of steel mills. These two problems will be exacerbated by the sharp resource imbalance that exists between powerful corporate actors and challengers to the status quo. Continued inability of the SVA to command the resources necessary to accomplish its main objectives may ultimately negate its initial organizing successes. As Stone pointed out, people sign on to projects based on their assessment of the projects' "doability."[39] If the SVA cannot deliver the goods while other organizations are receiving selective incentives from Pittsburgh's civic arena, it may very well lose its appeal. If, on the other hand, the SVA wants access to the resources of the governing regime, it will be forced to abandon its more "radical" proposals. Thus, the limits imposed by the corporatist structure and its consensual politics will either weaken the SVA organizationally or encourage it to pursue a unidimensional form of progressivism.

8
Toward a Conservative Progressivism?

> *Contemporary grass-roots activism is better captured by the term community politics than the term social movement, as urban groups have become more modest in their aims and less threatening to established power.*
> —Susan Fainstein and Norman Fainstein

Regime theory recently has come to occupy a central place within the urban politics literature. By focusing on the role of political choice within the confines of larger economic and structural constraints, regime theory offers an important antidote to both the "politics only" (i.e., pluralist) and the "economics only" (i.e., structuralist) interpretations of urban policy. Its novel political economy approach allows for much richer analyses of urban governance and policy than either of the alternative approaches. Its rejection of overly deterministic views of urban policy makes possible a normative critique of that policy and a holding accountable of policy-making officials. From a research perspective, it permits us to identify different policy scenarios.

As useful as regime theory has been, it suffers from several shortcomings that limit its explanatory powers. The emphasis on the internal dynamics of coalition building, maintenance, and decision making has drawn attention away from other important variables, in particular urban arenas, institutional frameworks, and political culture. The examination of Chicago and Pittsburgh has highlighted the critical role of urban arenas and the institutional frameworks and political cultures they house in influencing the opportunities for political participation by "nonelite" interests.

Unlike regime theory, which tends to hold a relatively static view of the balance of power between business elites and political elites within specific urban regimes, the preceding analysis shows considerable variance between them. This finding is critical since the balance of power between regime members influences the choice of arenas through which the regime principally operates. These shortcomings in regime theory make it difficult to discern the role that neighborhoods can be expected to occupy within a given regime, the prospects for progressive government, and the form that progressivism will assume.

Although Stone has developed a typology of regimes (caretaker, redevelopment, middle-class progressive, lower-class opportunity expansion), the key explanatory variable is the coalition. Thus, the redevelopment regime features a business-centered coalition, the progressive regime a middle-class progressive coalition, and so forth. Once again, attention is focused on the internal dynamics of the governing coalition; its composition, the nature of the accommodation process, and the selective incentives at its disposal explain the policy outputs of the regime.[1] What this typology fails to capture is variation within similar regime types. The examination here of Pittsburgh and Chicago has demonstrated that some redevelopment regimes can be much more progressive than others and allow a much larger role for neighborhoods in the policy-making structure.

Linking the concept of urban arenas to regime theory can overcome these limitations. By drawing our attention to institutional structures, patterns of resource distribution, and underlying political cultures, the incorporation of urban arenas into the analysis allows us to identify the opportunities for political mobilization and the form that such mobilization will take. We can identify some of the conditions favorable to neighborhood incorporation, the nature of that incorporation, and its significance for progressive government.

PITTSBURGH AND CHICAGO: SIMILAR REGIMES, DIFFERENT ARENAS

Neighborhood demands for resources and inclusion in the policymaking systems were received very differently in Pittsburgh and Chicago. In chapter 1 I noted key attributes of the regime, the arena in which it operated, and the institutional framework and political culture contained within the arena that would help to explain these differences. The following discussion elaborates on how these attributes operated in the two cities and the impact they had on neighborhood incorporation.

Governing Regimes

The study of Pittsburgh and Chicago has underscored the relationship between regime composition and the balance of power among regime members, on the one hand, and the selection of arenas within which a regime operates. In both cities, informal arrangements were established between public and private actors around aggressive agendas of bricks-and-mortar-style economic development.

Table 8.1. Governing Regimes: Pittsburgh and Chicago

Governing Regime	Pittsburgh	Chicago
Composition	Economic and political elites	Political and economic elites
Accommodation (balance of power)	Economic elites	Political elites
Objectives	Collective economic objectives	Accumulation of political power
Arena	Civic sector	Electoral
Form of governance	Social production	Social control

As Table 8.1 illustrates, the accommodation process between these actors varied markedly, with significant consequences.

Pittsburgh's regime was formed explicitly for purposes of economic development, with the major initiative coming from the most powerful member of the business community. As a result, economic elites dominated the regime. With economic objectives as the guide and economic elites at the helm, the regime steered much of its activity toward the civic-sector arena. Operating in an arena where the underlying logic is one of cooperation and civility, the regime adopted a form of governance resembling the social production model of power described by Stone. This type of governance is oriented toward "the capacity to assemble and use needed resources for a policy initiative" as opposed to the exercise of comprehensive control.[2] This cooperative orientation was reinforced by the regime's primary focus on large scale development projects that required substantial participation from public and private actors.

In Chicago, the early accommodation process catapulted political elites to a position of dominance. The overriding objective of the regime was the accumulation of political and electoral power, which often translated into a perceived need to eliminate and/or preempt potential rivals. Consequently, the regime practiced a form of governance resembling the social control model. This orientation reinforced the combative logic of the electoral arena within which the regime principally operated.

Institutional Framework

Institutional framework refers to the larger environment within which specific institutions operate. In chapter 1 I identified some of the critical elements that constitute this framework. The comparison of Chicago and Pittsburgh illustrated how these elements, and consequently the larger frameworks, affect participation in the political system. Table 8.2 provides an overview of these elements.

Orientation

In Pittsburgh, the early accommodation between economic and political elites resulted in a sharp party–government distinction. The existence of an at-

Table 8.2. Institutional Framework: Chicago and Pittsburgh

Element	Chicago	Pittsburgh
Orientation	Geographic Electoral	Functional Programmatic
Degree of formalization	Low	High
Decision making	Closed Conflictual	Open Consensual
Resource distribution	Individual Material exchange Bargaining Dispersed	Collective Programmatic Planning Targeted
Governing orientation	Social control	Social production

large, as opposed to district-based, electoral system probably facilitated this development.[3] The space between party and government was quickly filled by the creation of functionally oriented public authorities and private nonprofit organizations—moves that shifted power and resources to the civic-sector arena. Shielded from direct electoral pressures and guided by economic objectives, the institutional framework assumed a programmatic orientation.

In Chicago, party and government were indistinguishable. The primary institution, the political party, is geographically based, with its power rooted in the neighborhoods. This spatial dimension of power is reinforced by a district-based electoral system that has fifty city councillors. The tight integration of party and government infuses all agencies with an electoral orientation.

Formalization

Pittsburgh's institutional structure exhibits a much higher degree of formalization than does Chicago's. The ACCD, in its capacity as "unofficial leader" of the governing regime, directly or indirectly established numerous private, nonprofit institutions. The result was a powerful corporatist structure in the civic-sector arena that governed economic development in the central business district, the neighborhoods, and the region. In Chicago, by contrast, Richard J. Daley avoided any significant institution building for fear that such entities would become rivals for political power.

At the level of individual institutions, we find the same contrast. Pittsburgh's institutions tend to have more formal procedures, or at least to abide by more formal procedures, than their Chicago counterparts. The varying degrees of formalization bear directly on the role of individual leadership in the two cities. In Chicago, the absence of institutions meant that key actors had to deal directly with Richard J. Daley. The practice of institution building in Pittsburgh, by contrast, served to concentrate power within key organizations (e.g., ACCD, Urban Redevelopment Authority, Regional Industrial Development Corporation), thereby diminishing the importance of any single individual. One critical implication of this difference is that Chicago's political system contains a much greater potential for instability. To the extent that elites perceive this potential, they will tend to be more fearful of and hence resistant to any kind of change. This resistance and fear, in turn, reinforce the regime's social control orientation.

Decision Making

As one might infer from the preceding discussion, institutional decision making tends to be a more closed process in Chicago than in Pittsburgh. In Chicago, citizen participation requirements, as mandated by federal legislation, were routinely ignored, as were requests for public information from neighborhood groups or political activists. Chicago was the last big city to sign a Freedom of Information Act. The refusal to provide access to information resulted in a decision-making process that can be highly conflictual. Pittsburgh's decision-making process has tended to be much more open, and information is less zealously guarded. Corporatism's bias toward cooperative interactions, combined with the ACCD's rule that all of its decisions be unanimous, resulted in a highly consensual style of decision making.[4]

Resource Distribution

Resource distribution patterns reflect the underlying logic and objectives of the institutional framework. In Pittsburgh these led to a resource distribution system that encourages a collective orientation, a commitment to planning, and a programmatic orientation on behalf of those seeking resources. Protected from direct electoral pressures, the governing regime was able to concentrate resources in order to satisfy planning objectives. Chicago's institutional framework exhibited markedly different patterns. Operating according to a machine version of electoral logic, which exchanges resources for votes on an individual basis, resource distribution patterns contained a strong material, as opposed to programmatic, component. The system was also susceptible to a large amount of bargaining and a tendency to disperse resources in order to satisfy electoral needs.

Governing Orientation

To the extent that institutions provide opportunities as well as impose constraints, which most do, we can say that they contain both social production and social control elements; thus, the issue is which element predominates. In Pittsburgh, owing to the objectives of the regime, its operation in the civic-sector arena, and the logic of corporatism, the tendency has been toward social production. In Chicago, the regime's concern with accumulating political power and its operation in the electoral arena, where the primary logic is one of competition and conflict, has created a strong tendency toward social control.

Institutional Frameworks and Neighborhood Mobilization

Aggregating the various critical elements of the two institutional frameworks allows us to make some statements about their role in mediating organized neighborhood demands. Pittsburgh's institutional framework was favorable to neighborhood demands for resources and inclusion. The emphasis on institution building encouraged the formation of neighborhood organizations, especially those with economic development objectives. In theory, channeling resources through designated organizations would allow for comprehensive planning, a value central to the city's corporatist system. Thus, rather than contradicting the regime, neighborhood demands, if accommodated, could be an extension of the regime's orientation.

The overall orientation of Chicago's regime as reflected in its institutional structure does not bode well for organized neighborhood demands. Patterns of resource distribution discourage organizational development outside of the political machine. Neighborhood demands are seen as a direct challenge to the geographic orientation of the ward organizations. Supporting CBOs will not extend the regime's institutional framework but will create competitors. Similarly, allocating resources for economic development to CBOs will not extend the orientation of the regime; it will cut into its patronage supply. Within this context, neighborhood demands represented an effort to change the underlying logic of the electoral arena and its institutional framework. This created a zero-sum relationship between CBOs and the regime.

Political Culture

In Chicago and Pittsburgh, the political culture figures prominently in the political fortunes of neighborhood organizations. As Table 8.3 indicates, the differences are as stark as the ones encountered in institutional frameworks. Pittsburgh's political culture exhibits a somewhat deferential quality. The ACCD's successful handling of crisis situations in the forties and fifties gained it a favorable image early on; it appeared to be "above politics" and for the "collective interest." Its continued exercise of strong leadership further embellished its image while establishing a precedent of strong civic-mindedness within the city. These qualities have been nurtured by the city's institutional structure, which emphasizes and rewards cooperation, consensus, and compromise. This is not to

Table 8.3. Political Culture: Chicago and Pittsburgh

Element	Chicago	Pittsburgh
Social capital	Low	High
	Cynicism	Optimism
	Suspicion	Trust
Values	Individual	Communal
	Conflict	Compromise
		Cooperation
Civic attachment[a]	Low	High

[a] The term is used to connote feelings of attachment to the larger civic community. It does not refer to the number of organizations that form within a given city.

suggest that disagreement and conflict are absent. Rather, the weight of precedent and the lure of the incentive structure push strongly toward nonconflictual, accommodative behavior. Such behavior, in turn, reinforces the inclusionary orientation that permits the coexistence of numerous organizations, and the inclusion of neighborhood organizations does not represent a threat to the ultimate source of the dominant elite's power, wealth, or legitimacy.

In Chicago, the identification, in the minds of many, of politics with crass material exchange and of government with overt favoritism has bred an atmosphere of cynicism and mistrust. The pervasiveness of this outlook casts a dark shadow over any effort to change the system. Reform in Chicago is often interpreted as rewarding a new set of friends and punishing a new set of enemies. In such an environment it is enormously difficult to mobilize the requisite political support to alter the system.

The exchange model of politics has also helped to condition a market-oriented behavior that is much more individualistic than collective in outlook. This orientation places CBOs in a precarious situation. In contrast to Pittsburgh, where organizational development is viewed in a Tocquevillean manner as a necessary and positive component of civic life, such developments in Chicago are greeted with much ambivalence. The media, for instance, often portray CBOs as useless obstructionists, a view that is more generic in orientation than it is inspired by the actions of any specific organization.[5] In such a politicized environment, no entity can be above politics or serve the collective interest. The dominant elite takes potential competitors seriously, since this is not simply a dispute over policy or strategy but a direct threat to one's power.

At the neighborhood level, the machine's resistance to any outside organizing has fostered an adversarial relationship between CBOs and local government. The deep mistrust, suspicion, and cynicism that surround the relationship are exacerbated when the battles spill over into electoral politics, an arena that encourages conflict. Thus, the local political culture and the behavior it gives rise to further contribute to the zero-sum relationship that more often than not defines politics in Chicago. It also takes on a multidimensional character since the dispute is not over a particular issue or strategy but over the very locus of power and control of resources.

Political Culture and Neighborhood Mobilization

The attributes of cooperation and civility that characterize Pittsburgh's political culture circumscribe the range of activities within which CDCs can effectively engage. They cannot, for the most part, behave in a highly confrontational manner, nor can they push hard on issues that are seen as divisive; they are too tied into the institutional network that was built on, and continues to promote, cooperative, conflict-avoidant behavior. Hence, the predominant culture dictates which tactics are acceptable and which issues may be included on the agenda.

In Chicago, raucous behavior has always been a defining characteristic of the city's political culture, and thus there is more latitude in tactics. Moreover, the Alinsky tradition has appended to the city's political system a highly confrontational, aggressive, street-fighter component; however, this colorful folkloric quality can also constrain reform efforts. Largely because of this political history, Chicagoans are quite cynical about government and mistrustful of politicians. This cultural element played no small part in obstructing Harold Washington's efforts. As historian and noted Chicago politics commentator Paul Green observed, all mayors of Chicago ran as "reformers."[6] To many, Harold Washington was merely another in a long line of corrupt politicians carrying out the time-honored tradition of rewarding his friends and punishing his enemies, and policies such as affirmative action and contract set-asides supported this observation.

The discussion of political culture in Chicago and Pittsburgh is reminiscent of the dichotomy between a "public-regarding" and a "private-regarding" ethos elaborated on by, among others, Banfield and Wilson.[7] Amid the similarities there is one critical difference; Banfield and Wilson's distinction was based almost solely on socioeconomic class, while the distinction here is not. Proportionately, Pittsburgh has a larger working-class population than Chicago and a smaller professional class. If class were the key explanatory variable, the political cultures would be reversed. Rather, the differences in political culture are attributable to the nature of the respective regimes and the arena within and institutions through which they operate.

The persistence of these structures over time provides a continuity to the entire political system, making systemic change difficult to achieve. In Pittsburgh a powerful corporate interest centered on Richard K. Mellon created a distinctive set of institutions and culture. For a variety of reasons, that corporate interest no longer enjoys the commanding position it once held; for example, Mellon Bank has been overtaken by competitors, Gulf Oil has been sold, and the steel industry and U.S. Steel are not salient in a postindustrial, high-tech world. Nevertheless, the corporatist culture and corresponding institutions remain quite strong, permeating the politics of the city. Similarly, in Chicago the machine culture dominates large segments of political activity despite a substantial decrease in the machine's resource base and the declining influence of Chicago in the State of Illinois and national politics. This "halo effect" of regime-induced political culture has a powerful influence on political behavior, especially when patterns of resource distribution continue to reinforce a particular systemic logic.

Progressive Politics: Unidimensional Versus Multidimensional

The influence of this systemic logic and the institutional and cultural attributes that support it can also be seen in the form that progressive politics assumes. The term "progressive" has tended to be a catchall phrase for anything that appears to be left of center. Disagreements over where the "center" and "left" are located merely foreshadow the difficulties inherent in such an interpretation. Richard DeLeon, for instance, suggests that San Franciscans use the term "progressive" as a "synonym for 'leftist,' 'liberal,' 'libertarian,' 'antistatist,' 'populist,' 'environmentalist,' 'community activist,' and even 'Progressive' in the old-fashioned Hiram Johnson sense."[8] Such associations, which are not limited to San Franciscans, reflect the confusion surrounding the term. Rather than add to the proliferation of definitions, I propose that we add a new dimension: breadth.

Applying this categorization to Pittsburgh and Chicago reveals a unidimensional progressivism in Pittsburgh and efforts at a multidimensional progressivism in Chicago. In Pittsburgh, the dominant form of organizing was around neighborhood issues, and that was also where the governing regime was most responsive. Patterns of resource distribution encouraged such organizing. On the other hand, there were virtually no resources available for organizing around issues of race, the environment, or redistribution. Thus, Pittsburgh's institutional structure and its pattern of resource distribution contributed to the development of a narrow, almost unidimensional, progressivism.

In Chicago, by contrast, group mobilization took root around issues of neighborhood empowerment, race, redistribution of resources and power, overall governance, environmentalism, and a whole host of more minor issues. This situation had two sets of consequences for neighborhood organizations. First, since no single interest was strong enough to defeat the machine, progressive government in Chicago would have to be based on a coalition of diverse interests and, consequently, would have to assume a multidimensional character. Second, the instability within the electoral arena encouraged political elites to be even more resistant to group demands. Thus, whereas Pittsburgh's civic arena expanded to accommodate neighborhood interests, in Chicago accommodation was not perceived as an option.

Employing such distinctions enables us to better understand the difficulties in building and sustaining progressive coalitions and, ultimately, progressive urban regimes. As DeLeon argues, for example, "Success in building a new progressive regime depends in part on the capacity of progressive ideology to inspire a common vision, legitimate new power structures, give coherence and direction to policy, and embrace diverse and sometimes divergent constituency interests."[9] This would certainly be the case for a multidimensional progressive regime, but what about a unidimensional progressive regime? In Pittsburgh, neighborhood interests were successful in legitimating new power structures and in giving coherence and direction to neighborhood policy. On the other hand, they did not necessarily have an overt ideology that motivated their actions, nor did they try to embrace different interests. In Chicago, Harold Washington's attempts to establish a multidimensional progressive regime contained all of the elements cited by DeLeon except the legitimation of new power structures. While the case can be made that neighborhood interests in Pittsburgh did not create a new regime but instead got the existing regime to incorporate them, the larger point is still valid. As DeLeon's analysis of progressive politics in San Francisco and the experience of Harold Washington in Chicago make clear, it is easier to mobilize and sustain support for narrower movements.

This distinction between unidimensional and multidimensional progressivism, and the overall neighborhood experience in the two cities have broader implications for progressive politics and systems of political representation at the local level. It is to these issues we now turn.

POLITICAL REPRESENTATION: CORPORATISM VERSUS ELECTORAL POLITICS

The neighborhood experience in the two cities raises the thorny issue of representation. In Pittsburgh, neighborhood groups have been incorporated into the decision-making process to a much greater extent than in Chicago, but as the reintroduction of district elections for city council has highlighted, CDCs are not elected. In many ways this is counterintuitive to the underpinnings of a democratic society, where representation is associated with elections. Nevertheless, as Susan Clarke has argued, we need to consider forms of representation other than those produced through electoral politics. Interest groups and CBOs are two such entities.[10]

To put the discussion in more theoretical terms, we find two models of interest representation: interest incorporation, which is the electoral model, and interest designation, which is the corporatist model.[11] Each system is driven by an internal logic that advantages some and disadvantages others. The interest incorporation model, in which representation is achieved through competitive processes, requires successful coalition building in the electoral arena. However, the competitive logic, when combined with the relatively low level of institutionalization and the difficulties of sustaining coalitions over time, creates the potential for instability and relatively short-lived gains. To a large extent this was the tragedy of the Washington administration. On the other hand, the interest designation model, which often typifies politics in the civic arena, is driven by a logic of cooperation and institution building, thereby benefiting those groups "with resources essential to ensure sufficient cooperation."[12] Hence, the latter is a more elite model than the former and tends to be more stable.

These systems of representation influence the form that progressive politics can take. Electoral systems allow for a greater diversity of issues and interests than do corporatist systems, thus encouraging, indeed almost requiring, the development of a multidimensional progressivism. This was clearly the case with Harold Washington's coalition and administration. Multidimensional progressivism also characterized San Francisco's "anti-regime," Dennis Kucinich's short-lived administration in Cleveland, Ray Flynn's administration in Boston, and the five progressive administrations studied by Pierre Clavel (Hartford, Berkeley, Santa Monica, Burlington, and Cleveland).[13] Although these administrations may have varied in terms of their major emphasis, they all embodied diverse coalitions.

Corporatist systems, by contrast, foster both a narrowing of issues and a cooperative approach to organizational development. The former tends to promote a unidimensional progressivism, while the latter indirectly screens out more divisive issues. Thus, we are likely to find a "conservative" progressivism since governing regimes typically will not legitimate organizations that challenge their power or priorities.

Although both systems are usually operative in a city, one may tend to predominate. In Pittsburgh, where the governing regime operated primarily through institutions in the civic arena, the interest designation model was predominant, whereas in Chicago, with the regime's base in the electoral arena, the interest incorporation model was the primary system. At the micro level, different policy areas feature different systems of representation. Education policy, for instance, is characterized by systems of interest incorporation in cities that feature locally elected school councils. Economic development, on the other hand, at both the citywide and neighborhood levels, has been characterized more by interest designation to the extent to which development corporations are often the major players.

At the neighborhood level the trend has been toward an increasing reliance on CBOs and other private, nonprofit organizations. The 1980s witnessed a proliferation of these groups as federal retrenchment left a huge vacuum in neighborhoods. So far, the policy signals of the Clinton administration (emphasis on voluntarism, community banking, community partnerships) suggest a continuation of this pattern. These trends have major implications for progressive politics at the local level.

TOWARD A CONSERVATIVE PROGRESSIVISM?

The comparison of Pittsburgh and Chicago, combined with trends in the larger political economy, suggest that progressive politics at the local level generally will tend in the future to follow the Pittsburgh model of unidimensional progressivism centered around neighborhood economic development. This is likely to occur for several reasons. At the local level, the major reason is the difficulty of building and sustaining multidimensional progressive coalitions. Beyond the local level, the "neoconservative" political economy has influenced the pattern of resource distribution in ways that favor this unidimensional progressivism.

Efforts to build multidimensional progressive coalitions are plagued by the larger political culture and ideology, and also by the competing, and often conflictual, agendas of diverse coalition members. Political culture and ideology constrain progressive efforts to the extent that they deny them legitimacy and resources. Cities exist within the larger classical liberal culture of a political economy shaped by the ideology and practices of democratic capitalism. This produces a set of expectations regarding the roles of the public and private sectors. These expectations undermine certain progressive efforts, especially those geared toward public control of capital. The strong private-sector bias relegates all challengers to the prerogatives of capital as obstructionist. This legitimacy imbalance and the resource imbalance between opponents and proponents of the status quo reinforce the "privileged position of business."

Further strengthening this position is the anti-public-sector planning bias within the United States. For most of the twentieth century, and certainly before, most planning activities were conducted almost exclusively within the private sector, with local governments only recently assuming a role. This shift has not always been uncontested. When local governments supply planning staff to work on ideas generated in the private sector, as in Chicago under Richard J. Daley, or when they engage in public-sector building (schools, libraries, etc.), their role, for the most part, is innocuous to the business community. But when they meddle in the affairs of the private sector, for example, regarding regulations of business practices and land use, the arsenal of negative stereotyping (e.g., wasteful, inefficient, corrupt government) is unleashed. It is no accident that cities with fewer regulations and less interventionist governments, like those in the Sunbelt, are viewed as having "good business climates."

Ideology and culture also constrain progressive efforts through their influence on how policy is defined and evaluated. Nowhere is this more evident than in economic development, which has traditionally been defined in terms of "bricks and mortar." In the 1980s it was synonymous with real estate development. When Harold Washington's administration sought to redefine it in terms of job creation and to use public policy to direct the distribution of those jobs, it was going against the predominant culture (see chapter 6). Several observers of, and participants in, the Washington administration have commented on its use of language, slogans, and symbols.[14] For example, Chicago Works Together was not simply the name of a planning document; it came to symbolize the entire administration—featured prominently on all official documents and city signs and emblazoned on T-shirts. It was as if the administration was keenly aware of the role of language in social change.

Culture and ideology also influence the criteria used to evaluate public policy. One aspect of policy evaluation that is particularly damaging to progressive initiatives is scale. Community undertakings, almost by definition, operate on a small scale and thus they are easily written off as inconsequential. However, when compared with the reality, as opposed to the hype, of many "big-ticket" items, they are often more cost-efficient and productive. Cities continue to chase world's fairs, for instance, although apparently none has turned a profit since the "Century of Progress" in Chicago in 1933.[15]

With an ideology and political culture that promote a diminished role for government (i.e., except as supporter of private sector activity), that assume a definition of economic development policy limited almost exclusively to bricks and mortar, and that employ a narrow set of policy evaluation criteria, it is hardly surprising that urban policy agendas are still dominated by a growth machine mentality. This continued domination makes it exceedingly difficult for progressive movements to acquire a legitimacy that might enhance resource acquisition efforts. Pittsburgh's CDCs, for instance, were much more successful in acquiring resources than was the SVA, an organization with little legitimacy in the eyes of the business, civic, and foundation communities.

Efforts to build and sustain multidimensional progressive coalitions are also hampered by the competing agendas of coalition members. In Chicago, SONSOC's campaign revealed the underlying conflicts between the community empowerment and black empowerment agendas, while affirmative action and contract set-aside policies stimulated resentments between Hispanics and African Americans. Although Washington was able to hold his coalition together through the sheer force of his leadership, there were cracks in the coalition.

Harold Washington's premature death prevents us from saying with full accuracy what would have been, but Richard DeLeon's study of San Francisco can fill in some of the missing pieces. Perhaps the most enlightening, and at the same time disheartening, news is the failure of San Francisco's progressive movement. With its large middle and professional class, its sizable and highly politicized gay population which has tended to be quite liberal, and its significant social diversity, activist neighborhoods, and overall tolerance for alternative lifestyles, San Francisco clearly provides an environment that is much more conducive to progressive politics than Chicago. Nevertheless, the progressive movement in San Francisco was racked by internal class division and fragmentation along issue lines. Although DeLeon suggests that a coherent progressive ideology is necessary, an argument promoted by many social movement theorists as well, the experience of Chicago Works Together suggests that such an ideology may be necessary but insufficient. Chicago Works Together was the administration's "progressive manifesto,"[16] but it was insufficient to overcome the legacy of Chicago's institutional and political cultures. Overcoming this legacy, if it can be done, is a long-term process requiring that the coalition remain intact. Given the limits imposed by the larger political culture and the obstacles from competing agendas, this may not often be possible.

The difficulties of building and sustaining progressive coalitions will be magnified as the existing "small opportunities" continue to evaporate. The Republican-dominated Congress, if successful, will sharply curtail the amount of resources available to urban areas—resources that had been instrumental in progressive organizing activities. Recent decisions by the Supreme Court, constricting the use of affirmative action and contract set-aside programs, will have a debilitating effect on minority groups that organized around civil rights issues.

When the likelihood of acquiring resources is diminished, it becomes difficult to entice people to join political efforts. The tragedy, of course, is that as resources decline there is a greater need for organizing.

The decline in certain types of resources, such as affirmative action and contract set-asides, which were accessed through electoral politics, will diminish the significance of electoral control. As in Pittsburgh, other arenas will assume greater importance. With a narrower focus than the electoral arena, these other avenues, to the extent that they promote progressivism at all, will promote a unidimensional progressivism.

These local developments are being reinforced by larger trends in the national political economy. The militant conservatism that appended itself to the political economy in the 1980s affected patterns of resource distribution at the national and foundation levels. The most significant developments were the increased emphasis on economic development at the expense of advocacy and social services, and the overall cutback in federal funds. Both of these developments had a direct impact on local organizing efforts.

Substantively, there was a marked shift toward community economic development. The number of CBOs engaged solely in economic development activities increased from approximately two hundred in the mid-1970s to between fifteen hundred and two thousand by 1989.[17] Organizationally, there was a shift toward cooperative, consensual relations. As noted earlier, economic development activities require such relations. The cutback in federal funds reinforced this pattern as CDCs entered into partnerships with the local business community. Indeed, this was a major objective of the Reagan and Bush administrations and continues as a dominant theme in the Clinton administration despite a commitment to increased resources for urban areas. A central component of the Empowerment Zones, Clinton's major urban initiative, is local "partnerships."

Building these partnerships, obtaining resources for community economic development, and engaging in economic development are all activities that do not require broad-based coalition building. In fact, the territorial nature of such activities leads more in the direction of localism than globalism. To the extent that coalition building does take place, it will tend to be within economic development rather than across issue or policy areas. We may see, for example, a federation of neighborhood organizations. Thus, the urban trenches of community, workplace, and bureaucracy will give way to urban trenches delineated by their policy or issue area. In contrast to the earlier urban trenches, however, these newer forms will bypass the electoral arena, thereby reducing even further the significance of electoral control.[18]

The powerful influence of the neoconservative economy extends beyond CDCs. As Fisher observed, even Alinsky's Industrial Areas Foundation adopted a strategy of moderation in the 1980s.[19] This shift in organizing tactics does not mean that conflict will disappear from the urban scene. Rather, the dominant patterns of resource distribution will reward cooperative behavior and punish noncooperative behavior (neglect can be a brutal form of punishment!). Moreover, as economic development initiatives come to occupy a larger portion of community-based activities, systems of interest designation will replace electoral incorporation. This system of representation will selectively broaden the channels of participation while protecting the underlying structure of power within the city. As in Pittsburgh, it will encourage a conservative form of progressivism.

CHICAGO AND PITTSBURGH: THE IMPLICATIONS FOR POLITICAL PRACTICE

If, in fact, the trend is toward a conservative progressivism, what are the implications of this for political practice at the local level? My discussion in chapter 1 of some of the criticisms of community activism bears directly on this question. A major criticism leveled at many of the "neopopulist" urban movements is that their embrace of participatory democracy often occurs at the expense of any meaningful class-based analysis. Absent such analysis and the consequent agenda building that would occur, "neopopulists" are unable to effect any significant change in the structure of the underlying political economy.[20] This is certainly the major lesson of the Pittsburgh experience; following a cooperative path can yield some degree of neighborhood incorporation provided that such incorporation does not contradict the regime's primary objectives. It will become increasingly tempting for local activists to narrow their focus since that is where they will find the least resistance and the most resources.

Activists seeking broader structural changes, on the other hand, will have to develop an ideology or analytical framework capable of transforming "localized" issues into "public" issues.[21] In so doing they face the daunting task of changing the underlying ethos of the system in question. The experiences of the Washington administration and the Tri-State Conference on Steel offer some powerful insights into the contradictions and trade-offs encountered during this process.

First, transforming underlying cultures is a long-term venture; attitudes, perceptions, and ultimately behavior have to be changed. Developed over decades and deeply ingrained, these attributes will not change overnight and, in fact, may not change at all. Second, while these changes are being pursued, coalition maintenance must be tended to, and diverse interests have to be held together. But there is a fundamental Catch-22 in the choice of mechanisms. Distributing benefits based on group identification (e.g., African American, Hispanic, women, neighborhood, environmentalist) merely reinforces the parochialism that broad-based social movements seek to transcend (i.e., the objective is to unify around a common identity such as class). On the other hand, past practice often requires current compensation, and therefore a distribution scheme based on group identity. Exclusionary hiring practices in Chicago, for instance, which discriminated against African Americans, women, and Hispanics, required affirmative measures if parity were to be achieved. Finally, the failure to distribute such benefits may result in the breakup of the coalition.

The discussion of benefits, while identifying a real contradiction, assumes an availability of resources that is highly unrealistic. The more likely scenario—limited resources—points to another fundamental constraint on such movements. The conflicts over contract set-asides and affirmative action in Chicago illustrated the difficulties of redistributing benefits in an environment of shrinking resources. As resources decline, people become more sensitized to who is getting what, thereby reinforcing more parochial tendencies. On an organizational level, people will gravitate toward entities that are most able to acquire scarce resources. The CDCs in the Mon Valley enjoy much more support than does the Tri-State Conference or the Steel Valley Authority. Although there are numerous reasons for this, a primary one is the ability of CDCs to leverage significantly more resources than Tri-State or the SVA.

Another issue over which ideology and political expediency may come to loggerheads is participation. Although democratic participation is often central to progressive ideology, in practice such participation can result in conflicts that threaten the supporting coalition. These conflicts are particularly likely when coalition members come from the ranks of the previously "powerless," as the experience of the Washington administration demonstrated. Unfortunately, there is no "costless" way out of this dilemma.

In spite of these overwhelming odds, for a brief period Harold Washington was able to orchestrate a progressive government in Chicago. The fits, starts, and ultimate retreat of the Byrne administration, combined with the inability of subsequent candidates to forge a progressive coalition, are testimony to the critical role of political leadership. Through sheer force of leadership, Washington was able to overcome disunity within his coalition, to beat back city council opposition at critical junctures, and to inspire an administration made up largely of political neophytes. Without such leadership, Chicago's brief period of progressive government would not have occurred.

As important as it is, political leadership cannot indefinitely substitute for the institutionalization of reforms and political gains. Contrary to Browning, Marshall, and Tabb's initial findings, electoral victory "is not enough"[22] to secure political incorporation. It may be a necessary first step, but political gains, if they are to survive, require institutional protection. A major failing of the Washington administration was the lack of institutionalization. Although external opposition was a major impediment, some opportunities remained unclaimed. Not purging the city council of black machine members, for instance, was probably a major mistake. Had Washington replaced these aldermen with progressives, the revolution he sought might have had a better chance of surviving his passing.

In Pittsburgh, neighborhood gains have enjoyed considerable institutional protection. Neighborhood organizations have been recognized as part of the city's permanent organizational landscape for nearly twenty years. These arrangements have not only survived four mayoral administrations, but they have been strengthened with additional resources, authority, and responsibility. An "antineighborhood" administration would have an extremely difficult time rolling back these gains.

One of the dilemmas, though, is that powerful political leaders often do not engage in this type of institution building. Harold Washington's weakness in this area explains why this larger-than-life figure left little in the way of a permanent legacy. Contrast the Washington experience with that of Richard King Mellon, also a powerful leader but one who left a legacy of institution building that continues to dominate Pittsburgh's approach to policy and governance. The difference in time periods notwithstanding, institutions are important protectors of change, especially to the extent that they shape and sustain perceptions, alternatives, and political behavior.[23]

To sum up, building and sustaining a broad-based progressive movement requires, at a minimum, a combination of highly effective leadership skills, an ideology (or framework) capable of transcending divisional parochialisms, and a resource distribution system that can hold the coalition together while simultaneously avoiding contradicting the movement's ideology. These ambitious requirements, combined with the embeddedness of enclave consciousness and individualism within the larger American political culture, go a long way in explaining the disappointing experiences of urban progressive movements.[24]

Thus, the question becomes, is there a compromise between the conservative but stable form of progressivism found in Pittsburgh and the broad-based, multidimensional, but short-lived progressivism found in Chicago? It is to this question we now turn.

ADDRESSING THE LIMITATIONS OF URBAN ARENAS: THE JOB AHEAD

Linking regime theory to the concept of urban arenas provides a way to more thoroughly compare the political practices and norms of cities. From this study of Pittsburgh and Chicago we are able to generate some preliminary findings on the role of institutional and cultural factors in political participation and progressive politics. It would be useful to look at other cities and further test, modify, and expand these findings. For instance, electoral arenas share some common features (e.g., competitive logic, need for coalition building), but not all electoral arenas follow the Chicago model. San Francisco's electoral arena contains mechanisms for direct democracy (e.g., referenda and citizen initiative ballots) that have enabled well-organized groups to realize policy gains without changing the governing regime. The existence of such mechanisms does not eliminate the need for coalition building if the objective is regime change but instead provides alternative ways to alter policy. Given the difficulties involved in realizing wholesale regime change, such comparable knowledge is indispensable.

Future research should also explore the types of policies and politics that are possible within the various arenas. Since this study has demonstrated some fundamental limits to both the civic-sector arena and the electoral arena, we need to ask whether these limits are immovable. Can issues of race, for instance, be raised and addressed in the civic arena? The behavior of Pittsburgh's civic elites in education and housing offers some hope. Can such efforts be tapped to establish a meaningful dialogue on race? Put another way, can the boundaries of the civic arena be expanded? Can the electoral arena be modified so that it becomes a suitable vehicle for planning? Can an urban arena be expanded to address some of the limitations observed within Pittsburgh's civic arena and Chicago's electoral arena?

The existence of separate arenas also draws attention to the different forms that interest representation can and does take. There has been a strong tendency among political scientists to identify political representation with the electoral process. For example, Browning, Marshall, and Tabb's classic study, *Protest Is Not Enough,* placed electoral politics center stage as the central method for political incorporation. Even regime theory accords electoral representation disproportionate attention.[25] But, as the Pittsburgh case has amply demonstrated, there are other important systems of interest representation. Moreover, if issues continue to be moved out of the electoral arena and into other arenas, it will become necessary for us to learn about alternative systems of representation within those arenas. The case study of Pittsburgh has provided key insights into the operations of the civic arena and the potential for interest representation that it contains. The job now is to examine other arenas (e.g., intergovernmental, business) and their capacities for interest representation in terms of both degree and form.[26]

Although drawing on different literatures,[27] these research tasks are focused on the same important objective: improving the workings of a democratic polity. Measured against that objective, the political implications of the Chicago and Pittsburgh study are quite sobering. Perhaps most disheartening is the fact that many of this study's findings reflect the implications of the direction in which American politics appears to be heading more than they reflect any failure in political strategy. The American political climate has become openly hostile to the needs of poor people and minorities, the residents of many of these inner-city neighborhoods. Many years ago Lord Bryce observed that the "government of cities is the one conspicuous failure of the United States."[28] To the legacy of ill-conceived national policies and unregulated business practices, the 1980s and 1990s, at best, have added federal neglect of urban areas, thus ensuring that Bryce's observation remains current.

Notes

PREFACE

1. Pittsburgh did go through a reform period in the early 1900s, resulting in a charter change in 1911. This did not eliminate machine politics, however, and there was no subsequent reform period.

2. Two recent and very promising exceptions to this single case study approach that seek to broaden existing theories of urban policy/politics are Ester Fuchs, *Mayors and Money* (Chicago: University of Chicago Press, 1992), and Jeffrey Berry, Kent Portney, and Ken Thomson, *The Rebirth of Urban Democracy* (Washington, D.C.: The Brookings Institution, 1993). There are also some very rich efforts at cross-national comparative urban studies. See David Judge, Gerry Stoker, and Harold Wolman, eds., *Theories of Urban Politics* (London: Sage, 1995).

3. Stephen Elkin's work on regime theory, which contains a significant focus on the role of institutional structure, is the major exception to this pattern. See his *City and Regime in the American Republic* (Chicago: University of Chicago Press, 1987).

4. When public choice theory incorporates institutional analysis it is often around the concept of efficiency. For a good discussion of the role of institutional analysis in public choice theory and "reinventing government" literatures, see Harold Wolman, "Local Government Institutions and Democratic Governance," in *Theories of Urban Politics*, ed. David Judge, Gerry Stoker, and Harold Wolman (London: Sage, 1995), 135–159.

1. GOVERNING REGIMES

1. Todd Swanstrom, "Urban Populism, Uneven Development and the Space for Reform," in *Business Elites and Urban Development*, ed. S. Cummings (Albany: State University of New York Press, 1988).

2. Richard DeLeon, *Left Coast City: Progressive Politics in San Francisco, 1975–1991* (Lawrence: University Press of Kansas, 1992), 10.

3. Dennis Keating, "Linking Downtown Development to Broader Community Goals: An Analysis of Linkage Policy in Three Cities," *Journal of the American Planning Association* 52, no. 2 (Spring 1986).

4. Todd Swanstrom, *The Crisis of Growth Politics: Cleveland, Kucinich, and the Challenge of Urban Populism* (Philadelphia: Temple University Press, 1985).

5. Pierre Clavel, *The Progressive City* (New Brunswick, N.J.: Rutgers University Press, 1986).

6. Mark Kann, *Middle Class Radicalism in Santa Monica* (Philadelphia: Temple University Press, 1986).

7. Clavel, *The Progressive City;* Pierre Clavel and Nancy Kleniewski, "Space for Progressive Local Policy: Examples from the United States and the United Kingdom," in *Beyond the City Limits: Urban Policy and Economic Restructuring in Comparative Perspective,* ed. J. Logan and T. Swanstrom (Philadelphia: Temple University Press, 1990); Norman Krumholz and Pierre Clavel, eds., *Reinventing Cities: Equity Planners Tell Their Stories* (Philadelphia: Temple University Press, 1994); and Philip Nyden and Wim Wiewel, eds., *Challenging Uneven Development: An Urban Agenda for the 1990s* (New Brunswick, N.J.: Rutgers University Press, 1991).

8. The year 1955 was the beginning of the Richard J. Daley regime, and it is where I begin my political analysis of Chicago.

9. Stephen Elkin, "Twentieth Century Urban Regimes," *Journal of Urban Affairs* 7, no. 2 (Spring 1985): 11.

10. Clarence Stone, *Regime Politics: Governing Atlanta, 1946–1988* (Lawrence: University Press of Kansas, 1989), 6.

11. For a comparison of regime theory and pluralism, see Clarence Stone, "Urban Regimes: A Political Economy Approach," *Journal of Urban Affairs* 15, no. 1 (1993): 1–28.

12. Stone, *Regime Politics,* esp. chap. 11.

13. *Webster's Ninth New Collegiate Dictionary.*

14. Partisan is not meant entirely in the Democratic–Republican Party sense since many cities have nonpartisan electoral systems. Rather, it is used in the context of different groups representing different points of view.

15. The concept of arenas as developed here is analogous to the concept of "regime" as used in international politics. Although there are variants of this concept, I am thinking primarily of Stephen Krasner's and John Ruggie's use of the term. They see a regime as "sets of implicit or explicit principles, norms, rules, and decision-making procedures around which actors' expectations converge in a given area of international relations." Stephen Krasner, *International Regimes* (Ithaca, N.Y.: Cornell University Press, 1983), 2.

16. The attempt to assemble a policy typology has also been criticized for false distinctions—that is, distributive policies often have redistributive effects and so forth. See G. Greenberg, J. Miller, L. Mohr, and B. Vladeck, "Developing Public Policy Theory: Perspectives from Empirical Research," *American Political Science Review* 71 (1977): 1532–1543.

17. Elkin, "Twentieth Century Urban Regimes."

18. Susan Clarke, "Making a Difference: Interest Representation and Local Development Policy" (paper presented at the Midwest Political Science Association Meeting, Chicago, April 1992).

19. Robert Putnam, *Making Democracy Work: Civic Traditions in Modern Italy* (Princeton, N.J.: Princeton University Press, 1993), 8.

20. Charles Lindblom, "The Market as Prison," *Journal of Politics* 44 (1982): 324–336.

21. Ibid.

22. John Gray, "Does Democracy Have a Future?" *New York Times Book Review,* January 22, 1995, 25.

23. Paul Peterson, *City Limits* (Chicago: University of Chicago Press, 1981).

24. Putnam, *Making Democracy Work.*

25. The dates are a little fuzzy. The first regional councils were elected in 1970, but the central government did not issue the decrees for transferring money, power, and personnel to the regions until 1972. In 1975 more functions were decentralized to the regional governments, followed by additional reforms in 1977 that gave the regional governments still more authority. See Putnam, *Making Democracy Work,* chap. 2.

26. Putnam, *Making Democracy Work,* 167.

27. Jeffrey Henig, *Neighborhood Mobilization: Redevelopment and Response* (New Brunswick, N.J.: Rutgers University Press, 1982), 55.

28. Keating, "Linking Downtown Development to Broader Community Goals," 134.

29. CHAS is not a program but a requirement for local jurisdictions that apply for HUD funding. Beginning in fiscal year 1994, local jurisdictions applying for HUD money had to submit a CHAS that would outline the applicant's overall strategy for using the funds. The strategy had to incorporate community participation.

30. Sara Evans and Harry Boyte, *Free Spaces: The Sources of Democratic Change in America* (New York: Harper and Row, 1986).

31. Harry Boyte, *Commonwealth: A Return to Citizen Politics* (New York: Free Press, 1989), 12.

32. Sidney Plotkin, "Enclave Consciousness and Neighborhood Activism," in *Dilemmas of Activism: Class, Community, and the Politics of Local Mobilization,* ed. J. Kling and P. Posner (Philadelphia: Temple University Press, 1990).

33. Barbara Ferman, *Governing the Ungovernable City: Political Skill, Leadership, and the Modern Mayor* (Philadelphia: Temple University Press, 1985).

34. This is a play on Sayre and Kaufman's description of New York City as consisting of "functional islands of autonomy." Wallace Sayre and Herbert Kaufman, *Governing New York City: Politics in the Metropolis* (New York: Norton, 1965).

35. DeLeon, *Left Coast City.*

36. Swanstrom, *The Crisis of Growth Politics.*

2. CHANGING POLITICAL ECONOMY

1. Some public housing for senior citizens has been built in white areas.

2. Robin Jones, "Civic Capacity and Urban Education: Pittsburgh," Report for the Civic Capacity and Urban Education Project, 1995.

3. Paul Kleppner, *Chicago Divided: The Making of a Black Mayor* (DeKalb: Northern Illinois University Press, 1985).

4. Ward committeemen in Chicago are elected. The information on the increase in the number of ward committeemen is from William Grimshaw, *Bitter Fruit: Black Politics and the Chicago Machine 1931–1991* (Chicago: University of Chicago Press, 1992).

5. As a result of school reform efforts, Chicago now has locally elected school councils. These elections have been characterized by racial and ethnic division.

6. Barbara Ferman, "Chicago: Power, Race, and Reform," in *Big City Politics in Transition*, ed. H. V. Savitch and J. C. Thomas (Newbury Park, Calif.: Sage Publications, 1991).

7. Marc Weiss and John Metzger, "Planning for Chicago: The Changing Politics of Metropolitan Growth and Neighborhood Development," in *Atop the Urban Hierarchy*, ed. R. Beauregard (Totowa, N.J.: Rowman and Littlefield, 1989).

8. Ferman, "Chicago: Power, Race, and Reform."

9. Robert Alberts, *The Shaping of the Point: Pittsburgh's Renaissance Park* (Pittsburgh: University of Pittsburgh Press, 1980).

10. Rick Boyer and David Savageau, Rand McNally, *Places Rated Almanac: Your Guide to Finding the Best Places to Live in America* (Chicago: Rand McNally, 1985).

11. In 1966, for example, there were 293,000 jobs in manufacturing; in 1972, 256,000; in 1974, 266,000; in 1976, 218,000. Contrast these numbers with the 1979 to 1988 period: in 1979 there were 225,000 jobs; in 1987, 124,000, and in 1988, 125,000. Frank Giarratani and David Houston, "Structural Change and Economic Policy in a Declining Metropolitan Region: Implications of the Pittsburgh Experience," *Urban Studies* 26 (1989: 549–558.

12. Joan Fitzgerald Ely, "Economic Transformation in the Pittsburgh PMSA 1979–1986" (paper presented at the Midwest Restructuring Conference, Cleveland, 1988).

13. "Toward a Shared Economic Vision for Pittsburgh and Southwestern Pennsylvania 1992," a White Paper report prepared by Richard Florida and Robert Gleeson (Pittsburgh: Center for Economic Development, John Heinz III School of Public Policy and Management, Carnegie Mellon University, 1993).

14. See, for example, Marie Howland, *Plant Closings and Worker Displacement* (Kalamazoo, Mich.: W. E. Upjohn Institute for Employment Research, 1988).

15. Joan Fitzgerald, "Pittsburgh, Pennsylvania: From Steel Town to Advanced Technology Center," in *Economic Restructuring of the American Midwest: Proceedings of the Midwest Economic Restructuring Conference of the Federal Reserve Bank of Cleveland*, ed. R. Bingham and R. Eberts (Norwell, Mass:, Kluwer Academics, 1990).

16. Robert Lurcott and Jane Downing, "A Public–Private Support System for Community-Based Organizations in Pittsburgh," *Journal of the American Planning Association* 53, no. 4 (autumn 1987): 459–468.

17. Development Policies 1992–1997, City of Pittsburgh.

18. U.S. Bureau of the Census, *City and County Data Book*, 1992.

19. *Pittsburgh Press*, April 23, 1990.

20. Barbara Ferman and William Grimshaw, "Old Politics, New Politics: Divergence and Convergence Strategies" (paper presented at the annual meeting of the American Political Science Association, Washington, D.C., September 1991).

21. The first of the Shakman decrees prohibited "firing" for political reasons. A second Shakman decree, signed by Mayor Harold Washington in 1983, prohibited "hiring" on the basis of political affiliations.

22. Daley's votes declined by nearly 200,000 from 1971 to 1975, his last election. In

1971 Daley received 740,137 votes in the general election; in 1975 he received only 542,817. William Grimshaw, "The Daley Legacy: A Declining Politics of Party, Race and Unions," in *After Daley: Chicago Politics in Transition*, ed. S. Gove and L. Masotti (Urbana: University of Illinois Press, 1982).

23. Stone, *Regime Politics*.

24. In 1963, the height of Richard J. Daley's popularity among African Americans, 86 percent of the city's predominantly black wards were among the top ten vote producers. By 1967 this figure dropped to 30 percent; it fell to 14 percent in 1971 and 0 percent in 1975. Grimshaw, *Bitter Fruit*.

25. Paul Green, "Michael A. Bilandic: The Last of the Machine Regulars," in *The Mayors: The Chicago Political Tradition*, ed. P. Green and M. Holli (Carbondale: Southern Illinois University Press, 1987).

26. This was a top-to-bottom defeat: Byrne's candidate for president, Edward Kennedy, won only two black wards; Bernard Carey, her candidate for state's attorney, was defeated by her arch rival, Richard M. Daley; Independents Harold Washington and Gus Savage defeated machine-backed candidates in South Side congressional elections; five black organization committeemen lost to independents. See Michael Preston, "Black Politics in the Post-Daley Era," in *After Daley: Chicago Politics in Transition*, ed. S. Gove and L. Masotti (Urbana: University of Illinois Press, 1982).

27. See Milton Rakove, *Don't Make No Waves, Don't Back No Losers: An Insider's Analysis of the Daley Machine* (Bloomington: Indiana University Press, 1975). For a very romantic fictionalized account of machine politics, see Edwin O'Connor, *The Last Hurrah* (Boston: Little, Brown, 1985).

28. Barbara Ferman and William Grimshaw, "The Politics of Housing Policy," in *Politics of Policy Innovation in Chicago*, ed. Kenneth Wong (Greenwich, Conn.: JAI Press, 1992), 103–126; Robert Merton, *Social Theory and Social Structure* (New York: Free Press, 1957).

29. Basil Talbott, *Chicago Sun-Times*, April 5, 1979.

30. E. E. Schattschneider, *The Semisovereign People: A Realist's View of Democracy in America* (Hinsdale, Ill.: Dryden Press, 1960); V. O. Key, *Southern Politics in State and Nation* (New York: Knopf, 1949).

31. Although race was a factor in electoral politics since the mid-1960s, it was only since the 1970s that it became blatant.

32. Roy Lubove, *Twentieth-Century Pittsburgh* (New York: Wiley, 1969), 22.

33. Lawrence successfully ran for governor of Pennsylvania in 1958, which is why he picked a successor.

34. Appointments to the board of education were placed under court jurisdiction in 1911, the year the city produced its "reform" charter. Court control was lifted in 1976.

35. Morton Coleman, "Interest Intermediation and Local Urban Development" (Ph.D diss., University of Pittsburgh, 1983).

36. For good analyses of Daley's use of federal programs, see J. David Greenstone and Paul Peterson, *Race and Authority in Urban Politics: Community Participation and the War on Poverty* (Chicago: University of Chicago Press, 1976); and David Protess, "Banfield's Chicago Revisited: The Conditions for and Social Policy Implications of the Transformation of a Political Machine," *Social Service Review* 48 (June 1974): 184–202.

37. Louise Jezierski, "Neighborhoods and Public–Private Partnerships in Pittsburgh," *Urban Affairs Quarterly* 26, no. 2 (December 1990): 217–249.

38. For good analyses of the dilemmas that African Americans face in political organizing in Pittsburgh, see Laurence Glasco, "Double Burden: The Black Experience in Pittsburgh," in *City at the Point,* ed. S. Hays (Pittsburgh: University of Pittsburgh Press, 1989), 69–109; and Alberta Sbragia, "The Pittsburgh Model of Economic Development: Partnership, Responsiveness and Indifference," in *Unequal Partnerships,* ed. G. Squires (New Brunswick, N.J.: Rutgers University Press, 1989), 103–120.

39. Sbragia, "The Pittsburgh Model of Economic Development."

40. This does not include Section 8 housing.

41. The actual figure is 86 percent, but even this does not fully capture the extent of racial segregation. More than half of the whites living in public housing are in senior or elderly housing. Further, with the exception of some senior projects, the individual projects are not integrated. The data cited in the text were obtained from "The Local Community Fact Book Chicago Metropolitan Area, 1980" produced by the Chicago Fact Book Consortium c/o Sociology Department, the University of Illinois at Chicago.

42. Alton Fuller, "Powerless Politics: Blacks Evaluate Strategies after Setbacks in City Government," *Pittsburgh Press,* October 27, 1986.

43. Pittsburgh has three "Hill" districts: the Lower Hill, which was bulldozed; the Middle Hill, where protests stopped urban renewal; and the Upper Hill. The area discussed here encompasses the Middle Hill and the minor remains of the Lower Hill.

44. In 1980, East Liberty was 54 percent white and 46.3 percent black. Neighborhood Profiles, City of Pittsburgh, Planning Department. The ELDI was set up around 1981.

45. Stone, *Regime Politics.*

3. REGIME FORMATION

1. While most studies of corporatism have focused on Western Europe (see Schmitter, Panitch, Katzenstein, Lehmbruch), and while some scholars have attempted to explain the absence of corporatism in the United States (see Wilson, Salisbury), examples of this novel (novel for America) form of governance can be found at the local (Clarke, Coleman) and sometimes state, level (Ambrosius, Gray and Lowery, Hudson, Hyde, and Carroll). The works just cited are the following: Philippe Schmitter, "Modes of Intermediation and Models of Societal Change in Western Europe," *Comparative Political Studies* 10, no. 1 (April 1977): 7–38; Schmitter, "Still the Century of Corporatism?" *Review of Politics* 36 (January 1974): 85–131; Leo Panitch, "The Development of Corporatism in Liberal Democracies," *Comparative Political Studies* 10, no. 1 (April 1977): 61–90; Peter Katzenstein, *Small States in World Markets* (Ithaca, N.Y.: Cornell University Press, 1985); Gerhard Lehmbruch, "Liberal Corporatism and Party Government," *Comparative Political Studies* 10, no. 1 (April 1977): 91–126; Graham Wilson, "Why Is There No Corporatism in the United States?" in *Patterns of Corporatist Policymaking,* ed. G. Lehmbruch and P. Schmitter (London: Sage, 1982); Robert Salisbury, "Why No Corporatism in America?" in *Trends in Interest Intermediation,* ed. P. Schmitter and G. Lehmbruch (Beverly Hills, Calif.: Sage, 1979), 213–230; Susan Clarke, "Urban America, Inc: Corporatist Convergence of Power in American Cities?" in *Local Economies in Transition,* ed. E. Bergman (Durham, N.C.: Duke University Press, 1986), 37–58; Morton Coleman, "Interest Intermediation and Local Urban Development" (Ph.D diss., University of Pitts-

burgh, 1983); Margery Marzahn Ambrosius, "Meso-Corporatism, Pluralism or Preemptive Power?: Economic Development Policy Making in Three States" (paper presented at the Midwest Political Science Association Meeting, Chicago, April 1990); Virginia Gray and David Lowery, "The Corporatist Foundations of State Industrial Policy" (paper presented at the Midwest Political Science Association Meeting, Chicago, April 1989); William Hudson, Mark Hyde, and John Carroll, "Corporatist Policy Making and State Economic Development," *Polity* 19 (1987): 403–418.

2. Michael Weber, *Don't Call Me Boss: David L. Lawrence, Pittsburgh's Renaissance Mayor* (Pittsburgh: University of Pittsburgh Press, 1988).

3. Robert Alberts, *The Shaping of the Point: Pittsburgh's Renaissance Park* (Pittsburgh: University of Pittsburgh Press, 1980).

4. Jon Teaford, *The Twentieth-Century American City: Problem, Promise, and Reality* (Baltimore, Md.: Johns Hopkins University Press, 1986).

5. Quoted in Alberts, *The Shaping of the Point*, 65.

6. Jeanne Lowe, *Cities in a Race with Time: Progress and Poverty in America's Renewing Cities* (New York: Random House, 1967).

7. The idea for the ACCD was suggested to Mellon by one of his associates. Without Mellon's support, however, the idea probably would not have materialized.

8. Alberts, *The Shaping of the Point*.

9. Weber, *Don't Call Me Boss*.

10. Weber, *Don't Call Me Boss*.

11. Weber, *Don't Call Me Boss*.

12. Roy Lubove, ed., *Pittsburgh* (New York: New Viewpoints, 1976).

13. Initially, Lawrence did not want to head the URA, fearing that doing so would look like a power grab on his part. Republican businessmen, on the other hand, thought it politically expeditious for a popular Democrat to head an agency that would implement policies serving the interests of the business community. See Weber, *Don't Call Me Boss*, and Lubove, *Twentieth-Century Pittsburgh*.

14. Weber, *Don't Call Me Boss*, 172.

15. Even this number is somewhat misleading. Caliguiri, who died in midterm, was a very popular mayor and undoubtedly would have remained in office. Sophie Masloff, who filled out the rest of his term, won the regular election in 1989. At the age of seventy-six, she decided not to run for another term. She was succeeded by Tom Murphy in 1994.

16. Weber, *Don't Call Me Boss*.

17. Weber, *Don't Call Me Boss*.

18. Teaford, *The Twentieth-Century American City*, 120.

19. Quoted in Lubove, *Twentieth-Century Pittsburgh*, 59.

20. *National Municipal Review*, March 1955.

21. *Fortune Magazine*, June 1952.

22. Pittsburgh was the third-largest headquarters center, surpassed only by New York City and Chicago.

23. Within one year of implementation, Pittsburgh "received 39% more sunshine," while the "hours of 'moderate' and 'heavy' smoke decreased by approximately 50%." According to a poll of residents, the majority of Pittsburghers felt that conditions had improved. See Weber, *Don't Call Me Boss*, 247.

24. Lowe, *Cities in a Race with Time*.

25. Alberts, *The Shaping of the Point*, 104. The "radical new proposition" refers to

eminent domain, which had been intended for purposes of improvements that are in the "public interest." Since Gateway Center was to consist of office towers, the development was essentially "private." Hence, the reference to "not [having] been tested in the courts."

26. Quoted in Weber, *Don't Call Me Boss*, 262.
27. Weber, *Don't Call Me Boss*.
28. Lowe, *Cities in a Race with Time*, 115.
29. Weiss and Metzger, "Planning for Chicago."
30. Teaford, *The Twentieth-Century American City*.
31. Gregory Squires, Larry Bennett, Kathleen McCourt, and Philip Nyden, *Chicago: Race, Class, and the Response to Urban Decline* (Philadelphia: Temple University Press, 1987), 160.
32. Arnold Hirsch, *Making the Second Ghetto: Race and Housing in Chicago, 1940–1960* (Cambridge: Cambridge University Press, 1983).
33. Homer Hoyt was also the person who devised the underwriting guidelines for the Federal Housing Administration (FHA), which listed "Southern Italians," "Negroes," and "Mexicans" as the least desirable borrowers.
34. This area was not directly adjacent to the Loop, but it was chosen because of the existence of institutional anchors—Michael Reese and Mercy Hospitals and the Illinois Institute of Technology—and because the area was very run-down and virtually all black. Further, the ultimate objective was to redevelop the South Side from the Loop to Hyde Park, which is home to the University of Chicago. A major urban renewal project was undertaken several years later by the University of Chicago, which dramatically altered the residential and commercial makeup of Hyde Park. Thus, in the context of these longer-range plans, the logic of the Lake Meadows development is fairly apparent. There was and continues to be subsequent development in this South Side corridor, including the residential developments of Central Station, Dearborn Park I and II; the construction of a new Comiskey Park; efforts to remove the El tracks along State Street and build townhouses on the site; proposals to build a new football stadium that would replace the existing Soldier's Field and would remove much of the surrounding industrial outfits; the proposed but defeated 1992 World's Fair, which would have given a major boost to South Side development.
35. Hirsch, *Making the Second Ghetto*.
36. James Greer, "The Politics of Decline and Growth: Planning, Economic Transformation, and the Structuring of Urban Fortunes in American Cities" (Ph.D diss., University of Chicago, 1983).
37. Edward Banfield, *Political Influence: A New Theory of Urban Politics* (New York: Free Press, 1961), chap. 5.
38. Cermak was assassinated in 1933 at the Democratic National Convention when he caught a bullet intended for FDR. An alternative interpretation is that Cermak was assassinated by a member of Al Capone's gang. According to this legend, Cermak made the services of the Chicago police available to a rival gang to wipe out the Capone gang. He initiated this arrangement when Capone refused to increase the amount of money he was kicking back to city hall. In retaliation for Cermak's actions, Capone issued the assassination orders. See Sanford Horwitt, *Let Them Call Me Rebel: Saul Alinsky, His Life and Legacy* (New York: Vintage Books, 1992), 33–36.
39. Rakove placed the figure at 30,000 while other estimates have placed it between

20,000 and 30,000. Rakove, *Don't Make No Waves, Don't Back No Losers;* Len O'Connor, *Clout: Mayor Daley and His City* (Chicago: Henry Regnery Company, 1975).

40. Construction of the Kennedy and Eisenhower Expressways began prior to Daley's administration (1949 and 1947, respectively), but the Dan Ryan and Stevenson Expressways were built during his tenure; construction began in 1958 and 1963, respectively.

41. Weiss and Metzger, "Planning for Chicago."

42. McCormick Place burned down in 1967. Two years later, construction began on the same site for an even larger center.

43. Squires et al., *Chicago*, 162–163.

44. Loomis Mayfield, "The Decline of Chicago and the Rise of the 'Growth Machine': The Reorganization of Urban Politics" (paper presented to the Duquesne University History Forum, Pittsburgh, October 23, 1992).

45. Ferman, "Chicago: Power, Race, and Reform."

46. Mayfield, "The Decline of Chicago and the Rise of the 'Growth Machine.' "

47. Kleppner, *Chicago Divided.*

48. James Greer, "The Politics of Decline and Growth: Planning, Economic Transformation, and the Structuring of Urban Fortunes in American Cities" (Ph.D diss., University of Chicago, 1983).

49. Hirsch, *Making the Second Ghetto.*

50. Quoted in Hirsch, *Making the Second Ghetto,* 110.

51. Hirsch, *Making the Second Ghetto.*

52. Kleppner, *Chicago Divided.*

53. Ferman and Grimshaw, "The Politics of Housing Policy."

54. Hirsch, *Making the Second Ghetto;* Ferman and Grimshaw, "The Politics of Housing Policy."

55. Ferman and Grimshaw, "The Politics of Housing Policy"; Chicago Housing Authority Statistical Yearbook, 1984.

56. Kleppner, *Chicago Divided.*

57. Hirsch, *Making the Second Ghetto.*

58. Grimshaw, *Bitter Fruit.*

59. Squires et al., *Chicago.*

60. Hirsch, *Making the Second Ghetto;* Kleppner, *Chicago Divided.*

61. Stephen Elkin, *City and Regime in the American Republic* (Chicago: University of Chicago Press, 1987), 109.

62. Elkin, *City and Regime in the American Republic.*

4. PLANTING THE SEEDS OF DISCONTENT

1. Mike Royko, *Boss: Richard J. Daley of Chicago* (New York: Signet, 1971), 126.

2. This section draws heavily on George Rosen's exhaustive study, *Decisionmaking Chicago Style: The Genesis of a University of Illinois Campus* (Urbana: University of Illinois Press, 1980).

3. According to Rosen, this was "the only community in any of the sites considered that actively sought the campus." *Decisionmaking Chicago Style,* 67.

4. Rosen, *Decisionmaking Chicago Style,* 86.

5. Daley declared himself to be the "mayor of all neighborhoods" when he was sworn in, in 1955. Rosen, *Decisionmaking Chicago Style*, 64.

6. *Chicago Tribune*, March 2, 1992.

7. Saul Alinsky, *Reveille for Radicals* (New York: Vintage Books, 1969), 132.

8. The BYNC included seventy-six organizations.

9. The facility was in Davis Park, which was under the jurisdiction of the Park District. See Robert Slayton, *Back of the Yards: The Making of a Local Democracy* (Chicago: University of Chicago Press, 1986).

10. John Hall Fish, *Black Power/White Control: The Struggle of the Woodlawn Organization in Chicago* (Princeton, N.J.: Princeton University Press, 1973), 77.

11. Horwitt, *Let Them Call Me Rebel*.

12. Dawson's area was mostly west of Woodlawn. For an alternative assessment of Dawson's power, see Grimshaw, *Bitter Fruit*.

13. Fish, *Black Power/White Control*, 67.

14. Quoted in Ed Marciniak, *Reviving an Inner City Community* (Chicago: Discourses, Loyola University Department of Political Science, 1977), 21.

15. *Chicago Tribune*, June 7, 1973, N4A, 1.

16. *Chicago Tribune*, June 7, 1973, N4A, 1; *Chicago Tribune*, May 30, 1974, N4A, 1.

17. Squires et al., *Chicago*.

18. Jean Pogge and David Flax-Hatch, "The Invisible Lenders: The Role of Residential Credit in Community Economies," in *Challenging Uneven Development*, ed. P. Nyden and W. Wiewel (New Brunswick, N.J.: Rutgers University Press, 1991), 85–112.

19. Jean Pogge, "Reinvestment in Chicago Neighborhoods: A Twenty-Year Struggle," in *From Redlining to Reinvestment: Community Responses to Urban Disinvestment*, ed. G. Squires (Philadelphia: Temple University Press, 1992), 133–148.

20. Calvin Bradford, "Partnerships for Reinvestment: An Evaluation of the Chicago Neighborhood Lending Program" (report prepared for the National Training and Information Center, Chicago, September 1990).

21. Lowe, *Cities in a Race with Time*.

22. Weber, *Don't Call Me Boss*.

23. Weber, *Don't Call Me Boss*.

24. Donald Stevens Jr., "The Role of Nonprofit Corporations in Urban Development: A Case Study of ACTION-Housing, Inc. of Pittsburgh" (Ph.D diss., Carnegie-Mellon University, 1987).

25. The largest downtown in Pennsylvania is Center City in Philadelphia; the second largest is Pittsburgh's Golden Triangle. Oakland is not only the site of the University of Pittsburgh and its medical complexes, but also home to major museums, libraries, entertainment and recreational facilities, and numerous restaurants.

26. Lubove, *Twentieth-Century Pittsburgh*, 145.

27. Stevens, "The Role of Nonprofit Corporations in Urban Development."

28. Many of the residents displaced by the Lower Hill urban renewal moved into Homewood-Brushton.

29. Lubove, *Twentieth-Century Pittsburgh*.

30. Section 236 is a rental assistance program whereby the Federal Housing Administration (FHA) provides mortgage insurance in order to reduce the interest rates on the mortgage for rental units.

31. Stevens, "The Role of Nonprofit Corporations in Urban Development."

32. Stevens, "The Role of Nonprofit Corporations in Urban Development."
33. Urban Extension became the coordinator for CAP in four neighborhoods. See Stevens, "The Role of Nonprofit Corporations in Urban Development."
34. Quoted in Lubove, *Twentieth-Century Pittsburgh,* 161.
35. Quoted in Stevens, "The Role of Nonprofit Corporations in Urban Development," 177.
36. Stevens, "The Role of Nonprofit Corporations in Urban Development."
37. Quoted in Stevens, "The Role of Nonprofit Corporations in Urban Development," 199.
38. Lubove, *Twentieth-Century Pittsburgh,* 164.
39. Cynthia Horan, "Beyond Governing Coalitions: Analyzing Urban Regimes in the 1990s," *Journal of Urban Affairs* 13, no. 2 (1991): 120.
40. Horan, "Beyond Governing Coalitions," 132.

5. CHALLENGE AND RESPONSE

1. In their conception of the city as a "growth machine," Logan and Molotch argue that most conflicts within the city are over land-use issues, with the sides divided between those who derive an exchange value from their land (rentiers) and those who derive primarily a use value. See John Logan and Harvey Molotch, *Urban Fortunes* (Berkeley and Los Angeles: University of California Press, 1987).
2. Terry Clark and Lorna Ferguson, *City Money* (New York: Columbia University Press, 1983).
3. Official Election Returns, City of Pittsburgh, 1969.
4. Sbragia, "The Pittsburgh Model of Economic Development"; Shelby Stewman and Joel Tarr, "Four Decades of Public–Private Partnerships in Pittsburgh," in *Public–Private Partnerships in American Cities: Seven Case Studies,* ed. R. S. Fossler and R. A. Berger (Lexington, Mass.: D. C. Heath, 1982).
5. Bruce Campbell, Mayor's Executive Secretaries Oral History, 1989.
6. Clark and Ferguson, *City Money,* 199.
7. *New York Times,* February 26, 1977, S1, p. 8.
8. Clark and Ferguson, *City Money.*
9. Campbell, Mayor's Executive Secretaries Oral History Project.
10. Roger Ahlbrandt Jr., "Public–Private Partnerships for Neighborhood Renewal," *Annals of the American Academy of Political and Social Science* 488 (1986): 120–133; Robert Lurcott and Jane Downing, "A Public–Private Support System for Community-Based Organizations in Pittsburgh," *Journal of the American Planning Association* 53, no. 4 (autumn 1987): 459–468.
11. Stewman and Tarr, "Four Decades of Public–Private Partnerships in Pittsburgh."
12. The "evil cabal" consisted primarily of Edward Vrdolyak, Edward Burke, and Michael Bilandic, whom Byrne accused of destroying the city that her mentor, Richard J. Daley, had created. Ultimately, Byrne would promote Vrdolyak to party chair and support him, over Richard M. Daley, in the race for state's attorney.
13. Byrne also promised to secure collective bargaining rights for unions, a benefit long resisted by Richard J. Daley. Ultimately she would retreat from this promise as well, cre-

ating bad blood between herself and some of the unions. Between 1979 and 1980, Byrne was faced with strikes by the Transit Workers, Teachers, and Fire Fighters Unions.

14. Many white ethnics, especially Poles, voted for Byrne over Bilandic because of the frustration with the Southwest Side Irish, in particular the 11th ward, domination of the machine. Jane Byrne was Irish but from the Northwest Side, where many Poles lived. By contrast, the 11th ward had been home to mayors from 1933 to 1979. To many, it seemed like Chicago was an extension of Bridgeport (the 11th ward neighborhood where the Daleys and Bilandic lived); the budget director, corporation counsel, fire commissioner, patronage head, clerk of the circuit court, among others, came from Bridgeport. It was estimated that two thousand city employees lived in the 11th ward. This contrasts with the typical ward organization that had four to five hundred city jobs. See Gary Rivlin, *Fire on the Prairie: Chicago's Harold Washington and the Politics of Race* (New York: Henry Holt and Company, 1992), esp. 102.

15. Holli, "Ranking Chicago's Mayors," 202–211.

16. Renault Robinson, an informal adviser to Byrne whom she appointed to the CHA board, had, as director of the Afro-American Patrolmen's League, brought suit against the Chicago police department for hiring discrimination.

17. Bill Granger and Lori Granger, *Fighting Jane: Mayor Jane Byrne and the Chicago Machine* (New York: Dial Press, 1980), 222.

18. Quoted in *The Reader,* November 11, 1983.

19. Kenneth Reardon, "Local Economic Development in Chicago, 1983–1987: The Reform Efforts of Mayor Harold Washington" (Ph.D diss., Cornell University, 1990).

20. Byrne's megaprojects also included a major redevelopment of the North Loop area, a Rouse-like revitalization of Navy Pier and a new-town-in-town for the South Loop. See, City of Chicago, 1992 Plan.

21. Roughly 85 percent of the 144,000 people living in Chicago Housing Authority housing were African American. Of the 436,000 students in the public schools, 60.7 percent were African American, 20.4 percent Hispanic, and 16.3 percent white. See *New York Times,* January 12, 1983, 13.

22. The transition team's report documented enormous amounts of waste in city government. Although the Byrne administration tried to keep the report secret, it was leaked to the press several months later. Byrne responded by barring all reporters from city hall.

23. There were battles against some of the ward organizations, especially in the more liberal areas like Shadyside, but they tended to be isolated. Moreover, the ward presence within the overall political system was nowhere near as pervasive as it was in Chicago.

24. Quoted in Rivlin, *Fire on the Prairie,* 72–73.

25. In Chicago many aldermen are also ward committeemen.

26. The figures for Pittsburgh are for 1970 since Flaherty first ran in 1969. For Chicago the numbers are for 1980 since Byrne's election was in 1979. It should also be noted that in Chicago Hispanics accounted for 12.8 percent of the electorate, thus further reducing the significance of the white vote (see Kleppner, *Chicago Divided,* 67). In Pittsburgh the electorate consists almost entirely of whites and blacks. Pittsburgh data are from the Pittsburgh Department of City Planning.

27. Flaherty's stance may have lost him the governorship, though, as he did not get the African American vote in Philadelphia. Flaherty ran for governor of Pennsylvania in 1978.

28. Jezierski, "Neighborhoods and Public–Private Partnerships in Pittsburgh," 233.

29. Jezierski, "Neighborhoods and Public–Private Partnerships in Pittsburgh," 221.

30. Official Election Returns, City of Pittsburgh.
31. Penn Southwest was a continuation of the ACCD's institution building for economic development. It was established in 1972.
32. Ahlbrandt, "Public–Private Partnerships for Neighborhood Renewal." Funding for Pittsburgh's housing programs was a combination of residential mortgage bonds issued by the URA, UDAG grants, and CDBG money. See Ahlbrandt, "Public–Private Partnerships for Neighborhood Renewal"; Stewman and Tarr, "Four Decades of Public–Private Partnerships in Pittsburgh"; and Lurcott and Downing, "A Public–Private Support System."
33. *Neighborhoods Speak,* Newsletter of the Pittsburgh Neighborhood Alliance, February 1980.
34. Sbragia, "The Pittsburgh Model of Economic Development."
35. Interview, January 1988.
36. Interview, January 1988.
37. Quoted in Reardon, "Local Economic Development in Chicago, 1983–1987," 91.
38. Rivlin estimates the increase in black support to be 20 percent; see *Fire on the Prairie,* 161. Though this sounds somewhat high, there does seem to be a consensus that support in the African American community did go up as a result of Vrdolyak's comments. See, for instance, Grimshaw, *Bitter Fruit.*
39. Kleppner, *Chicago Divided.*
40. Washington received 80 percent of the black vote in the primary and approximately 97 percent of the black vote in the general election. And the turnout in some black middle-class wards exceeded the citywide figure of 82 percent. See Michael Preston, "The Resurgence of Black Voting in Chicago: 1955–1983," in *The Making of the Mayor, 1983,* ed. M. Holli and P. Green (Grand Rapids, Mich.: Erdmans, 1984), 39–52.
41. "Chicago Works Together," City of Chicago, 1984.
42. Ferman, "Chicago: Power, Race, and Reform."
43. Washington's proposal for a $300-million development of Navy Pier was defeated even though the council had approved a similar measure under Byrne. See John McCarron, "Is Chicago Ready for Reform?" *Planning,* September 1984. Additionally, a $1.25-billion airport expansion project was put on hold while battles over the awarding of contracts raged in council chambers.
44. Ferman and Grimshaw, "Old Politics, New Politics: Divergence and Convergence Strategies."
45. The legislation was actually passed during the Ford administration though it was assembled by the Nixon administration.
46. Housing and Community Development Act of 1974.
47. Swanstrom, *The Crisis of Growth Politics.*
48. Louise Jezierski, "Political Limits to Development in Two Declining Cities: Cleveland and Pittsburgh," in *Research in Politics and Society: Deindustrialization and the Economic Restructuring of American Industry,* ed. J. Rothschild and M. Wallace (Greenwich, Conn.: JAI Press, 1988), 173–189.
49. Although there is some speculation that Mayor Tom Murphy may try to alter the partnership, to date (1996), he has not taken such actions. Moreover, it is doubtful that he will try to overturn the entire system.
50. This amounted to $786 million. Development Draft, 1989–1994, City of Pittsburgh.
51. Capital Budget, City of Chicago.

52. Chicago held its first capital improvements workshops in 1987, and another one was also held during the Sawyer administration. Richard M. Daley set up the Capital Improvements Advisory Committee (CIAC) in 1991, which was largely ineffective, as the administration made capital budgeting decisions and reprogramming decisions without any input from the CIAC. Further, experiences of the Neighborhood Capital Budgeting Group, a private, nonprofit organization, indicated that even aldermen were not well informed on capital spending priorities. Interview, March 21, 1991.

53. Ahlbrandt, "Public–Private Partnerships for Neighborhood Renewal."

54. The original director of North Side Civic Development Council was there for ten years. He left to take a position in Cleveland and then returned to Pittsburgh to work in the Murphy administration. Sandra Philips, head of the Pittsburgh Partnership for Neighborhood Development, headed the Oakland Planning and Development Corporation for its first eight years. Bloomfield-Garfield Corporation has had only one director.

55. "Help All neighborhoods," *Pittsburgh Press*, editorial, December 5, 1985.

56. In addition to the operating monies, these CDCs also got project funds from a variety of sources, including LISC, the URA, and the planning department.

57. Robin Jones, "The CDC Experience of Pittsburgh" (paper presented at the annual meeting of the American Collegiate Schools of Planning, Portland, Oregon, October 1989).

58. Northside Civic Development Corporation, for example, is an umbrella organization representing many smaller organizations and several neighborhoods on the city's North Side.

59. The CBO fund and the Neighborhood Fund have since been collapsed. The reason for this merger was largely the realization that grants of less than ten thousand dollars were usually too small to produce any meaningful results. Interview, Robin Jones.

60. Initially, the Neighborhood Fund, Inc., made allocation decisions. When HUD discovered some conflicts of interest among some board members, the Neighborhood Fund was dissolved and ACCBO formed. See Jones, "The CDC Experience of Pittsburgh."

61. Teamworks, Evaluation Draft Report, 7.

62. Jezierski, "Neighborhoods and Public–Private Partnerships in Pittsburgh."

63. Between 1975 and 1984, 58.2 percent of the city's CDBG allocation went for housing activities, while only 29.2 percent of Chicago's did during that time despite neighborhood demands for such use. The perfunctory public hearings during the Daley, Bilandic, and Byrne administrations showed housing was a major priority. From 1987 to 1989 housing was the single largest expenditure in Pittsburgh's capital budget, accounting for one-third in 1987. Sources for this data are, in order, City of Pittsburgh, "Community Development in Pittsburgh: A Ten-Year Commitment to the Neighborhoods, 1975–1984"; Leonard Rubinowitz, "Chicago, Illinois," in *Decentralizing Urban Policy: Case Studies in Community Development,* ed. P. Dommel and Associates (Washington, D.C.: Brookings Institution, 1982), 120–165; Development Policies, 1992–1997, City of Pittsburgh.

64. Pittsburgh Partnership for Neighborhood Development, Annual Report, 1993.

65. Urban Development Action Grants (UDAGs), initiated during the Carter administration, were intended to leverage private sector dollars for urban development.

66. With membership limited to CEOs of the major corporations, the ACCD had an enormous resource base in terms of access, reputation, financial resources, and connections.

67. Quoted in Gary Rivlin, "City Hall: Understanding the Community Development Squabble," *The Reader,* June 6, 28, 1985.

68. *Chicago Defender,* May 25, 1983.

69. Hank De Zutter, "Putting the Community in Community Development," *The Reader,* May 27, 1983.

70. "The Truce on Block Grants" *Chicago Tribune,* editorial, May 28, 1983.

71. Chicago had evaded guidelines on housing, CDBG, and Model Cities funding. Perhaps the most notorious example was Daley's refusal to implement school desegregation orders. When the U.S. Department of Education threatened to cut off all federal school aid, Daley phoned his "good friend" President Lyndon Johnson. The threat was promptly dropped.

72. "Mayor Byrne's IOU," *Chicago Tribune,* editorial, April 22, 1983.

73. De Zutter, "Putting the Community in Community Development."

74. Byrne spent $4 million on snow removal and $1.7 million on TV advertising, allocated $16.8 million to the schools to cover a shortfall, and spent $10 million for a summer jobs program that created 3,800 jobs. See Stanley Ziemba, "U.S. Agency Bars Byrne's Use of Funds," *Chicago Tribune,* April 9, 1983.

75. Chicago had exceeded HUD's limit for public service expenditures. In fact, Chicago's percentage in this category was the largest of any city. In defense, Byrne argued that a lot of what the feds called "public service" items were not. See *Chicago Tribune,* April 22, 1983.

76. The battles ended in 1986, when, after special aldermanic elections, Washington had a 25–25 city council vote, with his vote as the tiebreaker.

77. The Department of Housing staff went from 363 to 7, while the Department of Economic Development staff decreased from 118 to 8. See Gary Rivlin, "City Hall: Understanding the Community Development Squabble," *The Reader,* June 28, 1985.

78. These aldermen also used race in an attempt to break the African American–Hispanic coalition. The council, for example, axed twenty-nine of thirty-six applications from Latino CBOs. Alderman Miguel Santiago, the one Hispanic on the city council in 1985, was a member of the Vrdolyak 29 and voted with them to cut funding for the Latino CBOs. Rivlin, *Fire on the Prairie,* 353; Clarence Page, "Block Grants and Blockages," editorial, *Chicago Tribune,* June 9, 1985.

79. The new guidelines, issued in February 1984, said eligible areas were those where at least 51 percent of the households had incomes of less than $19,650. Carol Oppenheim, "City to Cut Neighborhood Share of Community Aid," *Chicago Tribune,* May 15, 1984.

80. Alderman Burke stated, "We feel that all areas of the city are entitled to funds to stop growing blight and slum conditions in their neighborhoods." Quoted in James Strong, "Majority Bloc Shifts Funds to Its Members' Wards," *Chicago Tribune,* May 29, 1985.

81. Rivlin, "City Hall: Understanding the Community Development Squabble."

82. During the mayoral campaign many accusations were hurled and rumors started regarding Washington's managerial competency and what would happen if a black were elected. Washington's failure to file income tax returns for several years was used to show he was not competent. The competency issue was also couched in racial terms, suggesting that a black couldn't possibly run the city. Among the more prevalent rumors were that Washington would give the city away to blacks and that he would raise taxes on white homeowners.

83. Harry Golden, "Mayor, Foes Finally Agree on Spending of Federal Aid," *Chicago Sun-Times,* July 3, 1985.

84. Unlike most cities, where general obligation bonds require a two-thirds voter approval, in Chicago they only require city council approval.

85. Quoted in Gary Rivlin, "City Hall: How Low They Can Go," *The Reader,* July 26, 1985.

86. Rivlin, "City Hall: How Low They Can Go."

87. Interview with city council person allied with the mayor, June 24, 1991.

88. John McCarron, "Streets Resurface in Council Warfare," *Chicago Tribune,* May 16, 1985.

89. Rivlin, "City Hall: How Low They Can Go."

90. Quoted in McCarron, "Streets Resurface in Council Warfare."

91. These demands included guarantees that police services would not be cut on the Northwest and Southwest Sides, that the city implement a linked development program, and that the city adopt special program funding for schools. Ann Grimes, "Community Organizing in Black and White: The New Victims Raise Their Voices," *The Reader,* May 4, 1984.

92. Interview with community activist from Southwest Side, June 13, 1991.

93. Some of the member organizations had been involved in protests against Martin Luther King Jr.'s open housing march. Further, Marquette Park, one of the neighborhoods represented by SONSOC, was the headquarters for the Nazi Party.

94. The researchers were not part of SONSOC.

95. Interview with one of the researchers for the Home Equity proposal, May 23, 1991.

96. Grimshaw, *Bitter Fruit.*

97. Interviews with Home Equity proposal researchers, May 23, 1991. See also Rod McCullom, "Home Equity Proposal Fuels Racial Tensions as White Neighborhoods Struggle for Stability," *Chicago Reporter,* May 1988.

98. Quoted in McCullom, "Home Equity Proposal."

99. Madigan was also the ward committeeman for the area.

6. CHICAGO

1. Paul Johnston and William Holt, "Urban Public Organization as Obstacle to Regime Change: The Case of New Haven" (paper presented at the annual meeting of the Urban Affairs Association, Portland, Oregon, May 1995).

2. Johnston and Holt, "Urban Public Organization."

3. Johnston and Holt, "Urban Public Organization," 6.

4. Norman Krumholz, Patrick Costigan, and Dennis Keating, book review of Chicago Works Together: 1984 Development Plan, *Journal of the American Planning Association* 51, no. 3 (summer 1985): 395–396.

5. The exact figures were the following: the total six-year amount was $2,703,135,618; the annual average was $450,522,603; the six-year total for construction was $1,156,423,359. See David Ranney and Patricia Wright, "Employment Impacts of City of Chicago Purchasing Contracts" (Chicago: Center for Urban Economic Development, University of Illinois at Chicago, 1989).

6. Ranney and Wright, "Employment Impacts of City of Chicago Purchasing Contracts."

7. Study of Minority and Women Owned Business Enterprise Procurement Programs for the City of Chicago. Prepared by James H. Lowry and Associates, March 1985.

8. Lowry Report.

9. Dean Baquet, "Mayor Scores Coup on Contract Issue," *Chicago Tribune,* November 24, 1985.

10. The administration also sought to reform the purchasing practices by implementing a "Buy Chicago" program, which encouraged city agencies to purchase from local vendors. Information was also provided to the private sector in order to increase its purchases from Chicago vendors. Reardon estimates that "local purchases by all city agencies increased from 40% to 60% during Washington's first term" as a result of this program. He also suggests that approximately two thousand jobs were retained and/or created as a result. Reardon, "Local Economic Development in Chicago, 1983–1987," 140.

11. Even prior to the Lowry Report on city contracting practices, Washington informally pursued a minority set-aside program. As a result, 17.4 percent of city contracts were awarded to minorities. Bacquet, "Mayor Scores Coup on Contract Issue." Under Byrne, by contrast, 6 percent of city contracts went to minority businesses. *Chicago Defender,* February 3, 1986. Data on Byrne are for 1982.

12. The classification "minority" includes blacks, Hispanics, and Asians.

13. Lowry Report.

14. City of Chicago, Executive Order 85-2: Minority Purchasing Program. Although the city council did not approve Washington's set-aside proposal, they did pass an ordinance proposed by Councilman Roman Pucinski (a member of the "Vrdolyak 29") for a 30 percent set-aside. Under this ordinance four groups would share the 30 percent: "disadvantaged," "women," "small business," and "local" (*Chicago Tribune,* March 26, 1985). Pucinski's ordinance was reflective of a common practice of the Vrdolyak 29, who would often pass legislation either to preempt Washington's initiatives or to embarrass him. The CDBG episodes discussed in chapter 5 illustrate this practice.

15. *Chicago Defender,* February 3,1986. When Ware died, the program moved much faster.

16. Report of Blue Ribbon Panel to the Honorable Richard M. Daley, Mayor of the City of Chicago. March 29, 1990.

17. *Chicago Tribune,* October 27, 1985. Good-faith efforts carried no penalties, but instead relied on an honor system.

18. Merrill Goozner, "Genesis of a Fraud: Where the City Failed," *Crain's Chicago Business,* March 25, 1985.

19. Goozner, "Genesis of a Fraud."

20. Official Report of the Task Force on Affirmative Action, City of Chicago, December 1985, 2. This conclusion was arrived at by comparing the representation of minorities and women in city government with their availability in the workforce. Thus, in 1973, minorities (i.e., African Americans, Hispanics, and Asians) equaled 25 percent of the city's workforce and 25.4 percent of the external workforce (1970 census). In 1983 minorities constituted 32 percent of city government but 51 percent of the external workforce (1980 census). In 1973 women made up 16 percent of city workers and 33.3 percent of the external workforce. In 1983, women were 19.5 percent of city government and 44.2 percent of the external workforce.

21. Official Report of the Task Force on Affirmative Action, City of Chicago, December 1985.
22. Mattie Smith Colin, "Key Jobs for Women Part of Mayor's Legacy," *Chicago Defender*, November 28, 1987.
23. David Fremon, "Latinos Greatly Overlooked in City Hiring, Says Report," *W.S. Times–Lawndale News*, June 3, 1984.
24. Fremon, "Latinos Greatly Overlooked."
25. Maria de los Angeles Torres, "The Commission on Latino Affairs: A Case Study of Community Empowerment," in *Harold Washington and the Neighborhoods: Progressive City Government in Chicago, 1983–1987*, ed. P. Clavel and W. Wiewel (New Brunswick, N.J.: Rutgers University Press, 1991).
26. Development Plan, City of Chicago, 1984, 7.
27. Lisa Goff, "Despite Woes, Mayor Firm on Minority Jobs," *Crain's Chicago Business*, March 23, 1987.
28. Illinois had just signed a Freedom of Information Act as well in 1983. It was the last state to do so. John Kretzman, "Opening Up a Closed City," in *Harold Washington and the Neighborhoods: Progressive City Government in Chicago, 1983–1987*, ed. P. Clavel and W. Wiewel (New Brunswick, N.J.: Rutgers University Press, 1991).
29. *Blueprint of Chicago Government: A Study for Mayor Harold Washington*, by the Agency Review Unit of the Transition Team, May 1983, p. 2. A comparable report with similar findings was produced for the Byrne administration as well. Unlike Washington, however, who moved on numerous recommendations, Byrne ignored the report altogether.
30. Simpson also ran twice, unsuccessfully, against Dan Rostenkowski in the Democratic primary for U.S. Congress (1992 and 1994).
31. Kretzman, "Opening Up a Closed City."
32. The city council did not even number its ordinances. Often aldermen did not even see the legislation prior to voting on it. This was especially true under Richard J. Daley. Tom Keane, Daley's floor manager, instructed aldermen how to vote. This was one of the major factors that led to the revolt of the Young Turks (see chapter 3).
33. City of Chicago, Planners Digest, December 1984, 3.
34. This was especially true of the Department of Economic Development. Rob Mier, who was appointed commissioner, had a long history of working with CBOs through the Center for Urban Economic Development at the University of Illinois-Chicago. Art Vazquez, a deputy commissioner, had been the head of the Eighteenth Street Development Corporation, a CBO in Pilsen, the city's Mexican neighborhood. Robert Giloth, deputy commissioner for research in the Department of Economic Development, also had significant involvement with CBOs.
35. Ferman and Grimshaw, "The Politics of Housing Policy"; Arthur Lyons, Spenser Staton, and Dianne Kallenback, "When Everything Works and Nothing Is Right," Chicago 1992 Committee: Institute on Taxation and Economic Policy. 1986.
36. Prior to that designation, neighborhood infrastructure expenditures were rolled into transportation under the category "local streets." In Byrne's 1983 capital budget, $40,700,000 was allocated for "local streets." In 1984 Washington allocated $148,539,000 for neighborhood infrastructure. Washington's capital budget for 1984 was nearly double Byrne's 1983 budget. Capital Improvement Plan, City of Chicago, 1983–1987, 1984–1988.
37. Capital Improvement Plan, City of Chicago, 1986–1990.

38. Wim Wiewel and Nicholas Rieser, "The Limits of Progressive Municipal Economic Development: Job Creation in Chicago, 1983–1987," *Community Development Journal* 24, no. 2 (1989): 111–119,
39. Clavel, *The Progressive City.*
40. *Chicago Sun-Times,* April 30, 1983.
41. The information on block grants is from Michael Rich, "Community Politics and the New Federalism: Implementation of the Community Development Block Grant Program in Chicago" (paper presented at the annual meeting of the American Political Science Association, Chicago, August 1987). The information on Chicago's federal aid is from Ester Fuchs, *Mayors and Money: Fiscal Policy in New York and Chicago* (Chicago: University of Chicago Press, 1992).
42. For a good example of this critique, see Robert Brehm, "Learning to Live with Friends in City Hall," in *Harold Washington and the Neighborhoods: Progressive City Government in Chicago, 1983–1987,* ed. P. Clavel and W. Wiesel (New Brunswick, N.J.: Rutgers University Press, 1991).
43. Grimshaw, *Bitter Fruit.*
44. Several Washington aides advised against the formation of MACLA, and even Washington himself would have preferred a different type of arrangement. However, after several Hispanic leaders seized the initiative and moved ahead with forming a group, it was politically difficult for Washington to publicly rebuke their efforts.
45. Stone, *Regime Politics,* 242.

7. PITTSBURGH

1. Robert Fisher, *Let the People Decide: Neighborhood Organizing in America,* rev. ed. (New York: Twayne, 1994), 189.
2. John Portz, *The Politics of Plant Closings* (Lawrence: University Press of Kansas, 1990).
3. For a good examination of the Mon Valley CDCs, see Ross Gittell, *Renewing Cities* (Princeton, N.J.: Princeton University Press, 1992).
4. Note that there are other universities as well, most notably Duquesne, but that, in size and role, the University of Pittsburgh and Carnegie Mellon University overshadow them. The city is also home to a major heath care industry, which has significantly bolstered the economy.
5. The Pittsburgh figure is from the U.S. Census; the Duquesne figure is from Portz, *The Politics of Plant Closings.*
6. Mellon Bank had investments in foreign steel companies at the same time it was foreclosing on loans in the Mon Valley. Mellon's foreclosure on a thirteen-million-dollar loan to Mesta Machine Company, for example, precipitated its shutdown, which resulted in over one thousand jobs lost. See Plotkin and Scheuerman, "Two Roads Left," 193–217.
7. In the ACCD's 1983 report, "A Strategy for Growth: An Economic Development Program for the Pittsburgh Region," there were strong acknowledgments that the steel industry was dead and that the Mon Valley needed to diversify its economy.
8. *State of the Region: Economic, Demographic and Social Trends in Southwestern*

NOTES TO PAGES 126-132

Pennsylvania, ed. Ralph Bangs and Vijai Singh (Pittsburgh: University Center for Social and Urban Research, University of Pittsburgh, 1988).

9. Portz, *The Politics of Plant Closings.*

10. Morton Coleman, "Decline of the Mon Valley Viewed in a Global Context," in *Steel People: Survival and Resilience in Pittsburgh's Mon Valley,* ed. Jim Cunningham and Pamela Martz (Pittsburgh: University of Pittsburgh Press, 1986), 1-8.

11. Coleman, "Decline of the Mon Valley Viewed in a Global Context."

12. John Hoerr, *And the Wolf Finally Came: The Decline of the American Steel Industry* (Pittsburgh: University of Pittsburgh Press, 1988).

13. Portz, *The Politics of Plant Closings.*

14. Coleman, "Decline of the Mon Valley Viewed in a Global Context," 4.

15. Portz, *The Politics of Plant Closings.*

16. Staughton Lynd, "The Genesis of the Idea of a Community Right to Industrial Property in Youngstown and Pittsburgh, 1977-1987," *Journal of American History* 74, no. 3 (December 1987): 948.

17. This was not like other companies that relocated facilities overseas. U.S. Steel was getting out of the industry and into other activities such as oil, real estate, and banking.

18. Portz, *The Politics of Plant Closings;* Sbragia, "The Pittsburgh Model of Economic Development."

19. Portz, *The Politics of Plant Closings.*

20. In 1977 there were organizing efforts in Youngstown, Ohio, around the idea of worker-owned steel mills. The Ecumenical Coalition, formed in October of that year, began a major organizing drive at the local, state, and federal levels. Although it raised over four million dollars locally and got HUD and Federal Commerce Department backing on the project, the announcement of additional steel mill closings led the Commerce Department to withdraw its support. See John Russo and Brian Corbin, "A System of Interpretation: Catholic Social Teaching and American Unionism," in *Conflict* 11 (October-December 1991): 237-266.

21. The nine municipalities, in descending order of population size, were Pittsburgh, McKeesport, Munhall, Swissvale, Turtle Creek, Glassport, Homestead, Rankin, and East Pittsburgh (this is not part of the city of Pittsburgh).

22. The best exposé of Robert Moses's power is Robert Caro's *The Power Broker: Robert Moses and the Fall of New York City* (New York: Vintage Books, 1975).

23. Duquesne was a one-industry town since 1898. During the early 1980s, 44 percent of the municipality's real estate taxes and 60 percent of its wage taxes came from U.S. Steel. See Portz, *The Politics of Plant Closings,* esp. 102.

24. Portz, *The Politics of Plant Closings,* 86.

25. Quoted in Portz, *The Politics of Plant Closings,* 96.

26. A Community Plan to Save Pittsburgh's Steel Industry, the Steel Valley Authority, 6.

27. Quoted in Lynd, "The Genesis of the Idea of a Community Right to Industrial Property in Youngstown and Pittsburgh, 1977-1987," 933-934.

28. Portz, *The Politics of Plant Closings.*

29. Interview with SVA director, July 13, 1990.

30. Interview with labor activist, February 20, 1992.

31. Interview with labor activist, February 20, 1992.

32. Quoted in Portz, *The Politics of Plant Closings,* 98.

33. Interview with SVA director, July 13, 1990.

34. In its 1984 Report, "A Strategy for Growth: An Economic Development Program for the Pittsburgh Region," the ACCD declared as one of its guiding principles that the "strategy should recognize the inevitability of change" (8). This was a direct reference to the decline of the steel industry and heavy manufacturing.

35. The ACCD hired Mike Eichler to organize CDCs in the Mon Valley. His efforts resulted in the Mon Valley Development Team and then the Mon Valley Initiative.

36. Michael Lipsky, "Protest as a Political Resource," *American Political Science Review* 62 (December 1968): 1144–1158.

37. Interview with SVA director, July 13, 1990.

38. Plotkin, "Enclave Consciousness and Neighborhood Activism."

39. Clarence Stone, "Urban Regimes and the Capacity to Govern: A Political Economy Approach," *Journal of Urban Affairs* 15, no. 1 (1993): 1–28.

8. TOWARD A CONSERVATIVE PROGRESSIVISM?

1. Clarence Stone, David Imbroscio, and Marion Orr, "The Reshaping of Urban Leadership in U.S. Cities: A Regime Analysis," in *Urban Life in Transition*, ed. M. Gottdiener and C. Pickvance (Beverly Hills, Calif.: Sage, 1991), 222–239.

2. Stone, *Regime Politics*, 227.

3. Pittsburgh had an at-large system from 1911 until 1987.

4. The rule was that all decisions of the executive committee, which is the central committee, had to be unanimous.

5. In 1988, for instance, the *Chicago Tribune* issued a scathing indictment of CBOs in a seven-part series entitled "Chicago on Hold: The Politics of Poverty," August 8 to September 4, 1988.

6. Paul Green, "The Chicago Political Tradition: A Mayoral Retrospective," in *The Mayors: The Chicago Political Tradition*, ed. Paul Green and Melvin Holli (Carbondale and Edwardsville: Southern Illinois University Press, 1987), 212–214.

7. Edward Banfield and James Q. Wilson, *City Politics* (New York: Vintage Books, 1963).

8. DeLeon, *Left Coast City*, 32.

9. DeLeon, *Left Coast City*, 32.

10. Clarke, "Making a Difference."

11. Clarke, "Making a Difference."

12. Clarke, "Making a Difference," 12.

13. Clavel, *The Progressive City*.

14. Robert Mier and Joan Fitzgerald, "Managing Economic Development," book review essay, *Economic Development Quarterly* 5, no. 3 (August 1991): 268–279; Pierre Clavel and Wim Wiewel, "Introduction," in *Harold Washington and the Neighborhoods: Progressive City Government in Chicago, 1983–1987*, ed. P. Clavel and W. Wiewel (New Brunswick, N.J.: Rutgers University Press, 1991).

15. R. C. Longworth, "It's Still Not Certain Who'll Pay for Fair," *Chicago Tribune*, May 9, 1983, 1.

16. DeLeon, *Left Coast City*, 175.

17. "Against All Odds: The Achievements of Community-Based Development Orga-

nizations," National Congress for Community Economic Development, March 1989. The number refers to community development corporations (CDCs), CBOs that engage almost exclusively in economic development activities.

18. Although Katznelson argued that the existence of urban trenches weakened electoral politics (or party politics), the "community" trench was rooted in electoral (i.e., machine) politics. Moreover, workplace issues did involve elections, albeit of union officials as opposed to municipal officials. Urban trenches that develop around different policy or issue areas, by contrast, will totally bypass electoral politics.

19. Fisher, *Let the People Decide.*

20. On this argument, see Kling and Posner, "Class and Community in an Era of Urban Transformation," 23–45.

21. Kling and Posner, "Class and Community in an Era of Urban Transformation."

22. This, of course, is a play on their title: Rufus Browning, Dale Rogers Marshall, and David Tabb, *Protest Is Not Enough: The Struggle of Blacks and Hispanics for Equality in Urban Politics* (Berkeley and Los Angeles: University of California Press, 1984).

23. Of course, the flip side of this is that while these institutions may initially protect these changes, whatever they may be, the changes ultimately become the status quo and institutions, in protecting them, become a conservative force.

24. Although progressive coalitions have come into power through electoral victory in numerous cities, their tenure has usually been short-lived.

25. Clarke, "Making a Difference."

26. For a good start in this direction, see Clarke, "Making a Difference."

27. This literature includes the "new institutionalism" (see Walter Powell and Paul DiMaggio, eds., *The New Institutionalism in Organizational Analysis* [Chicago: University of Chicago Press, 1991]); corporatism; interest group; social movement; empirical work on cities; and regime theory in international politics. For a good discussion of the relationship between regime theory in international politics and its use in urban politics, see Shama Bole and Andrew McFarland, "The Concept of Regime: Urban Politics, International Relations, and Policy Studies" (paper presented at the annual meeting of the American Political Science Association, Washington, D.C., 1993).

28. James Bryce, *The American Commonwealth,* vol. 1, 3d rev. ed. (New York: Macmillan, 1924), 642.

Bibliography

Ahlbrandt, Roger, Jr. "Public–Private Partnerships for Neighborhood Renewal." *Annals of the American Academy of Political and Social Science* 488 (1986): 120–133.
Alberts, Robert. *The Shaping of the Point: Pittsburgh's Renaissance Park.* Pittsburgh: University of Pittsburgh Press, 1980.
Alinsky, Saul. *Reveille for Radicals.* New York: Vintage, 1969.
Allegheny Conference on Community Development. "A Strategy for Growth: An Economic Development Program for the Pittsburgh Region." 1984.
Ambrosius, Margery Marzahn. "Meso-Corporatism, Pluralism or Preemptive Power?: Economic Development Policy Making in Three States." Paper presented at the Midwest Political Science Association Meeting, Chicago, April 1990.
Banfield, Edward. *Political Influence: A New Theory of Urban Politics.* New York: Free Press, 1961.
Banfield, Edward, and James Q. Wilson. *City Politics.* New York: Vintage, 1963.
Bangs, Ralph, and Vijai Singh. *State of the Region: Economic, Demographic and Social Trends in Southwestern Pennsylvania.* Pittsburgh: University Center for Social and Urban Research, University of Pittsburgh, 1988.
Baquet, Dean. "Mayor Scores Coup on Contract Issue." *Chicago Tribune,* November 24, 1985.
Beauregard, Robert, ed. *Atop the Urban Hierarchy.* Totowa, N.J.: Rowan and Littlefield, 1989.
Bergman, Edward, ed. *Local Economies in Transition.* Durham, S.C.: Duke University Press, 1986.
Berry, Jeffrey, Kent Portney, and Ken Thomson. *The Rebirth of Urban Democracy.* Washington, D.C.: Brookings Institution, 1993.
Bingham, Richard, and R. Eberts, eds. *Economic Restructuring of the American Midwest.* Norwell, Mass.: Kluwer Academics, 1990.
Blueprint of Chicago Government: A Study for Mayor Harold Washington. 1983. Harold Washington Transition Team, Agency Review Unit, City of Chicago.
Bole, Shama, and Andrew McFarland. "The Concept of Regime: Urban Politics, Interna-

tional Relations, and Policy Studies." Paper presented at the annual meeting of the American Political Science Association, Washington, D.C., 1993.

Boyer, Rick, and Daivd Savageau. *Places Rated Almanac: Your Guide to Finding the Best Places to Live in America.* Chicago: Rand McNally, 1985.

Boyte, Harry. *Commonwealth: A Return to Citizen Politics.* New York: Free Press, 1989.

Bradford, Calvin. "Partnerships for Reinvestment: An Evaluation of the Chicago Neighborhood Lending Program." Report prepared for the National Training and Information Center, Chicago, September 1990.

Brehm, Robert. "Learning to Live with Friends in City Hall." In *Harold Washington and the Neighborhoods,* edited by P. Clavel and W. Wiewel. New Brunswick, N.J.: Rutgers University Press, 1991.

Browning, Rufus, Dale Rogers Marshall, and David Tabb. *Protest Is Not Enough: The Struggle of Blacks and Hispanics for Equality in Urban Politics.* Berkeley and Los Angeles: University of California Press, 1984.

Bryce, James. *The American Commonwealth.* 3d rev. ed. New York: Macmillan, 1924.

Capital Improvement Plan, City of Chicago. 1983–1987.

———. 1984–1988.

———. 1986–1990.

Caro, Robert. *The Power Broker: Robert Moses and the Fall of New York City.* New York: Vintage, 1975.

"Chicago on Hold: The Politics of Poverty." *Chicago Tribune,* August 28–September 4, 1988.

"Chicago Works Together." City of Chicago, 1984.

City of Chicago. Planners Digest. December 1984.

City of Pittsburgh. "Community Development in Pittsburgh: A Ten-Year Commitment to the Neighborhoods, 1975–1984."

Clark, Terry, and Lorna Ferguson. *City Money.* (New York: Columbia University Press, 1983.

Clarke, Susan. "Urban America, Inc.: Corporatist Convergence of Power in American Cities?" In *Local Economies in Transition,* edited by Edward Bergman, 37–58. Durham, N.C.: Duke University Press, 1986.

———. "Making a Difference: Interest Representation and Local Development Policy." Paper presented at the Midwest Political Science Association Meeting, Chicago, April 1992.

Clavel, Pierre. *The Progressive City.* New Brunswick, N.J.: Rutgers University Press, 1986.

Clavel, Pierre, and Nancy Kleniewski. "Space for Progressive Local Policy: Examples from the United States and the United Kingdom." In *Beyond the City Limits: Urban Policy and Economic Restructuring in Comparative Perspective,* edited by John Logan and Todd Swanstrom, 199–234. Philadelphia: Temple University Press, 1990.

Clavel, Pierre, and Wim Wiewel, eds. *Harold Washington and the Neighborhoods: Progressive City Government in Chicago, 1983–1987.* New Brunswick, N.J.: Rutgers University Press, 1991.

Coleman, Morton. "Interest Intermediation and Local Urban Development." Ph.D diss., University of Pittsburgh, 1983.

———. "Decline of the Mon Valley Viewed in a Global Context." In *Steel People: Survival and Resilience in Pittsburgh's Mon Valley,* edited by J. Cunningham and P. Martz, 1–8. Pittsburgh: University of Pittsburgh Press, 1986.

Colin, Mattie Smith. "Key Jobs for Women Part of Mayor's Legacy." *Chicago Defender,* November 28, 1987.
Cummings, Scott, ed. *Business Elites and Urban Development.* Albany: State University of New York Press, 1988.
Cunningham, Jim, and Pamela Martz, eds. *Steel People: Survival and Resilience in Pittsburgh's Mon Valley.* Pittsburgh: River Communities Project, School of Social Work, University of Pittsburgh, 1986.
DeLeon, Richard. *Left Coast City: Progressive Politics in San Francisco, 1975–1991.* Lawrence: University Press of Kansas, 1992.
Development Draft, 1989–1994. City of Pittsburgh.
Development Policies, 1992–1997. City of Pittsburgh.
De Zutter, Hank. "Putting the Community in Community Development." *The Reader,* May 27, 1983.
Dommel, Paul, and Associates, eds. *Decentralizing Urban Policy: Case Studies in Community Development.* Washington, D.C.: Brookings Institution, 1982.
Elkin, Stephen. "Twentieth Century Urban Regimes." *Journal of Urban Affairs* 7, no. 2 (spring 1985): 11–27.
_____. *City and Regime in the American Republic.* Chicago: University of Chicago Press, 1987.
Ely, Joan Fitzgerald. "Economic Transformation in the Pittsburgh PMSA 1979–1986." Paper presented at the Midwest Restructuring Conference, Cleveland, 1988.
Evans, Sara, and Harry Boyte. *Free Spaces: The Sources of Democratic Change in America.* New York: Harper and Row, 1986.
Ferman, Barbara. *Governing the Ungovernable City: Political Skill, Leadership, and the Modern Mayor.* Philadelphia: Temple University Press, 1985.
_____. "Chicago: Power, Race, and Reform." In *Big City Politics in Transition,* edited by H. V. Savitch and J. C. Thomas, 47–63. Newbury Park, Calif.: Sage, 1991.
Ferman, Barbara, and William Grimshaw. "Old Politics, New Politics: Divergence and Convergence Strategies." Paper presented at the annual meeting of the American Political Science Association, Washington, D.C., September 1991.
_____. "The Politics of Housing Policy." In *Politics of Policy Innovation in Chicago,* edited by Kenneth Wong, 103–126. Greenwich, Conn.: JAI Press, 1992.
Fish, John Hall. *Black Power/White Control: The Struggle for the Woodlawn Organization in Chicago.* Princeton, N.J.: Princeton University Press, 1973.
Fisher, Robert. *Let the People Decide: Neighborhood Organizing in America.* Rev. ed. New York: Twayne, 1994.
Fitzgerald, Joan. "Pittsburgh, Pennsylvania: From Steel Town to Advanced Technology Center." In *Economic Restructuring of the American Midwest,* edited by R. Bingham and R. Eberts, 237–254. Norwell, Mass.: Kluwer Academics, 1990.
Florida, Richard, and Robert Gleeson. "Toward a Shared Vision for Pittsburgh and Southwestern Pennsylvania 1992." White Paper. Pittsburgh: Center for Economic Development, John Heinz III School of Public Policy and Management, Carnegie Mellon University, 1993.
Fossler, Scott, and Renee Berger, eds. *Public–Private Partnerships in American Cities: Seven Case Studies.* Lexington, Mass.: D. C. Heath, 1982.
Fremon, David. "Latinos Greatly Overlooked in City Hiring, Says Report." *W. S. Times–Lawndale News,* June 3, 1984.

Fuchs, Ester. *Mayors and Money: Fiscal Policy in New York and Chicago.* Chicago: University of Chicago Press, 1992.
Fuller, Alton. "Powerless Politics: Blacks Evaluate Strategies After Setbacks in City Government." *Pittsburgh Press,* October 27, 1986.
Giarratani, Frank, and David Houston. "Structural Change and Economic Policy in a Declining Metropolitan Region: Implications of the Pittsburgh Experience." *Urban Studies* 26 (1989): 549–558.
Gittell, Ross. *Renewing Cities.* Princeton, N.J.: Princeton University Press, 1992.
Glasco, Laurence. "Double Burden: The Black Experience in Pittsburgh." In *City at the Point,* edited by S. Hays, 69–109. Pittsburgh: University of Pittsburgh Press, 1989.
Goff, Lisa. "Despite Woes, Mayor Firm on Minority Jobs." *Crain's Chicago Business,* March 23, 1987.
Golden, Harry. "Mayor, Foes Finally Agree on Spending of Federal Aid." *Chicago Sun-Times,* July 3, 1985.
Goozner, Merrill. "Genesis of a Fraud: Where the City Failed." *Crain's Chicago Business,* March 25, 1988.
Gottdiener, Marc, and Chris Pickvance, eds. *Urban Life in Transition.* Beverly Hills, Calif.: Sage, 1991.
Gove, Samuel, and Louis Masotti, eds. *After Daley: Chicago Politics in Transition.* Urbana: University of Illinois Press, 1982.
Granger, Bill, and Lori Granger. *Fighting Jane: Mayor Jane Byrne and the Chicago Machine.* New York: Dial Press, 1980.
Gray, John. "Does Democracy Have a Future?" *New York Times Book Review,* January 22, 1995.
Gray, Virginia, and David Lowery. "The Corporatist Foundations of State Industrial Policy." Paper presented at the Midwest Political Science Association Meeting, Chicago, April 1989.
Green, Paul. "The Chicago Political Tradition: A Mayoral Retrospective." In *The Mayors: The Chicago Political Tradition,* edited by P. Green and M. Holli, 212–214. Carbondale and Edwardsville: Southern Illinois University Press, 1987.
———. "Michael A. Bilandic: The Last of the Machine Regulars." In *The Mayors: The Chicago Political Tradition,* edited by P. Green and M. Holli, 164–171. Carbondale and Edwardsville: Southern Illinois University Press, 1987.
Green, Paul, and Melvin Holli, eds. *The Mayors: The Chicago Political Tradition.* Carbondale and Edwardsville: Southern Illinois University Press, 1987.
Greenberg, George, Jeffrey Miller, Lawrence Mohr, and Bruce Vladeck. "Developing Public Policy Theory: Perspectives from Empirical Research." *American Political Science Review* 71 (1977): 1532–1543.
Greenstone, J. David, and Paul Peterson. *Race and Authority in Urban Politics: Community Participation and the War on Poverty.* Chicago: University of Chicago Press, 1976.
Greer, James. "The Politics of Decline and Growth: Planning, Economic Transformation, and the Structuring of Urban Fortunes in American Cities." Ph.D diss., University of Chicago, 1983.
Grimes, Ann. "Community Organizing in Black and White: The New Victims Raise Their Voices." *The Reader,* May 4, 1984.

Grimshaw, William. "The Daley Legacy: A Declining Politics of Party, Race and Unions." In *After Daley: Chicago Politics in Transition,* edited by S. Gove and L. Masotti, 57–87. Urbana: University of Illinois Press, 1982.

———. *Bitter Fruit: Black Politics and the Chicago Machine, 1931–1991.* Chicago: University of Chicago Press, 1992.

Hays, Samuel. *City at the Point.* Pittsburgh: University of Pittsburgh Press, 1989.

Henig, Jeffrey. *Neighborhood Mobilization: Redevelopment and Response.* New Brunswick, N.J.: Rutgers University Press, 1982.

Hirsch, Arnold. *Making the Second Ghetto: Race and Housing in Chicago, 1940–1960.* Cambridge: Cambridge University Press, 1983.

Hoerr, John. *And the Wolf Finally Came: The Decline of the American Steel Industry.* Pittsburgh: University of Pittsburgh Press, 1988.

Holli, Melvin. "Ranking Chicago's Mayors: Mirror, Mirror, on the Wall, Who Is the Greatest of Them All?" In *The Mayors: The Chicago Political Tradition,* edited by P. Green and M. Holli, 202–211. Carbondale and Edwardsville: Southern Illinois University Press, 1987.

Holli, Melvin, and P. Green, eds. *The Making of the Mayor, 1983.* Grand Rapids, Mich.: Erdmans, 1984.

Horan, Cynthia. "Beyond Governing Coalitions: Analyzing Urban Regimes in the 1990s." *Journal of Urban Affairs* 13, no. 2 (1991): 119–136.

Horwitt, Sanford. *Let Them Call Me Rebel: Saul Alinsky, His Life and Legacy.* New York: Vintage, 1992.

Howland, Marie. *Plant Closings and Worker Displacement.* Kalamazoo, Mich.: W. E. Upjohn Institute for Employment Research, 1988.

Hudson, William, Mark Hyde, and John Carroll. "Corporatist Policy Making and State Economic Development." *Polity* 19 (1987): 403–418.

Jezierski, Louise. "Political Limits to Development in Two Declining Cities: Cleveland and Pittsburgh." In *Research in Politics and Society: Deindustrialization and the Economic Restructuring of American Industry,* edited by J. Rothschild and M. Wallace, 173–189. Greenwich, Conn.: JAI Press, 1988.

———. "Neighborhoods and Public–Private Partnerships in Pittsburgh. *Urban Affairs Quarterly* 26, no. 2 (December 1990): 217–249.

Johnston, Paul, and William Holt. "Urban Public Organization as Obstacle to Regime Change: The Case of New Haven." Paper presented at the annaul meeting of the Urban Affairs Association, Portland, Oregon, May 1995.

Jones, Robin. "The CDC Experience of Pittsburgh." Paper presented at the annual meeting of the American Collegiate Schools of Planning. Portland, Oregon, October 1989.

———. "Civic Capacity and Urban Education: Pittsburgh." Report for the Civic Capacity and Urban Education Project. 1995.

Judge, David, Gerry Stoker, and Harold Wolman, eds. *Theories of Urban Politics.* London: Sage, 1995.

Kann, Mark. *Middle Class Radicalism in Santa Monica.* Philadelphia: Temple University Press, 1986.

Katzenstein, Peter. *Small States in World Markets.* Ithaca, N.Y.: Cornell University Press, 1985.

Katznelson, Ira. *City Trenches.* New York: Pantheon, 1981.

Keating, Dennis. "Linking Downtown Development to Broader Community Goals: An Analysis of Linkage Policy in Three Cities." *Journal of the American Planning Association* 52, no. 2 (spring 1986): 133–141.

Key, V. O. *Southern Politics in State and Nation.* New Yorl: Knopf, 1949.

Kleppner, Paul. *Chicago Divided: The Making of a Black Mayor.* DeKalb: Northern Illinois University Press, 1985.

Kling, Joseph, and Prudence Posner. "Class and Community in an Era of Urban Transformation." In *Dilemmas of Activism: Class, Community, and the Politics of Local Mobilization,* edited by Joseph Kling and Prudence Posner, 23–45. Philadelphia: Temple University Press, 1990.

———, eds. *Dilemmas of Activism: Class, Community, and the Politics of Local Mobilization.* Philadelphia: Temple University Press, 1990.

Krasner, Stephen. *International Regimes.* Ithaca, N.Y.: Cornell University Press, 1983.

Kretzman, John. "Opening Up a Closed City." In *Harold Washington and the Neighborhoods,* edited by P. Clavel and W. Wiewel. New Brunswick, N.J.: Rutgers University Press, 1991.

Krumholz, Norman, and Pierre Clavel, eds. *Reinventing Cities: Equity Planners Tell Their Stories.* Philadelphia: Temple University Press, 1994.

Krumholz, Norman, Patrick Costigan, and Dennis Keating. Book review of Chicago Works Together: 1984 Development Plan. *Journal of the American Planning Association* 51, no. 3 (summer 1985): 395–396.

Lehmbruch, Gerhard. "Liberal Corporatism and Party Government." *Comparative Political Studies* 10, no. 1 (April 1977): 91–126.

Lehmbruch, Gerhard, and Philippe Schmitter, eds. *Patterns of Corporatist Policymaking.* London: Sage, 1982.

Lindblom, Charles. "The Market as Prison." *Journal of Politics* 44 (1982): 324–336.

Lipsky, Michael. "Protest as a Political Resource." *American Political Science Review* 62 (December 1968): 1144–1158.

Local Community Fact Book Chicago Metropolitan Area. Chicago: Chicago Fact Book Consortium c/o Department of Sociology, University of Illinois, 1980.

Logan, John, and Harvey Molotch. *Urban Fortunes.* Berkeley and Los Angeles: University of California Press, 1987.

Logan, John, and Todd Swanstrom, eds. *Beyond the City Limits: Urban Policy and Economic Restructuring in Comparative Perspective.* Philadelphia: Temple University Press, 1990.

Longworth, R. C. "It's Still Not Certain Who'll Pay for Fair." *Chicago Tribune,* May 9, 1983, 1.

Lowe, Jeanne. *Cities in a Race with Time: Progress and Poverty in America's Renewing Cities.* New York: Random House, 1967.

Lowry, James H., and Associates. Study of Minority and Women Owned Business Enterprise Procurement Programs for the City of Chicago, 1985.

Lubove, Roy. *Twentieth-Century Pittsburgh.* New York: Wiley, 1969.

———. ed. *Pittsburgh.* New York: New Viewpoints, 1976.

Lurcott, Robert, and Jane Downing. "A Public–Private Support System for Community-Based Organizations in Pittsburgh." *Journal of the American Planning Association* 53, no. 4 (autumn 1987): 459–468.

Lynd, Staughton. "The Genesis of the Idea of a Community Right to Industrial Property

in Youngstown and Pittsburgh, 1977–1987." *Journal of American History* 74, no. 3 (December 1987): 926–957.
Lyons, Arthur, Spenser Staton, and Dianne Kallenback. "When Everything Works and Nothing Is Right." Chicago 1992 Committee: Institute on Taxation and Economic Policy, 1986.
McCarron, John. "Is Chicago Ready for Reform?" *Planning,* September 1984.
―――. "Streets Resurface in Council Warfare." *Chicago Tribune,* May 16, 1985.
McCullom, Rod. "Home Equity Proposal Fuels Racial Tensions as White Neighborhoods Struggle for Stability." *Chicago Reporter,* May 1988.
Marciniak, Ed. *Reviving an Inner City Community.* Chicago: Discourses, Loyola University Department of Political Science, 1977.
Mayfield, Loomis. "The Decline of Chicago and the Rise of the 'Growth Machine': The Reorganization of Urban Politics." Paper presented to the Duquesne University History Forum, Pittsburgh, October 23, 1992.
Merton, Robert. *Social Theory and Social Structure.* New York: Free Press, 1957.
Mier, Robert, and Joan Fitzgerald. "Managing Economic Development." Book review essay. *Economic Development Quarterly* 5, no. 3 (August 1991): 268–279.
National Congress for Community Economic Development. "Against All Odds: The Achievements of Community-Based Development Organizations." March 1989.
Neighborhoods Speak. Newsletter of the Pittsburgh Neighborhood Alliance. February 1980.
Nyden, Philip, and Wim Wiewel, eds. *Challenging Uneven Development: An Urban Agenda for the 1990s.* New Brunswick, N.J.: Rutgers University Press, 1991.
O'Connor, Edwin. *The Last Hurrah.* Boston: Little, Brown, 1985.
O'Connor, Len. *Clout: Mayor Daley and His City.* Chicago: Henry Regnery Company, 1975.
Oppenheim, Carol. "City to Cut Neighborhood Share of Community Aid." *Chicago Tribune,* May 15, 1984.
Page, Clarence. "Block Grants and Blockages." *Chicago Tribune,* editorial, June 9, 1985.
Panitch, Leo. "The Development of Corporatism in Liberal Democracies." *Comparative Political Studies* 10, no. 1 (April 1977): 61–90.
Peterson, Paul. *City Limits.* Chicago: University of Chicago Press, 1981.
Pittsburgh Partnership for Neighborhood Development. Annual Report, 1993.
Plotkin, Sidney. "Enclave Consciousness and Neighborhood Activism," In *Dilemmas of Activism: Class, Community, and the Politics of Local Mobilization,* edited by Joseph Kling and Prudence Posner, 218–239. Philadelphia: Temple University Press, 1990.
Plotkin, Sidney, and William Scheuerman. "Two Roads Left: Strategies of Resistance to Plant Closings in the Monongahela Valley." In *Dilemmas of Activism: Class, Community, and the Politics of Local Mobilization,* edited by J. Kling and P. Posner, 193–217. Philadelphia: Temple University Press, 1990.
Pogge, Jean. "Reinvestment in Chicago Neighborhoods: A Twenty-Year Struggle." In *From Redlining to Reinvestment: Community Responses to Urban Disinvestment,* edited by Gregory Squires. Philadelphia: Temple University Press, 1992.
Pogge, Jean, and David Flax-Hatch. "The Invisible Lenders: The Role of Residential Credit in Community Economies." In *Challenging Uneven Development: An Urban Agenda for the 1990s,* edited by P. Nyden and W. Wiewel, 85–112. New Brunswick, N.J.: Rutgers University Press, 1991.

Portz, John. *The Politics of Plant Closings.* Lawrence: University Press of Kansas, 1990.
Powell, Walter, and Paul DiMaggio, eds. *The New Institutionalism in Organizational Analysis.* Chicago: University of Chicago Press, 1991.
Preston, Michael. "Black Politics in the Post-Daley Era." In *After Daley: Chicago Politics in Transition,* edited by S. Gove and L. Masotti, 88–117. Urbana: University of Illinois Press, 1982.
———. "The Resurgence of Black Voting in Chicago: 1955–1983." In *The Making of the Mayor, 1983,* edited by M. Holli and P. Green, 39–52. Grand Rapids, Mich.: Wm. B. Erdmans, 1984.
Protess, David. "Banfield's Chicago Revisited: The Conditions for and Social Policy Implications of the Transformation of a Political Machine." *Social Science Review* 48 (June 1974): 184–202.
Putnam, Robert. *Making Democracy Work: Civic Traditions in Modern Italy.* Princeton, N.J.: Princeton University Press, 1993.
Rakove, Milton. *Don't Make No Waves, Don't Back No Losers: An Insider's Analysis of the Daley Machine.* Bloomington: Indiana University Press, 1975.
Ranney, David, and Patricia Wright. "Employment Impacts of City of Chicago Purchasing Contracts." Chicago: Center for Urban Economic Development, University of Illinois-Chicago, March 1989.
Reardon, Kenneth. "Local Economic Development in Chicago, 1983–1987: The Reform Efforts of Mayor Harold Washington." Ph.D diss., Cornell University, 1990.
Rich, Michael. "Community Politics and the New Federalism: Implementation of the Community Development Block Grant Program in Chicago." Paper presented at the annual meeting of the American Political Science Association, Chicago, 1987.
Rivlin, Gary. "City Hall: Understanding the Community Development Squabble." *The Reader,* June 28, 1985.
———. "City Hall: How Low They Can Go." *The Reader,* July 26, 1991.
———. *Fire on the Prairie: Harold Washington and the Politics of Race.* New York: Henry Holt and Company, 1992.
Rosen, George. *Decisionmaking Chicago Style: The Genesis of a University of Illinois Campus.* Urbana: University of Illinois Press, 1980.
Rothschild, Joyce, and Michael Wallace, eds. *Research in Politics and Society: Deindustrialization and the Economic Restructuring of American Industry.* Greenwich, Conn.: JAI Press, 1988.
Royko, Mike. *Boss: Richard J. Daley of Chicago.* New York: Signet, 1971.
Rubinowitz, Leonard. "Chicago, Illinois." In *Decentralizing Urban Policy: Case Studies in Community Development,* edited by P. Dommel and Associates, 120–165. Washington, D.C.: Brookings Institution, 1982.
Russo, John, and Brian Corbin. "A System of Interpretation: Catholic Social Teaching and American Unionism." *Conflict* 11 (October–December 1991): 237–266.
Salisbury, Robert. "Why No Corporatism in America?" In *Trends in Interest Intermediation,* edited by P. Schmitter and G. Lehmbruch, 213–230. Beverly Hills, Calif.: Sage, 1979.
Savitch, Hank, and John Clayton Thomas, eds. *Big City Politics in Transition.* Newbury Park, Calif.: Sage, 1991.
Sayre, Wallace, and Herbert Kaufman. *Governing New York City: Politics in the Metropolis.* New York: Norton, 1965.
Sbragia, Alberta. "The Pittsburgh Model of Economic Development: Partnership, Re-

sponsiveness, and Indifference." In *Unequal Partnerships,* edited by Gregory Squires, 103–120. New Brunswick, N.J.: Rutgers University Press, 1989.
Schattschneider, E. E. *The Semisovereign People: A Realist's View of Democracy in America.* Hinsdale, Ill.: Dryden Press, 1960.
Schmitter, Philippe. "Still the Century of Corporatism?" *Review of Politics* 36 (1974) 85–131.
_____. "Modes of Intermediation and Models of Societal Change in Western Europe." *Comparative Political Studies* 10, no. 1 (1977): 7–38.
Schmitter, Phillippe, and George Lehmbruch, eds. *Trends in Interest Intermediation.* Beverly Hills, Calif.: Sage, 1979.
Slayton, Robert. *Back of the Yards: The Making of a Local Democracy.* Chicago: University of Chicago Press, 1986.
Squires, Gregory, ed. *Unequal Partnerships.* New Brunswick, N.J.: Rutgers University Press, 1989.
_____. ed. *From Redlining to Reinvestment: Community Responses to Urban Disinvestment.* Philadelphia: Temple University Press, 1992.
Squires, Gregory, Larry Bennett, Kathleen McCourt, and Philip Nyden. *Chicago: Race, Class, and the Response to Urban Decline.* Philadelphia: Temple University Press, 1987.
Stevens, Donald, Jr. "The Role of Nonprofit Corporations in Urban Development: A Case Study of ACTION-Housing, Inc., of Pittsburgh." Ph.D diss., Carnegie-Mellon University, 1987.
Stewman, Shelby, and Joel Tarr. "Four Decades of Public–Private Partnerships in Pittsburgh." In *Public–Private Partnerships in American Cities: Seven Case Studies,* edited by R. S. Fossler and R. A. Berger. Lexington, Mass.: D. C. Heath, 1982.
Stone, Clarence. *Regime Politics: Governing Atlanta, 1946–1988.* Lawrence: University Press of Kansas, 1989.
_____. "Urban Regimes and the Capacity to Govern: A Political Economy Approach." *Journal of Urban Affairs* 15, no. 1 (1993): 1–28.
Stone, Clarence, David Imbroscio, and Marion Orr. "The Reshaping of Urban Leadership in U.S. Cities: A Regime Analysis." In *Urban Life in Transition,* edited by M. Gottdiener and C. Pickvance, 222–239. Beverly Hills, Calif.: Sage, 1991.
Strong, James. "Majority Bloc Shifts Funds to Its Members' Wards." *Chicago Tribune,* May 29, 1985.
Swanstrom, Todd. *The Crisis of Growth Politics: Cleveland, Kucinich, and the Challenge of Urban Populism.* Philadelphia: Temple University Press, 1985.
_____. "Urban Populism, Uneven Development and the Space for Reform." In *Business Elites and Urban Development,* edited by Scott Cummings. Albany: State University of New York Press, 1988.
Teaford, Jon. *The Twentieth-Century American City: Problem, Promise, and Reality.* Baltimore, Md.: Johns Hopkins University Press, 1986.
Torres, Maria de los Angeles. "The Commission on Latino Affairs: A Case Study of Community Empowerment." In *Harold Washington and the Neighborhoods: Progressive City Government in Chicago, 1983–1987,* edited by P. Clavel and W. Wiewel. New Brunswick, N.J.: Rutgers University Press, 1991.
Tri-State Conference on Steel. "A Community Plan to Save Pittsburgh's Steel Industry." Pittsburgh, n.d.

Weber, Michael. *Don't Call Me Boss: David L. Lawrence, Pittsburgh's Renaissance Mayor.* Pittsburgh: University of Pittsburgh Press, 1988.

Weiss, Marc, and John Metzger. "Planning for Chicago: The Changing Politics of Metropolitan Growth and Neighborhood Development." In *Atop the Urban Hierarchy,* edited by R. Beauregard, 123–151. Totowa, N.J.: Rowan and Littlefield, 1989.

Wiewel, Wim, and Nicholas Rieser. "The Limits of Progressive Municipal Economic Development: Job Creation in Chicago, 1983–1987. *Community Development Journal* 24, no. 2 (1989): 111–119.

Wilson, Graham. "Why is There No Corporatism in the United States?" In *Patterns of Corporatist Policymaking,* edited by G. Lehmbruch and P. Schmitter. London: Sage, 1982.

Wolman, Harold. "Local Government Institutions and Democratic Governance." In *Theories of Urban Politics,* edited by David Judge, Gerry Stoker, and Harold Wolman. London: Sage, 1995.

Wong, Kenneth. *Politics of Policy Innovation in Chicago.* Greenwich, Conn.: JAI Press, 1992.

Ziemba, Stanley. "U.S. Agency Bars Byrne's Use of Funds." *Chicago Tribune.* April 9, 1983.

Index

ACCBO. *See* Advisory Committee on Community-Based Organizations
ACCD. *See* Allegheny Conference on Community Development
ACTION-Housing, Inc. (Pittsburgh), 38, 40, 74–82, 83, 87, 109
Advisory Committee on Community-Based Organizations (ACCBO) (Pittsburgh), 101
Affirmative action, 115, 121, 122, 147, 150, 169(n20)
Affirmative Neighborhood Information Program (Chicago), 119
African Americans, 20–21, 22, 23, 40–42. *See also under* Chicago; Pittsburgh
AHRCO. *See* Allegheny Housing Rehabilitation Corporation
Alberts, Robert, 52
Alcoa (firm), 45
Alinsky, Saul, 13, 66–67, 70, 71, 72–73, 74, 142, 148
Allegheny Conference on Community Development (ACCD) (1943), 31, 38, 39, 40, 46–47, 48, 50, 52, 53–54, 75, 76, 77, 78, 82, 86, 94, 95, 100, 101, 125, 127, 131, 132, 133, 138, 165(n31)
Allegheny County Sanitation Authority, 49
Allegheny Housing Rehabilitation Corporation (AHRCO), 82
American Standard Corporation, 130
Arenas. *See under* Institutional framework
Arvey, Jake, 68
Asians, 20, 21
Atlanta, 42, 113

Bach, Ira, 62
Back of the Yards Neighborhood Council (BYNC) (Chicago), 70–71, 74

Banfield, Edward, 57, 142
Barr, Joseph, 37(table), 38, 78, 87, 88
Bauler, Paddy, 90
Bickerdike Redevelopment Corporation, 74
Biesczat, Matthew, 73
Bilandic, Michael, 34, 35, 89, 98, 119, 163(n12)
Blighted Areas Act (Ill.) (1947), 56, 57, 61
Bloom, Larry, 104, 105
Boston (Mass.), 2, 14, 144
Bottom-up strategy, 132
Boyte, Harry, 12, 13
Brophy, Paul, 94
Browning, Rufus, 150, 152
Bryce, James, 152
Burke, Edward, 91, 106, 107, 163(n12)
Burnham, Daniel, 55, 59, 90
Burnham Plan (1909) (Chicago), 55–56
Bush, George, 14, 148
Business arena, xi, 152
Business community, 8, 11(fig.), 65, 146. *See also under* Chicago; Pittsburgh
BYNC. *See* Back of the Yards Neighborhood Council
Byrne, Jane, 34, 35, 86, 96, 108, 118
 administration (1979–1983), 88–92, 93, 103, 105, 107, 110, 121, 150, 163–164(n13)
 and development, 90, 120
 and minorities, 115–116, 117(table)
 and neighborhoods, 88–89, 90, 91, 93, 104, 107, 110, 167(n74)

Caliguiri, Richard, 18, 37(table), 38, 39, 40, 93
 administration (1977–1988), 94–95, 109
 and neighborhoods, 94, 99, 100, 103
 and steel industry, 127

185

186   INDEX

Campaign Against Pollution. *See* Citizen's Action Program
CAP. *See* Citizen's Action Program
Capital Improvement Plan (CIP) (Chicago), 120
Capital Improvements Advisory Committee (CIAC) (Chicago), 166(n52)
Carbone, Nicholas, 2
Carter, Marlene, 108
CBD. *See* Central Business District
CBO Fund (Pittsburgh), 100, 101
CBOs. *See* Community-based organizations
CCAC. *See* Chicago Central Area Committee
CDAC. *See* Community Development Advisory Committee
CDBG. *See* Community Development Block Grant
CDCs. *See* Community development corporations
Central Business District (CBD), 11(fig.). *See also* Downtown
Cermak, Anton, 58, 160(n38)
CHA. *See* Chicago Housing Authority
CHAS. *See* Comprehensive Housing Affordability Strategy
Chicago
  African Americans, 20, 21–22, 23, 26–27(fig.), 33, 34, 35, 55, 57, 61–63, 71–72, 75, 84, 89, 90, 92, 95, 96, 108, 114, 115–116, 117, 122, 150
  age, median, 21(table), 30
  air pollution, 73
  Asians, 20, 21
  blizzard (1978–1979), 35
  business community, 54–55, 58, 59, 60, 61, 97, 113, 114, 117
  CBOs, ix, x, xi, 1, 16, 17, 18, 32, 36, 66, 67, 71, 72–74, 84, 105, 119, 120, 140, 170(n34)
  city council, 33–34, 35, 58, 59, 68, 74, 91–92, 97, 103, 104, 105, 106, 107, 115, 119, 138, 150, 170(n32)
  civic beautification (1909–1930), 55–56
  Department of City Planning, 60, 89
  Department of Economic Development, 105, 170(n34)
  Department of Housing, 5, 34, 41, 62, 89, 105 (*see also* Chicago Housing Authority)
  Department of Neighborhoods, 89, 119
  Department of Purchasing, 114
  Department of Public Works, 114
  Department of Urban Renewal (DUR), 72, 73
  development, 16, 19, 28, 29, 31, 32, 54, 55, 56–63, 69–70, 114, 120, 138
  Development Plan (1958), 59–60, 61, 67
  Development Plan (1984), 111, 112–113, 117, 146
  Development Plan (1987), 119–123
  downtown, 1, 28–29, 33, 57, 58, 60–61, 67, 68, 90, 95, 120, 138
  economy, 28, 30, 54
  education, 21, 22, 28, 71–72, 156(n5)
  electoral arena, xi, 5, 23, 32, 34, 37, 42, 44, 54, 84, 92, 137, 139
  elites, 16, 20, 23, 35, 36, 43, 44, 55, 57, 61, 96, 137
  ethnic groups, 28, 31, 91
  expenditures, 113–114, 120, 168(n5)
  and federal programs, 38, 98, 103, 104–106, 114, 121, 125, 167(n71)
  governing regime, 1, 16, 17, 22–23, 28, 33, 34, 44, 54, 58, 66, 67, 89, 91, 137, 139, 145
  growth machine, 1, 29, 32, 44, 54, 55, 66, 69, 98
  Hispanics, 20, 21, 90, 96, 164(n21)
  home equity proposal, 108–109
  housing, 21, 22, 41, 56, 57, 62–63, 66, 71, 74, 90, 104, 120, 155(n1)
  income, 21(table)
  infrastructure, 59, 73
  institutional framework, 42, 54, 61, 67, 84, 112, 115, 121–122, 138, 139, 140
  Loop, 57, 59, 60, 61, 161(n42)
  machine politics, 19, 32–33, 34, 35, 36–37, 43, 54, 58, 60, 63, 67, 70, 73, 84, 88, 89, 90, 91, 93, 95, 97, 103, 109, 118, 138, 142
  manufacturing jobs, 19, 28, 54, 55–56
  mayors, 17, 37(table), 58, 63 (*see also* individual names)
  neighborhoods, 22, 26–27(fig.), 28, 29, 30, 34, 36–37, 43, 66–75, 88–89, 90, 95, 103–110, 120, 141, 147
  neighborhoods, funding, 99, 104, 106–107, 166(nn52&63), 170(n36)
  Parks Department, 98
  political culture, 20, 112, 115, 122, 140, 141, 142
  politically oriented research, ix–x
  population, 20, 21, 26–27(fig.), 28, 57
  poverty, 21(table), 29
  progressivism, 143, 147, 150, 151 (*see also* Washington, Harold)
  race issue, 15, 16, 20, 21–22, 23, 28, 33, 34–35, 37, 61–63, 64, 72, 84, 85, 90, 92, 95, 96, 105, 106, 107–109, 143, 149–50, 167(n82)
  railroads, 68
  real estate, 29, 31, 58
  and reform, 90, 121–123, 141

INDEX   187

school board, 34, 92
service economy, 19, 28, 29
and social control, 28, 137, 138(table)
stability, 16
taxes, 107
tourism, 29
transit authority, 35
unemployment, 21(table), 29, 30
urban renewal, 57, 62, 66, 68, 69, 98
wards, 23, 36, 42, 67, 68, 73, 82, 84, 90–91, 92, 103–104, 106–107
see also Chicago and Pittsburgh
Chicago and Pittsburgh
differences, 20, 21, 22–23, 28, 38, 63, 82, 83–84, 109, 123, 137–142, 143
similarities, 19, 28
Chicago Association of Neighborhood Development Organizations, 36
Chicago Central Area Committee (CCAC), 58, 59
Chicago First, 117–118, 120
Chicago Housing Authority (CHA), 34, 61–62, 63, 90, 92
Chicago Municipal Depository Ordinance (1974), 74
Chicago Park District, 68
Chicago Rehab Network, 36
Chicago Title and Trust Company, 56
Chicago Tribune, 104, 118
Chicago Works Together (CWT). *See* Chicago, Development Plan (1984); Chicago, Development Plan (1987)
CIAC. *See* Capital Improvements Advisory Committee
CIP. *See* Capital Improvement Plan
Citizen Participation Conference (1969) (Pittsburgh), 94
Citizen's Action Program (CAP) (Chicago), 73–74
"City limits" theory, 9
Civic arena, xi, 5, 11(fig.), 152. *See also under* Pittsburgh
Civic attachment, 8, 9, 10, 140(table)
Civil rights, 23, 72, 147
Clark, Terry, 89
Clarke, Susan, 144
Class issues, 14, 23, 95, 142, 147
Clavel, Pierre, 121, 144
Cleveland (Ohio), 2, 15, 99, 144
Clinton, Bill, 148
Coalitions. *See* Governing regime, coalitional needs; Regime theory, accommodation and cooperation; Washington, Harold, coalition
Commercial Club (Chicago), 55, 56
Community Action Board (Pittsburgh), 38

Community-based organizations (CBOs), ix, x, 1, 12, 13, 14, 145, 148, 152. *See also under* Chicago; Pittsburgh
Community Development Advisory Committee (CDAC) (Chicago), 89, 104, 119
Community Development Block Grant (CDBG), 12, 88, 89, 90–91, 97–98, 99, 100, 101, 102, 104–105, 106, 119, 121
Community development corporations (CDCs), 40, 41, 74, 95, 99, 144, 148. *See also under* Chicago; Mon Valley; Pittsburgh
Community Outreach Partnership Center (COPC), 12
Community Planning Program (Pittsburgh), 87
Community Reinvestment Act (CRA) (1977), 12, 74
Community Technical Assistance Center (Pittsburgh), 94
Comparative analysis, xi–xii, 7, 10, 11(fig.)
Comprehensive Housing Affordability Strategy (CHAS), 12, 155(n29)
Consensual politics, 126, 132, 140. *See also* Pittsburgh, CDCs
Consolidation Coal (firm), 51
Contract set-asides, 114, 115, 122, 148, 150
COPC. *See* Community Outreach Partnership Center
Corporate culture, 31–32
Corporatism, 46, 93, 94, 98, 109, 124, 132, 138, 139, 158–159(n1)
challenge to (*see* Steel Valley Authority)
and progressive politics, 144, 145
CRA. *See* Community Reinvestment Act
Cunningham, James, 81
CWT (Chicago Works Together). *See* Chicago, Development Plan (1984); Chicago, Development Plan (1987)

Daily News (Chicago), 73
Daley, Richard J., x, 5, 20, 22, 32, 33, 59, 60, 74, 167(n71)
administration (1955–1976), 33–35, 36, 58, 92, 138, 156–157(n22)
and African Americans, 34–35, 157(n24)
death (1976), 33
and development, 54, 55, 58, 60, 62, 67, 68, 146
son (*see* Daley, Richard M.)
Daley, Richard M., 35, 37(table), 91, 96, 116, 163(n12), 166(n52)
Daniels, John, 111
Daniels, Mary Lou, 94
D'Arco, John, 68
Dawson, "Boss," 72
Decision making, xi, 6, 7, 8(table), 42, 138(table), 139

INDEX

DeLeon, Richard, 2, 14, 142–143, 147
Democratic Party, 33, 34, 38, 46, 47, 70, 86, 96
Democratic political systems, 8, 15, 152
Denomination Ministry Strategy (DMS), 127
Development, 2, 3, 16, 32, 85, 148, 149
　community, 2, 11(fig.), 16 (*see also* Neighborhoods)
　See also under Chicago; Pittsburgh
Disinvestment, 28, 31, 125, 127
DMS. *See* Denomination Ministry Strategy
Dorothy Six (blast furnace), 127, 128
Downtown, 12, 13, 15, 65, 162(n25). *See also under* Chicago; Pittsburgh
Dual-state structure, 39, 42
Duquesne (Pa.), 125, 127, 129, 172(n23)
DUR. *See* Chicago, Department of Urban Renewal

Economic elite, 3, 6, 11, 19, 131, 137. *See also* Chicago, elites; Pittsburgh, elites
Economy, 2, 132. *See also under* Chicago; Pittsburgh
Electoral arena, xi, 5, 6, 11(fig.), 144, 151, 152, 154(n14). *See also under* Chicago
Elkin, Stephen, 7, 63–64, 153(n3)
Eminent domain, 52, 56, 61, 69, 125, 129, 130, 131, 132
Empowerment Zones, 12, 148
Enclave consciousness, 13, 14, 133, 151
Environmental concerns, 14, 45, 50, 51, 73, 75
Epton, Bernard, 96
Equitable Life Assurance Society (firm), 51
Ethnic groups, 23, 28, 31, 91
Evans, Sara, 12
Exclusivity, 1, 3, 13

Federal aid, 14, 38, 63, 79, 98, 100, 148. *See also* Chicago, and federal programs; Pittsburgh, and federal programs
Federal Housing Administration (FHA), 79, 82, 120
Federalist structure, 2, 11(fig.)
Ferguson, Lorna, 87
FHA. *See* Federal Housing Administration
Field, Marshall, III, 71
Field Foundation, 71
Field Museum of Natural History (Chicago), 56
Fish, John Hall, 72
Fisher, Robert, 124–125, 148
Flaherty, Peter, 18, 37(table), 38–39, 40
　administration (1969–1977), 86, 90, 92–93, 98, 109
　and neighborhoods, 86–88, 92, 93, 99, 100
　and party-government distinction, 87–88

Flynn, Ray, 144
Foerster, Thomas, 94
Ford Foundation, 100
Freedom of Information Act (Chicago), 118–119, 139
Free spaces, 12–13
Front companies, 114–115
Frost, William, 35

Gateway Center (Pittsburgh), 50–51, 52, 159–160(n25)
Gautreaux v. CHA (1969), 63
Gentrification, 31, 60
Globalism, 2, 11(fig.), 148
Governing regime
　arenas, 5–6, 7(table), 154(n15)
　coalitional needs, 4, 6, 15, 136, 151
　and neighborhoods, 3, 6, 11(fig.), 13, 15, 18
　and policy, 6–7, 11(fig.), 12, 146–147
　power, 5, 6, 11(fig.), 138, 139
　prior, 111
　pro-growth, 16
　typology, 136
　see also under Chicago; Pittsburgh
Gray, John, 8, 9
Great Depression (1930s), 56, 57
Green, Paul, 142
Greer, James, 57
Grimshaw, William, 122
Growth machine, xi, xii, 1, 2, 12, 15, 17–18. *See also under* Chicago; Pittsburgh
Gulf Oil (firm), 31, 142

Hartford, (Conn.), 2, 144
Heinz, John, 127
Henig, Jeffrey, 10
HILP. *See* Housing Improvement Loan Program
Hinz, Greg, 89
Hispanics, 20, 21. *See also under* Chicago; Pittsburgh
HMDA. *See* Home Mortgage Disclosure Act
Holt, William, 111
Home Mortgage Disclosure Act (HMDA) (1975), 74
Horan, Cynthia, 83
Horn, Stanley, 41
Housing, 5, 12, 23. *See also under* Chicago; Pittsburgh
Housing Act (1954), 56
Housing and Redevelopment Act (1945) (Pa.), 51–52, 104, 105, 106
Housing and Urban Development, Department of (HUD), 105, 155(n29)
Housing Improvement Loan Program (HILP) (Pittsburgh), 94

Hoyt, Homer, 56, 61, 160(n33)
HUD. *See* Housing and Urban Development, Department of

IAF. *See* Industrial Areas Foundation
Inclusivity, 3, 122, 140
Individualism, 8, 10, 151
Industrial Areas Foundation (IAF), 70, 71, 148
Institutional framework, xi, 4, 6, 9, 15, 63–64, 135, 151, 153(nn3&4)
  arenas, 4–5, 6, 7, 136, 139, 148, 152 (*see also* Business arena; Civic arena; Electoral arena; Intergovernmental arena)
  defined, 7
  formalization, 7, 8(table), 138–139
  orientation, 7, 8(table), 137–38
Interest groups, 144. *See also* Community-based organizations
Intergovernmental arena, xi, 152
Italy, 9

Jackson, Jesse, 128
Jackson, Maynard, 113
J & L. *See* Jones and Laughlin project
Jezierski, Louise, 39, 93, 99, 102
Johnson, Hiram, 143
Johnston, Paul, 111
Jones & Laughlin (J & L) project (Pittsburgh), 52–53, 77, 126

Katznelson, Ira, 13, 174(n18)
Kaufmann, Edgar, 76
Kaufmann Foundation, 76
Keating, Dennis, 12
Kelly, Edward, 58, 63
Kennelly, Martin, 58
Key, V. O., 37
King, Martin Luther, Jr., 35, 79
King, Robert, 76
Kramer, Fred, 56
Kretzman, John, 118
Krumholz, Norman, 112
Kucinich, Dennis, 2, 15, 144

Land Clearance Commission (LCC) (Chicago), 57, 61, 62
Lawrence, David Leo, 32, 33, 37(table), 38, 47, 48, 153(n33)
  economic restructuring, 44, 45, 48, 49, 50, 52, 76, 77, 78, 159(n13)
  and party-government distinction, 38, 47, 48, 49, 50
LCC. *See* Land Clearance Commission
Lindblom, Charles, 8
Lipsky, Michael, 133

LISC. *See* Local Initiatives Support Corporation
Local Initiatives Support Corporation (LISC), 100
Localism, 15, 148, 149
Logan, John, 85
Los Angeles (Calif.), 20
Loshbough, Bernard, 80, 81, 82
Lowe, Jeanne, 53
Lowi, Theodore, 6
Lowry Report (1985), 113–114
LTV Corporation, 126, 130–131
Lubove, Roy, 78, 81

Machine politics, ix, 19. *See also under* Chicago; Pittsburgh
MACLA. *See* Mayor's Advisory Committee on Latino Affairs
McNair, William, 47
Madigan, Michael, 109
MAHA. *See* Metropolitan Area Housing Alliance
Manpower Demonstration and Training Act (1962), 38
Marshall, Dale Rogers, 150, 152
Marshall Field (firm), 56
Marsh and McClennan (firm), 71
Martin, Edward, 47
Maryland, 115
Masloff, Sophie, 18, 37(table), 99
Mayor's Advisory Committee on Latino Affairs (MACLA) (Chicago), 117, 122, 171(n44)
Mayor's Committee for Economic and Cultural Development (MCECD) (Chicago), 60
Mayor's Office of Employment and Training (MET) (Chicago), 118
MBE. *See* Minority business enterprise
MCECD. *See* Mayor's Committee for Economic and Cultural Development
Meatpacking industry, 54
Mell, Richard, 103, 106
Mellon, Andrew, 46
Mellon, Richard King, 31, 44, 45, 46, 47, 49, 51, 52, 53, 76, 78, 142, 151
Mellon Bank and Trust Company, 31, 38, 46, 100, 126, 127, 142, 171(n6)
Mencken, H. L., 50
MET. *See* Mayor's Office of Employment and Training
Metcalfe, Ralph, 33
Metropolitan Area Housing Alliance (MAHA) (Chicago), 73–74
Metropolitan Housing and Planning Council (MHPC) (Chicago), 56

MHPC. *See* Metropolitan Housing and Planning Council
Minority business enterprise (MBE), 113, 114
Model Cities program, 63, 98
Molotch, Harvey, 85
Montgomery, James, 113
Mon Valley (Pa.), 125, 126–128
 CDCs, 133, 150, 173(n35)
Mortgage Banker Act (Ill.), 74
Mumford, Milton, 56, 62
Municipalities Authorities Act (1945), 129
Murphy, Tom, 18, 37(table), 99, 165(n49)

Nash, Patrick, 58
National People's Action (NPA), 74
NCO. *See* Northwest Community Organization
Neighborhood Fund, Inc. (Pittsburgh), 100, 101
Neighborhoods, x, xii, 1, 12–13, 14, 65, 152
 mobilization, 10, 11(fig.), 16, 18, 36–37, 40, 107, 139–140, 141–142, 148, 149, 174(n18)
 see also under Chicago; Pittsburgh
New Haven (Conn.), 111
New York City, 13
New York Life Insurance Company, 57
Nixon, Richard, 97–98
Northwest Community Organization, 72–74
NPA. *See* National People's Action

Patronage, 5, 32, 39, 58, 89, 90, 98, 104, 140
Pease, Robert, 31
Pennsylvania Railroad, 51
Peterson, Paul, 6
Pettibone, Holman, 56, 58, 62
Philadelphia (Pa.), 15, 115, 130
Philips, Sandra, 103
Pittsburgh (Pa.)
 African Americans, 20–21, 22, 23, 24–25(fig.), 40–42, 76, 77, 79, 92
 age, median, 21(table), 30
 antipoverty program, 81
 Asians, 20, 21(table)
 business community, 38, 40, 45, 47, 53, 75, 90, 94, 99, 124–125, 133
 CBOs, ix, x, 1, 16, 18, 40, 43, 66, 75, 76, 77, 80, 83, 94, 95, 99, 100, 124, 140
 CDCs, 40, 41, 99, 100, 102, 109, 124–125, 126, 140, 141, 147
 chamber of commerce, 41
 city council, 38, 41, 48, 49, 92, 101, 109
 civic arena, xi, 5, 20, 23, 33, 38, 41, 42, 43, 44, 50, 83, 88, 101–102, 110, 134, 137, 138 (*see also* Corporatism)
 Department of City Planning, 40, 87, 94, 98, 100, 101, 124

Department of Housing, 94
development, 16, 19, 31, 39, 44–53, 90, 99, 138
district councils, 102
downtown, 46, 51, 52, 77, 138
economy, 28, 30, 44–49, 125, 126
education, 21(table), 22, 23, 38
elites, 16, 19, 23, 38, 43, 44, 49, 109, 137
environmental problems, 45, 50, 51, 75
and federal programs, 38, 100
Golden Triangle, 52, 57, 77, 162(n25)
governing regime, 16, 17, 28, 38, 44, 45, 48–49, 66, 83, 86–88, 91, 137, 139, 143, 145 (*see also* Social production)
growth machine, 44, 45, 49–53, 132
Hispanics, 20, 21(table)
housing, 5, 40, 41, 75–82, 94, 102
income, 21(table), 29, 126
infrastructure, 45
institutional framework, 19, 33, 42, 43, 45, 49, 53–54, 109, 137–138, 139, 143
machine politics, 19, 32, 33, 37–39, 40, 86, 90
manufacturing jobs, 19, 28, 37–38, 47, 50
mayors, 18, 32, 37–38, 47, 50 (*see also individual names*)
neighborhoods, 19, 22, 24–25(fig.), 39, 40–42, 43, 66, 75, 77, 78–80, 86–88, 90, 94–95, 99–103, 109, 139, 140, 141, 143, 149, 150–151, 158(n44)
neighborhoods, funding, 99, 100–101, 102, 124, 166(n63)
party politics, 46, 47–48, 86
and policy-oriented research, ix
political culture, 20, 43, 140–141
population, 19, 20, 21(table), 24–25(fig.), 28, 30
progressivism, 17, 124, 134, 143, 148, 151
race issue, 22, 40, 42, 79, 109
ranking as most livable city, 29
reform, ix, 37, 48, 153(n1)
renaissance, ix, 50, 52, 94, 132
Renaissance I, 46, 47 52–53, 94
service economy, 19, 29, 30
stability, 16, 20
taxes, 87
unemployment, 21(table), 30–31, 125, 126–127
universities, 125, 171(n4)
Urban Redevelopment Authority (URA) (1946), 40, 49, 52, 76, 77, 87, 94, 95, 98, 99–100, 101, 124, 138
urban renewal, 18, 39–40, 66, 75, 76, 80
wards, 23, 41, 82, 95, 109
see also Chicago and Pittsburgh
Pittsburgh National Bank, 38

Pittsburgh Partnership for Neighborhood
  Development (PPND) (1988), 1, 40, 99,
  100, 101, 102–103, 109, 124
Pittsburgh Plate and Glass (firm), 31
Pittsburgh Regional Planning Association
  (PRPA), 76
Planning policy, 3, 55, 60, 146, 152
Plotkin, Sidney, 13, 133
Policy development, 2, 3–4, 6–7, 11(fig.), 12,
  15
Political culture, xi, 4, 6, 7, 9–10, 11(fig.), 15,
  133, 135, 140–142
  defined, 8
Political economy, 2, 3, 135
Political elite, 3, 5, 6, 11, 16, 19, 137. *See also*
  Chicago, elites; Pittsburgh, elites
Political mobilization, xi, 6. *See also*
  Neighborhoods, mobilization
Political participation, xi, 3, 8, 11, 15, 97, 135,
  139, 144, 152. *See also* Community-based
  organizations
Political party, 11(fig.). *See also* Democratic
  Party; Machine politics; Republican Party
Populism, 14–15, 129–130, 149
Portz, John, 129
Postindustrial cities, 28, 55, 142
PPND. *See* Pittsburgh Partnership for
  Neighborhood Development
Progressive policy, xii, 1, 2, 7, 17, 84, 112,
  124, 136, 142–144, 151
  characteristics, 3, 143–144, 151, 174(n24)
  conservative, 145–149
  and electoral and corporatist systems,
  144–145
  limits to, 8, 9, 14, 121, 134, 145–149
  *Protest Is Not Enough: The Struggle of Blacks
  and Hispanics for Equality in Urban
  Politics* (Browning et al.), 152
PRPA. *See* Pittsburgh Regional Planning
  Association
Public choice theory, xi, 9, 153(n4)
Public-private partnerships, ix, 3, 32, 49, 53,
  57, 82, 86, 129–130, 131, 146, 148
Putnam, Robert, 9, 10

Racial minorities, 11(fig.), 13, 14, 15,
  149–150, 152. *See also* African
  Americans; Asians; Hispanics
Reagan, Ronald, 14, 148
Redlining, 28, 73
Reform, 2, 90, 121–123, 141. *See also*
  Progressive policy; *under* Chicago;
  Pittsburgh
Regime theory, xi, xii, 3, 7, 153(n3)
  accommodation and cooperation, 4, 7(table),
  135, 136, 137–138, 151, 174(n27)

and governing regime, 4, 6, 136, 151, 152
and policy, 3–4, 135
see also Arenas
Regional Industrial Development Corporation,
  94, 138
Republican Party, 47, 96, 147
Resource distribution, xi, 2, 5, 6, 14, 33, 43,
  66, 103, 138(table), 139, 140, 143
  patterns, 6, 7, 8(table), 38, 110, 138(table),
  147–148, 150
Rice, Charles Owen, 130
Rizzo, Frank, 15
Robins, John, 95
Robinson, Renault, 89
Rosen, George, 69
Rostenkowski, Daniel, 105, 120
Royko, Mike, 67, 73

San Francisco (Calif.), 2, 14, 15, 143, 144,
  147, 151
Save Our Neighborhoods, Save Our City
  (SONSOC), 107–109, 121, 147
Sawyer, Eugene, 37(table), 109, 166(n52)
Scala, Florence, 69
Schattschneider, E. E., 37
School integration, 22–23
Scully, Cornelius, 47–48
Service sector, 19, 28, 29, 30
Shakman decrees, 33, 115, 156(n21)
Shelley v. Kramer (1948), 62
Simpson, Dick, 118
Smith, Dutch, 71
Social capital, 10, 140(table)
Social control, 4, 8(table), 28, 32, 33, 42, 137,
  138(table)
Social learning, 122
Social production, 4, 8(table), 10, 33, 38, 43,
  137, 138(table)
SONSOC. *See* Save Our Neighborhoods, Save
  Our City
Specter, Arlen, 127
Squires, Gregory, 56, 60
Steel industry, 29, 30, 45, 125–134, 142
Steel Valley Authority (SVA), 17, 30, 125,
  126, 128–134, 147, 172(n21)
Stoddard, Evan, 95
Stone, Clarence, 4, 32, 42, 134, 136
Sun-Times (Chicago), 36
SVA. *See* Steel Valley Authority
Swanstrom, Todd, 2, 15, 99

Tabb, David, 150, 152
Talbott, Basil, 36
The Woodlawn Organization (TWO)
  (Chicago), 71, 72, 74
Trickle-down theory, 2, 132

INDEX

Tri State Conference on Steel (Ohio, W. Va., Pa.), 125, 149
TWO. *See* The Woodlawn Organization
UDAG. *See* Urban Development Action Grant
UIC. *See* University of Illinois, Chicago
University of Chicago, 57, 70–71
University of Illinois, Chicago (UIC), 60, 66, 67, 68, 69, 70
URA. *See* Pittsburgh, Urban Redevelopment Authority
Urban Community Conservation Act (1953) (Ill.), 56
Urban Development Action Grant (UDAG), 103
Urban politics, xii, 2, 152, 174(n27)
Urban renewal, 14, 51, 82
  and displacement, 61, 65, 75, 77
  and neighborhood organizing, 18, 39, 65–66, 69, 83
  see also under Chicago; Pittsburgh
U.S. Steel (firm), 45, 73, 125, 126, 127, 128, 129, 131, 133, 142

Van Buskirk, Arthur, 52
Voluntary associations, 13
Von Hoffman, Nicholas, 72
Vrdolyak, Edward, 33, 91, 95–96, 104, 105, 106, 163(n12)

Walker, Dan, 73
Wall Street Journal, 29, 45
Wards, 23. *See also under* Chicago; Pittsburgh
Ware, Bill, 113
Washington, Harold, ix, x, 1, 3, 15, 17, 18, 35, 106, 151, 167(n32)
  administration (1983–1987), 105, 111–112, 115, 150, 169(n11)
  coalition, 96, 97, 143, 144, 147, 149, 150
  death (1987), 37
  and minorities, 96, 114, 116–117, 119, 122, 142, 146, 147, 165(n40)
  and neighborhoods, 96, 97, 103–104, 105, 106, 107–109, 110, 119, 120, 122
  U.S. congressman, 96
Weber, Michael, 50, 76
Westinghouse (firm), 45
White flight, 71, 79
Willis, Benjamin, 72
Wilson, James Q., 142
Women, 114, 115, 116, 169(n20)
Wood, Elizabeth, 61, 62
Worker-ownership arrangements, 17, 127, 131, 172(n20)
World's fairs (Chicago) (1893, 1933), 55, 146
Wright, Frank Lloyd, 50